I0046647

The Stationers' Company

The Stationers' Company (1960) examines the corporate existence, under one name or another, of the Stationers' Company over five hundred and fifty years. At some periods of its life it was of importance only to its own members, while at others it played parts of consequence in the history of the City of London and even in the history of England.

The Stationers' Company

A History, 1403–1959

Cyprian Blagden

Routledge
Taylor & Francis Group

First published in 1960
by George Allen & Unwin Ltd

This edition first published in 2025 by Routledge
4 Park Square, Milton Park, Abingdon, Oxon, OX14 4RN

and by Routledge
605 Third Avenue, New York, NY 10017

Routledge is an imprint of the Taylor & Francis Group, an informa business

© 1960 George Allen and Unwin Ltd

Publisher's Note
The publisher has gone to great lengths to ensure the quality of this reprint but points out that some imperfections in the original copies may be apparent.

Disclaimer
The publisher has made every effort to trace copyright holders and welcomes correspondence from those they have been unable to contact.

A Library of Congress record exists under LCCN 61002340

ISBN: 978-1-032-90565-5 (hbk)
ISBN: 978-1-003-55858-3 (ebk)
ISBN: 978-1-032-90572-3 (pbk)

Book DOI 10.4324/9781003558583

THE STATIONERS' COMPANY

1 *An eastern window in the hall, 1960*

THE STATIONERS' COMPANY

A HISTORY, 1403-1959

BY CYPRIAN BLAGDEN

Ruskin House

GEORGE ALLEN & UNWIN LTD

MUSEUM STREET LONDON

First Published in 1960

This book is copyright under the Berne Convention.
Apart from any fair dealing for the purposes of private
study, research, criticism or review, as permitted under
the Copyright Act 1956, no portion may be reproduced
by any process without written permission. Enquiries
should be addressed to the publisher.

© *George Allen and Unwin Ltd, 1960*

Printed in Great Britain
in 12 on 13 pt. Fournier type
by Unwin Brothers Limited
Woking and London

To Jane

PREFACE

T HE Stationers' Company has had a corporate existence, under one name or another, for over five hundred and fifty years. At some periods in its life it was of importance only to its own members; at others it played parts of some consequence in the history of the City of London and even in the history of England. For some periods the records of its activities do not exist; for others the records are almost embarrassingly full. Certain of its archives, particularly those dealing with copyright ownership in Elizabethan and Jacobean times, have been combed with great thoroughness by scholars who have published their findings; other records, like the Court Books of the early nineteenth century, have scarcely been looked at and never written about.

Variations in quantities of evidence and in degrees of a subject's importance present the historian of any corporation with one of the problems of balance; but the variation in the weight of past attention—by the printing of documents or by the publication of monographs—poses a special problem of balance for the historian of the Stationers' Company. I have been able to give to the first 150 years a mere 20 pages because there is evidence for no more. To the century from 1557—admittedly the most important in the life of the Company—I have chosen to allot only 120 pages because the material already in print is considerable; but the next 150 years—roughly from 1660 to 1810—receive almost as much space because they have hitherto attracted little notice. To the last 150 years of waning power I have devoted only 30 pages.

The harmonizing of narrative with analysis poses another problem of balance, for analysis presupposes the breaking down of the whole into its components. The separate parts of the organism must be studied at different stages of development and in their changing relationships with all the other parts; yet sight must not be lost of the complete body and of the alterations in its general character as one century succeeds another. Even such an apparently self-contained aspect of a corporation's activities as the management of property

9

impinges on the general prosperity of the Company and on the provision for the poor; and, in its turn, it is affected by the Company's need for cash and by the City's planning policy. How much more completely woven into the texture of a corporation's everyday life are the changing rules by which it governs itself, the varying rate and method of entry into the society, the speed of promotion and the attitude to the holding of office, the fluctuations in the power of the trading interests and in their policies of trade control, the changes in corporate feeling and in the relationships with other companies, with the City and even with the central Government. Over and above these elements, which are common to all corporations, there are in the Stationers' Company two unique strands of overwhelming importance: the control of copyright and the management of the trading concerns known as the Stocks. Both were invented by the Stationers; the first gave them the necessary urge to combine, without which they might never have achieved Government recognition; the second gave them unusual—and long lasting—economic inducements to support their Company in the usual gild ways. Each demands much space; but because the first—copyright—has already received considerable attention and the second little, I have treated the Stocks in greater detail.

It is one thing to be aware of these problems of balance and quite another to solve them satisfactorily. I will only say that I have tried to avoid subservience either to the unenterprising narrative which records each event in its chronological place without admitting any other context, or to the repetitious, card-index, method which covers the ground as many times as there are aspects of the subject; and that the attempt to employ the best of both techniques is the most difficult balance to achieve. With the inevitable emphasis on the corporation and with the interweaving of the different strands in its development, the individual Stationer tends to be forgotten. I have therefore interposed the careers of a few men, partly because they played roles of some importance in their Company but chiefly because each exemplifies the manner in which, at a certain stage of the Company's growth, a man might make his way.

A high proportion of the evidence for this study is housed at Stationers' Hall and a high proportion of the evidence up to the year 1640 is in print; what exists at the Hall and what has been published I have set out in a 'Note on the records and on secondary sources'.

The records are those of the Company; other primary sources include items at the British Museum, the Public Record Office, the Guildhall Record Office and Library, the Universities of Oxford and Cambridge, Somerset House, Lambeth Library and the House of Lords; most of the secondary works deal with specific aspects of the Company's history. The rules I have followed, in order to keep footnotes in their proper place as servants, are: firstly, where the ground has been covered in detail by one of these secondary works, with full references to the sources used (as, for instance, in the relationship between the Company and the Universities of Oxford and Cambridge), I have not repeated the evidence but referred to the appropriate publications; and secondly, I have omitted all references to the Company's archives when these sources are self-evident, and I have provided the references to other primary sources only when these are not given in the secondary authorities. The 'Note on records' also takes the place of a bibliography, select or otherwise.

'The future historian of the Stationers' Company . . . will be grateful for the first-fruits here ingathered', wrote Edward Arber in the Introduction to the second volume of his *Transcript* (p. 11). This is an understatement. Not only did he transcribe and annotate many hundreds of pages of the early records, but he dug out of the British Museum and the Public Record Office many pieces of relevant material—some printed but most in manuscript—which he incorporated (on a highly idiosyncratic plan) in the *Transcript*. The more I use his work and compare it with the originals, the more I admire it and am grateful to him. To the late Sir Walter Greg and to Professor William A. Jackson I am proportionately grateful for their editing of the Court minutes, which were denied to Arber. To Mr Graham Pollard I owe two debts; the first is his pioneer study of the Company in the fifteenth, and the first half of the sixteenth, century, without which I would have found it even more difficult to write Chapter I and part of Chapter II; the second is the stimulating—and often highly critical—interest he has shown in my own work on hitherto neglected aspects of Company history. I am grateful, too, to the late Dr John Johnson both for his published work and for his generous encouragement; to Mr Ellic Howe who first took me to Stationers' Hall and from whose generosity to the Company I have derived more benefit than anyone else; to Mr Sidney Hodgson, who has always made me feel that the work was worth doing; to Mr T. F. Reddaway for his guidance in matters relating to the history of London; to Mr Mettrop, the late Beadle, and to Mr Osborne for their friendliness and willingness to help. I would like to express more formal thanks to a succession of Masters and Wardens of the Company for permission to publish articles based on the Stationers' records; to the Trustees of the Leverhulme Foundation for generous assistance in making my researches easier and to Messrs Longmans, Green, my own company, for enabling me to take advantage of this help.

CONTENTS

CONTENTS

ILLUSTRATIONS

FIGURES

Originals at Stationers' Hall unless otherwise stated

PLATES

CHAPTER I

THE CHARTER—AND BEFORE

THE NEW HALL AND THE CHARTER

TWO important events in the life of the Stationers' Company occurred during the short reign of Mary Tudor. In the late autumn of 1554 it moved its headquarters from Milk Street, in the parish of St Mary Magdalen, to Peter's College. This second building, on which a good deal of money was spent to make it suitable for its new functions, lay on the south side of St Paul's Churchyard and towards the western end; it was in the parish of St Gregory-by-St Paul and in the very centre of the area which for so long was associated with the buying and selling of books. About two and a half years later—on May 4, 1557—the privy seal was set to the Charter of incorporation.

It is tempting to exaggerate the importance of these two events. The move was made in expectation of the enhanced status which the Charter would confer, and the significance which the Stationers themselves attached to the twofold change is reflected in the making of a fresh start in the keeping of records. One of the duties which the Beadle of the Company undertook in the months following the incorporation was the fair copying, in a folio volume for which one senior Stationer[1] provided the paper and another the binding, of the details of receipts and expenditure from December 1554. Since all traces of earlier transactions have disappeared, this first surviving record of the Company's activities—Register A it was labelled—has, understandably, been reckoned of the greatest importance. But it must have taken the place of another account book, which could hardly have been the first of its kind. Furthermore, the granting of the Charter was only an incident, albeit unique, in the life of the brother-

---

[1] I have throughout distinguished between a Stationer (with a capital S) who was a member of the Stationers' Company but may have traded as a draper, and a stationer (with a lower-cases) who dealt in paper but may have been a Draper (i.e. a member of the Drapers' Company).

hood and should be regarded rather as the attainment of majority than as the day of birth. The analogy between the growth of an organization and the growth of a man cannot be pressed very far; but it is safe to say that, just as a man reaches a political and legal status at the age of twenty-one without any change in his personality, so the Company of Stationers, in spite of the move to St Paul's Churchyard and the achievement of a Charter, was fundamentally the same after these events as it had been ten years before them.

We cannot, however, escape the fact that the Charter which Philip and Mary granted in 1557 is the first official document to go beyond a mere mention of the gild's existence; it must therefore be closely scrutinized for every scrap of evidence which it can be compelled to reveal. The first point to notice is that almost exactly eighty years had passed since Caxton began to print at Westminster. I am concerned with the history of the Company and not with that of the book trade; but the two histories were closely involved, particularly so up to the beginning of the eighteenth century; and, though Caxton was not a Stationer, his introduction into England of the mechanical method of reproducing the written word created in the book trade the conditions which moulded the terms of the Stationers' Charter.

These terms fall into two groups: those likely to be found in grants to other companies and those which could occur only in a grant to the Stationers. The first gave to ninety-seven named 'free men[1] of the mistery or art of Stationery', of the City of London and its suburbs, the right for ever to be a corporate body with perpetual succession, the power to take legal action and to make rules for their own governance, the right to meet together and to elect a Master and two Wardens (who are named in the Charter) and the right to own property in the City or suburbs to the annual value of £20. There is also a proviso tucked in that the Master—and in his absence the elder Warden—shall have a casting vote in elections. The lack of any more detailed provisions for the choosing of officers led to trouble later on.

Much more interesting are the reasons given for the making of the grant and the later clauses about printers and the products of their

[1] There were a dozen or more freemen whose names, for one reason or another, do not appear in the list; moreover, no mention is made of the inferior grade of Brothers (see below, p. 35). A freeman of a London company (or gild) was a full member of that company; the advantages and ways of becoming a freeman are discussed below, p. 34. In the sixteenth century a man could not become a freeman of the City of London unless he were free of a company; again, the advantages and ways of achieving full citizenship are discussed below, p. 26. All freemen of companies were supposed to take up the freedom of the City, but not all did.

presses. The preamble declares that the King and Queen, wishing to provide a suitable remedy against the seditious and heretical books which were daily printed and published, gave certain privileges to their beloved and faithful lieges, the ninety-seven Stationers, in addition to the normal rights of a company. It was laid down, firstly that no one in the realm should exercise the art of printing, either himself or through an agent, unless he were a freeman of the Stationers' Company of London or unless he had royal permission to do so; and secondly that the Master and Wardens of the Company were to have the right to search the houses and business premises of all printers, bookbinders and booksellers in the kingdom for any printed matter, to seize (and treat as they thought fit) anything printed contrary to any statute or proclamation, and to imprison anyone who printed without the proper qualification or resisted their search; such offenders were to remain in gaol for three months without trial and be fined £5, half of which was to go to the Crown and half to the Company.

The rule that all printers should be members of the Stationers' Company or specially privileged meant an overwhelming concentration of power in the London Company, even if it did not mean that printing outside the capital was impossible. Moreover, it applied to one group only of the craftsmen comprising the Stationers and it cut across the tradition of the City that a freeman was entitled to practise any craft even though he were not free of the company which supervised that craft; the result was a good deal of friction in the years to come, both within the Company and between the Company and the City. The nation-wide right of search—a privilege allowed earlier to the Goldsmiths and the Pewterers—is the earliest formal evidence of an association between the Crown and the Company which lasted 150 years. How far these two important provisions were answers to Stationers' ambitions or part of royal policy to stifle criticism of Church and State can be decided only by a survey of the previous 150 years.

THE STATIONERS AND THEIR CRAFT GILDS

As early as the thirteenth century the word *stationarius*[1] was being used in Oxford and Cambridge; and it appears in the records of York

---

[1] What follows is largely based on the first of two articles by Graham Pollard, 'The Company of Stationers before 1557'. (*The Library*, 4th ser., xviii, 1938.)

and London at the beginning of the fourteenth century. It described a man who had a fixed place of business, a stall-holder rather than a hawker; and it first became regularly attached to members of the book trade—no one has explained why it adhered to this trade and not to any others—in University towns where academic authorities kept an eye on the supply of reading matter to their students. In the course of the fourteenth century the word achieved general use in London along with, or as an alternative to, the words describing the four craftsmen who between them created a medieval book: the parchminer who supplied the parchment, the scrivener who wrote the text, the lymner who added the illuminations, and the bookbinder. The 'stationer' may have been trained in one of these crafts, but he was primarily a shop-keeper; he arranged for the manufacture of a book to a customer's order and he may have carried a stock of second-hand books and even of a few lines, like service books, for which there was a sure demand.

By 1357 there was a craft gild in London to which the scriveners and the lymners belonged. In 1373 those scriveners who specialized in writing legal documents—writers of court hand rather than writers of texts—petitioned for and obtained from the City the right to a separate organization; and thus began the independent existence of the Scriveners' Company. Shortly after this, the other branch of the scriveners also parted from the lymners and each is distinguished in the City records as a separate gild with its own ordinances. But no more is known of these ancestors of the present Company than the fact of their existence and the names of some of their members.

The separation of the crafts must have weakened their usefulness for, on July 12, 1403, 'the reputable men of the Craft of Writers of Text-letter, those commonly called "Limners", and other good folks, citizens of London, who were wont also to bind and sell books' petitioned the Mayor and Aldermen for the right of electing each year a lymner and a text-writer to be joint Wardens of these trades. The two Wardens so elected were to be sworn before the Mayor that they would oversee the behaviour and the work of these craftsmen, in the interests both of the City and of the law-abiding members of the fellowship; and they were empowered to present 'bad and disloyal' men to the Chamberlain at Guildhall for punishment. With the granting of this request in the reign of Henry IV begins the unbroken history of the present corporation, though many years passed before it became known as the Stationers' Company. It was the gild to which, as the 1403 petition declares, the writers of text-letter, the lymners, the bookbinders and the booksellers belonged; it is a reasonable guess that the parchminers were in it too.

PRINTING IN ENGLAND

About sixty years later, books printed on the Continent began to find their way into this country, and in November 1477 Caxton published the first book printed in England. Printed books, whether of home or foreign origin, had to be distributed by wholesalers, men with the capital and the organization to handle books in bulk; it was impossible for a printer and difficult for an importer to sell all his stock over his own counter to retail customers. With printing, therefore, came wholesaling, which had hitherto been unnecessary in the book trade; and the earlier printers—Caxton and Wynkyn de Worde and Julian Notary—were also importers. How did the Stationers react to the process by which the printed slowly took the place of the hand-written book? It was an easy step for a shop-keeper, living on a 'made-to-measure' trade with a few ready-made articles on his shelves, to begin stocking printed books which he could have bound, and even illuminated, by the old craftsmen in his own workshop or, if he employed none, by the tradesmen he had previously patronized. Booksellers welcomed the fall in price and the growth in turnover; bookbinders welcomed the increase in business; for many years there was enough work for illuminators. Even parchminers and text-writers were only gradually squeezed out of the book business, and, though Caxton claimed to have many enemies and few friends, there is no evidence of unemployment or of organized opposition to the new machines in this country, as there was, for instance, at Toulouse in 1477, a year after the introduction of printing in that city.[1] The opposition in England, when it did come, was to the continental craftsman rather than to the continental craft.

Though we know a little about individual Stationers, we are almost completely in the dark about the gild during the fifteenth century. There are brief testamentary mentions and there are references in the City records to the part played by the Stationers', along with other

[1] P. Mellottée, *Histoire Economique de l'Imprimerie*, Paris, 1905, pp. 23-4.

companies, in royal welcomes or in paying its share of assessments,[1] in presenting its members for freedom of the City or its Wardens for swearing in. We may, however, assume the official gild attitude on one important matter. In 1484 an Act was passed to restrict the conditions under which those who were not English by birth could trade or work in this country; but none of the restrictions was to affect 'any artificer or merchant stranger, of what nation or country he be', if he were engaged in the book trade; this applied equally to 'any books written or printed' for retail or wholesale business, and to setting up as text-writer, illuminator, binder or printer. I cannot believe that one group of craftsmen and shop-keepers would have been so pointedly excluded from the main provisions of the Act, which suited the general run of London citizens, unless the organization to which the native craftsmen and shop-keepers belonged—the fellowship of Stationers—had approved of the exclusion.

In the first forty years of the sixteenth century the pattern completely changed. Though it is difficult to trace in detail how the alteration came about, it is possible to see five different but related developments which led the Stationers first to work for and finally to achieve a Charter with the basic provision that printers must be freemen of the Company or royally privileged.

In the first place there developed a new kind of specialization in which men were differentiated not only by the functions they performed but by the manner in which they invested their money. Caxton was a printer who distributed the productions of his press by wholesale and by retail; he was also an importer of books which he disposed of in the same ways as his own; he was also what we would call a publisher and what, in the seventeenth century, the trade called an undertaker, who paid another printer to produce books for him. All these functions require, and lock up, capital in varying degrees; with the increase in the trade and the resulting competition, economic pressure forced all but the wealthiest printers to limit their activities. Some gave up the importation of foreign books; some could only survive by printing not on their own account but largely on behalf of men with more money to invest—often wholesalers and not always

---

[1] Such as that of 1488 for a loan to the King; the Stationers were assessed at £20, along with the Linendrapers, the Weavers, the Glovers and the Girdlers. This is the lowest rate among the first thirty fellowships, which the Mercers head with £740. Below the Stationers came forty-six which had to lend from £18 to £1, and below them six assessed at nil. (*Acts of the Court of the Mercers' Company 1453–1527*, Cambridge, 1936, pp. 187–9.)

Stationers. Each function abandoned by a printer was a function gained by a bookseller; and it is possible to detect thus early the beginning of a battle among the Stationers which continued until the reign of Queen Anne. But though the printers lost some ground in the first half of the sixteenth century they remained the most powerful element in the trade.

Caxton was an Englishman, but most of his contemporaries and his immediate successors—printers and importers—came from France, from the Low Countries or from Germany; they were welcomed by the Government and, at first, by the gild of Stationers; they brought much-needed skill and created good business. But they did not become members of the gild and they worked either outside the City—as Caxton did in Westminster and Pynson in St Clement Danes—or, if within the City, in a 'liberty' where they were beyond the reach of the City courts—as Machlinia did, by Fleet Bridge. Even before the end of the fifteenth century the men who worked for Pynson were being intimidated—by their neighbours in the parish of St Clement's and not, it seems, by rival craftsmen; but there is not enough additional evidence to show how far the siting of these printing houses was the result of the aliens' desire to keep clear of the City and how far it was the policy of the fellowship of Stationers, as it was of the City, to deny them the rights of citizens.

ALIENS AND FOREIGNERS

Those who came from the Continent to produce or to trade in printed books had been exempted from the restrictions of the 1484 Act only because their business was new and poorly developed in this country; but the general anti-alien feeling was bound sooner or later to affect native booksellers and the new generation of master printers, as it had earlier affected other tradesmen; it is only strange that it took so long. Three Acts of Parliament, passed within a dozen years, show how the feeling hardened. That of 1523 ordered that 'all . . . aliens born using any manner of handicraft' in the City and its immediate neighbourhood must be subject to the rules of the appropriate company and must even submit to search by its Wardens. That of 1529 extended this to their paying the quarterly dues levied on all members of a company, even though they were living in the suburbs. These two Acts were general but applied to printers and bookbinders. The third, that of 1534, applied solely to the book trade. By it the exceptions made in the Act of 1484 were withdrawn; in future it was an offence to buy a book which had been bound abroad or to buy a book retail from an alien. That this Act was passed only as a result of representations from an interested body is obvious; moreover, the officers of the gild of Stationers took action, less than three years later, against the importation of bound books from Rouen and, in a letter of 1538 to Thomas Cromwell, Coverdale accused 'the company of Booksellers in London' of ruining the business of a Paris stationer by refusing to allow him to sell books he had had printed specially for the English market. 'Protection', both for local production and for native craftsmen, was by the 1530s as much the policy of the gild of Stationers as it was of any other London company.

An alien printer or bookseller now had two choices: he could return to his own country or he could try to obtain citizenship of London. Many chose the second, partly because they had been some years in England and had, with royal or official backing, become free denizens; partly because there were economic and welfare advantages in membership of a gild; and partly because the gild itself aimed at maximum control over those who practised its crafts and might be expected to support, under certain conditions, applications for membership. But the City was jealous of the privileges of its citizens; the Lord Mayor told Thomas Berthelet, the King's Printer, that only one stranger had become a freeman in forty years, and, though Berthelet said he knew of at least six,[1] one admission every six or seven years is clear enough indication of policy.

What were these closely guarded privileges? They fell into two classes: those arising out of the control of a craft or mystery, and those inherent in a body of men, or fraternity, formed for mutual support. The main advantages of the former were the right to open a shop and sell retail within the City (aliens could deal only by wholesale and only with freemen) and exemption from toll throughout the kingdom. Among the benefits of the latter were the care of widows and orphans, the help which a freeman himself could expect in times of sickness or adversity, and organized conviviality. Only by purchase could these advantages be obtained by those whose fathers were not citizens or who were not prepared to serve a full apprenticeship. The

[1] In a letter to a Privy Councillor, c. 1540. *Letters and Papers of Henry VIII*, vol. 16, no. 1029.

26

City would not normally sell the right to be a citizen unless a man were sponsored by royalty or by a notable; and it insisted that a stranger could be admitted only as a member of the gild which controlled his craft.[1]

Whatever the Lord Mayor and the King's Printer may have said to each other, only one alien was allowed his freedom in the fellowship of the Stationers during the first thirty years of the sixteenth century. This was Thomas Baeldewyn, who was admitted early in 1525 for a fine of £10 after his substance had been valued by a committee of the corporation at under £200.[2] But from the early 1530s there was a steady stream of them. I get the impression from such evidence as survives in the City records that, of the three parties involved, the aliens found the conditions after 1534 too limiting for profitable business; the Stationers were ready to take them in at a price; and the City was forced to admit them by external pressure, usually from above. Each case seems to have been treated on its merits. In 1536 Queen Ann supported Reyner Wolfe, who was only accepted on condition that he took none but English apprentices.[3] Protector Somerset's letter on behalf of Thomas Gualtyer was referred to the Court of Common Council and no more heard of. John Gypkyn, with support from Edward VI, was admitted without payment.[4] A few, like Stephen Kevall in 1535,[5] were granted their freedoms without evidence of backing and without conditions except that they settle their fines with the Chamberlain. It is unlikely that the Stationers would take the trouble to win the support of the sovereign for an alien; it is equally unlikely that the City would miss the opportunity of denying the freedom to a man who was not approved of by his prospective fellowship.

The control of the alien is the second of the developments in the early part of the sixteenth century; the control of the 'foreign' printer is the third. To a citizen of London a foreigner was a shop-keeper or craftsman of English origin who was not free of the City. A member

[1] On February 7, 1433, in answer to a petition from the citizens, the Mayor and Aldermen laid it down that the Recorder was to admit no one by redemption 'in eny Felship of such craft as he hath verrily used to use' unless, in presenting him for freedom, the masters of his gild swear that his admission hurts no other craft and unless he lives in the City and pays scot and lot. (*Calendar of Letter Book K*, p. 165.) In August 1516 the Court of Aldermen resolved that no one was to be admitted to the freedom of the City by redemption for a period of five years. (Letter Book N, f. 17.)   [2] Repertories of the Court of Aldermen, vol. 7, f. 77b.
[3] Journals of the Court of Common Council, vol. 13, f. 471b.
[4] Repertories, vol. 12, ff. 78, 296b and 305.   [5] Ibid., vol. 9, f. 140b.

of the Stationers' Company of Chester, which had received a charter from the corporation in 1534, had no privileges outside his own city and was a foreigner in the eyes of the Stationers of London. As a bookseller he was a useful customer of the London wholesaler and a not very well stocked retail competitor at the Chester fairs; but if he threatened to set up as a printer he was immediately in competition with the London printers for a small piece of the still limited field. When it is remembered in how many French cities printing presses flourished in the sixteenth century it is surprising to find English provincial printing dying out in the 1520s; neither York nor Bristol, nor either of the Universities, was able to support a press in the second half of Henry VIII's reign. That printing was well established on the Continent before it got a footing in this country and that the English market early became a profitable one for French printers and exporters are two of the reasons; London's economic dominance of England is a third. But it must have been the London gild of Stationers which, taking advantage of these tendencies, applied the necessary pressures first to make provincial printing an unprofitable business and then to have included in its Charter a clause by which all printers in the kingdom must be members of the Company unless licensed by the Crown. The visit in 1539 of three Stationers to St Albans and their return to London with one of the Abbey printers, who was accused of printing a book of heresies, looks like an opportunity well taken, since at St Albans was one of the few presses outside the capital;[1] the abbot's protest makes it look like a put-up job.

GOVERNMENT INTERFERENCE

Although the Stationers did not finally obtain their Charter until 1557 they were ready with one fifteen years earlier. At a session of the Convocation of Canterbury in March 1542 a book containing a Charter for the Company was debated and referred to the King. The terms of this document are not known but, in view of the success which the gild had achieved in the previous eight years, they may not have been very different from those of the Charter as granted, and may have been rejected by the King because he considered the powers asked for were too wide. Within a day or two of the meeting of Convocation a

---

[1] From 1549 John Oswen had a press at Worcester on which, for a year or two, he printed books mainly for distribution in Wales, and John Mychell had a press at Canterbury.

proclamation[1] was drafted against the reading of any Bible except that printed by Grafton in 1540 and against the possession of works by Wycliffe, Tyndale, Coverdale and other dangerous authors. There are three important points in the draft 1542 proclamation. The first is that bishops and others who are to supervise the handing in and burning of the forbidden works are not to 'be curious to mark who bringeth forth such books'; the attack was against doctrines rather than against men. The second is that printing in the provinces is clearly envisaged in the provision that a printer is not only to set his own name and the name of the author and the date of printing on every English book he puts out but to present a copy to the mayor of the town where he lives two days before he begins general distribution. The third is that no English books on religious subjects printed abroad can be imported without royal licence. Royal sympathy did not yet extend to the full demands of the Stationers (if they made them at this time) but the Crown had for some time been fully aware of dangers from the products of continental presses.

This proclamation leads straight into the fourth development—the change in the Government attitude to the printed word. The Act of 1484 suggests, by its exclusions, a desire to foster in this country the distribution of the products of the exciting new invention. The Act of 1534, though it was aimed at a certain kind of man—one who was taking business away from worthy citizens—made it more difficult to bring into the country a certain kind of publication—one that might put wrong ideas into the heads of the King's loyal subjects. Even before this, the dangerous possibilities of the printed word had begun to worry the Government. The heretical doctrines of Luther were, it is true, spread by word of mouth; but printed books and pamphlets could be produced and distributed in their hundreds—secretly; they did not disappear but remained for second readings and for passing on to friends; they were difficult to answer back. Closely related to the fear of theological heterodoxy in the printed word went fear of criticism of the Government; the adjectives heretical and seditious appear over and over again in official pronouncements up to the beginning of the eighteenth century. Henry VIII was vulnerable; the Governments of Edward VI were even more obvious targets of criticism; Mary had, perhaps, most need to fear the press.

From 1528, for the next thirty years, there appeared a stream of

[1] *Letters and Papers of Henry VIII*, vol. 17, no. 177.

royal proclamations against seditious and heretical books; sometimes they were in general terms, sometimes—as in the 1542 draft—aimed at particular authors; sometimes the attack was on local printing—as in that of November 16, 1538—sometimes on English books printed abroad. In 1549 the Privy Council made an order against papistical books; four years later Mary was attacking the printers and Stationers who were dealing in Protestant publications for 'an evyle zeale for lucre and [being] covetous of vyle gaine', phrases strongly reminiscent of those used by Coverdale about popish books in a letter to Cranmer in 1539.[1] On February 17, 1554, a proclamation ordered all aliens who were not denizens or established merchants to leave the country within twenty-four days and drew particular—and interesting—attention to booksellers, printers and preachers. In 1539 Cochlaeus had explained in a letter to Cardinal Contarini[2] how he had been sent from Liège a book by the learned Albertus Pighius 'written last year against the King—yea! tyrant—of England', to be printed at Leipzig; how the printer there had failed to get a licence from the Duke of Saxony, a Lutheran; how the author had then sent the book to a printer at Cologne who was willing to print secretly in some village but the Senate, coming to hear of it, had forbidden his printing it on pain of death because it was against the King of England. It is not surprising that a watch was kept on books in English printed on the Continent.

In the course of the campaign, pre-publication censorship appeared for the first time in this country. The Council of Latran, in 1515, decreed that no book should be printed before it had been submitted to and approved by the bishop of the diocese or by his delegate. Six years later Francis I forbade publication in France without the authority of the University of Paris. In 1524 and 1526 the Bishop of London had tried by straight talks to booksellers to stop the importation of Lutheran books and to oversee the printing of new works,[3] but it was not until June 1530 that a proclamation, aimed mainly at 'pestiferous errors and blasphemies' in books printed abroad, quietly ordered at the end that new theological books in English were not to be sent to the press before they had been examined by the bishop of the diocese. By the proclamation of 1538 no book in English was to

[1] *Letters and Papers of Henry VIII*, vol. 14, no. 4. [2] Ibid., no. 818.
[3] Arthur W. Reed, 'The Regulation of the Book Trade before the Proclamation of 1538', *Trans. Bib. Soc.*, xv, 1920, pp. 162–72.

be printed in England without the approval of a royal licenser. The significance of these orders in the history of the book trade and for individual Stationers is considerable; their significance for the corporation is as further moves towards the control of the press in which the Company was to play a part. The gild had, perhaps, in 1542 offered its assistance to the ecclesiastical authorities in their attempts to establish this control; it may be that it offered its assistance, either to the civil Government or again to the bishops, in the early part of 1551, when Randle Cholmondeley of Lincoln's Inn promised 'to be of counsaile with the companie of Stationers when they shuld conuenientlye Desyre him', in their negotiations: it is certain that six years later Queen Mary's Government accepted the Company's organization as a piece of machinery useful to it, in spite of the hard things said in the 1553 proclamation about the behaviour of some of its members.

It would have been possible to trace in detail the stiffening of royal and ecclesiastical attitudes against an unfettered use of the printing press; but though this would tell us about certain printers and booksellers, whose misdeeds are referred to in correspondence or against whom action was taken by the Privy Council or the Court of Star Chamber, it would reveal nothing of the brotherhood to which most of them belonged; though there is mention of 'printers' and 'booksellers' and 'bookbinders' in Acts of Parliament and in royal proclamations, there is no mention of the gild of Stationers. It is not until Mary, having seen the failure of other methods, agreed to the Stationers' own proposals for control by conferring on them the powers they required for their own purposes, that the corporation was officially recognized and at once given, not only the ordinary privileges of a City company but also—so far as printing was concerned—nation-wide powers, almost as if it were an executive arm of the Government.

COPYRIGHT

The fifth and last of the developments before 1557 is as undocumented as the fourth abounds in evidence, and it is the one in which the importance of tracing the evolution would have been the greatest; for it is the early history of copyright, which the Company invented and of which it was the record-keeper until 1911. But all we know is that a freeman could have 'the empression of any Copye, peculier to hym' either by a royal grant 'or by the ordenaunces of this Companye'. These phrases, from a resolution of the governing body taken in December 1565, refer to the two methods by which a kind of copyright could be secured: by letters patent or by the gild rule which made it an offence not to present to the Wardens—for putting on record—every publication not protected by royal privilege. The evidence for grants from the King can often be found in the books to which they refer, and though the 1565 memorandum is the earliest reference which links the two methods and which tells us anything about the practice of registration, an ordinance for registration existed before incorporation and a senior printer was fined for breaking it.

In the days before printing a 'stationer' provided his customer with a new book, written, illuminated and bound to that customer's order; a single sale completed the transaction and gave the 'stationer' his profit. A printer, on the other hand, had to make as many sales as there were copies in his impression of a book before the transaction was at an end and the profit fully earned. To lie easy at night he wanted no reduplication of his book by another printer, no more hundreds of copies chasing an already limited number of customers. But the early printers in London were quite ready to profit by the enterprise of others. Redman took advantage of Pynson's trouble and expense in preparing the manuscript, setting the type and printing off Littleton's *Tenures*, a complicated legal treatise, and was probably able to sell his edition more cheaply than the original; but Pynson had behaved in the same way to Caxton. The first answer to be thought of was the royal grant of the sole right to print and sell a particular book for a given number of years, within which it was expected that the whole impression could be disposed of. As usual, English lagged behind continental practice; a Venetian printer had obtained a privilege as early as 1469, and printers in Paris had won similar concessions at least as early as 1507. It was not until 1518 that Pynson and Rastell obtained the first grants to protect books printed in England; within the next few years such grants were fairly common, the greater part of Pynson's output being privileged. It was a short step to the similar protection of whole classes of books—those of common law, for instance, and the official publications which only the King's Printer was permitted to produce.

But as the demand for reading matter became more varied and the number of printers increased, royal protection could not be obtained for every sermon and almanack and ballad; those interested in uninterrupted enjoyment of the profit from an impression of a book were therefore compelled to agree to respect each other's claims on these little monopolies. The gild of Stationers was the obvious organization through which such agreement could be worked and the register of claims to 'copies' was the written record to which another claimant could be referred and by which disputes might be settled. A new ordinance, therefore, of an unknown date before 1557, made it an offence for a Stationer to put out a book before he had shown it to the Wardens and had it entered in the register; the fees for entrance were a small but useful addition to the income of the gild.

This simple-seeming arrangement which gave a form of copyright protection, not of course to authors or translators but to printers and booksellers, was a great step forward in the organization of the book trade, and out of it much has grown; for about 350 years it was, in the eyes of the English-speaking world, the *raison d'être* of the Stationers' Company. But its importance here is that it concentrates within itself the developments which I have been discussing and which culminated in the granting of the Charter, when the Government could no longer control the press without the aid of a specialized and interested organization. The copyright system of this organization would break down if aliens in the suburbs or foreigners in the provinces could print—unchallenged except by the invoking of a London gild's ordinance—the books to which the London Stationers laid claim; but it might be made to work if all the potential breakers of the agreement were in London or (at worst) members of the London Company. The very concentration of printers which the Stationers desired was a supreme advantage in the eyes of the Government. And so it came about that the Stationers obtained their Charter on their own terms but at a time when it suited the Crown to make use of their organization for other purposes.

CHAPTER II

THE EARLY STATIONERS
AND THEIR GOVERNANCE

THE PATTERN OF MEMBERSHIP

THE ninety-seven men whose names are in the Charter can be differentiated in three ways: by their trades, by their standing in the Company and by their relationship one to another. There were printers, bookbinders and booksellers; there were suppliers of parchment and paper and stationery, and there may even have been illuminators; there were certainly a few whose business was of another kind altogether: the first Master, Thomas Dockwray, was an ecclesiastical lawyer. Standing in the Company was most strictly by seniority; it ranged from the group of ex-Wardens and near-Wardens like Stephen Kevall (who purchased his freedom in 1535, was Warden in 1551 and number 9 in the Charter list) to those whose admission occurred in the thirty months between the move to the new Hall and the grant. From odd surviving records of presentations (by the Wardens of the Stationers) for freedom of the City, it appears that Richard Lant (number 35) was free in 1537 and that Richard Tottell (number 67) was free in 1552. This kind of seniority had little to do with a man's relations with his fellows; John Allde (number 85) was in business, soon after his admission to the freedom, as a master printer binding apprentices, and employing journeymen who may have been twenty years his senior and who probably died as wage-earners.

But all entered the Company by one of four doors: servitude, patrimony, redemption or translation. In Appendix I are the numbers of freemen, year by gild year, from 1557 to 1959; the changes in the popularity of the methods of entry are indicative, as I shall hope to make clear, of various changes in the attitude to, and in the functions of, the Stationers' Company. At the time of the Charter, the intake was almost entirely of those who had served their apprenticeship with independent masters free of the Company; the formal contract was by a pair of indentures which were drawn up by the Clerk and which the apprentice, his parent or sponsor, and his master brought to Stationers' Hall for formal enrolment within three months of the date of signature;[1] the length of service was not less than seven years and, according to an Act of Common Council in 1556, at least as much longer as would make the apprentice free only at the age of twenty-four. The sons of a Stationer could be admitted by patrimony, provided their father was a freeman of the Company at the time of their birth; I get the impression that in the sixteenth century fathers preferred their sons to learn a trade along with young men of their own age and would take advantage of the right to present them *per patrimonium* only when their training was completed before their indentured years of service were up; freedom by patrimony seems to have been allowed before a man reached his twenty-fourth birthday, and the rule of the City referred specifically to freedom by appenticeship or redemption.

This freedom by purchase was the manner in which aliens and foreigners came into the gild.[2] It was a method much more freely used for gaining admission to the more important companies in which chances of success in City politics were greater. For those already free of the City in another company the method of becoming a Stationer was by translation.[3] This meant obtaining the permission of both companies and such permission was naturally much more difficult to get from the company a man was leaving; any arguments with the company to which he was being translated were over his admission fee and the degree of seniority he was to be allowed.

The main body of freemen, by whatever method they had gained admission, was the 'Commonalty' of the Charter and was known as the Yeomanry. In the Stationers' Company there was no theoretical differentiation between employers and employed, between masters and journeymen; and there was no Yeomanry organization such as is found in other companies. But there was a group of men known as 'Brothers'; these obtained some status—in the Company but not in the City—by an admission fine of any sum up to 10s, which was

[1] This rule was often broken, sometimes to the extent that a master enrolled his apprentice only on the day he presented him for his freedom. The City allowed twelve months.

[2] See above, p. 26.

[3] The number is not as small as the translation column in Appendix I suggests, for men were sometimes entered as free *per redemptionem* when they came from another company.

often kept back from their wages, and they had to obey the ordinances without having all the privileges of freemen. Their names proclaim them as aliens or foreigners, some of whom had learnt their craft abroad. The booksellers and bookbinders among them, since they were not competing with native printers, were allowed to be independent masters and employ free journeymen or other Brothers; but they could have apprentices only if these were officially bound to freemen.[1] If they were printers by trade they could work, under the terms of the Charter, only for full members of the Company; when Richard Schilders was discovered printing a book in 1578, the Court of Assistants invoked the Charter and arranged for Thomas Dawson to take over both the man and the work. The status of Brother is evidence of the change which had occurred in the standing of the Dutch and French printers and bookbinders in London—the result of the widespread anti-alien feeling—since the early part of the sixteenth century, and particularly since 1534; though their skill, and occasionally their capital, was an important element in the book trade, the Brothers were of no account in the Company. The records show that there were Brothers at the time of the Charter, but their names do not appear in the list; many of the aliens who obtained letters of denization after 1534—there was a large group in 1544—joined the fellowship as Brothers because, perhaps, the City refused them full citizenship. There was a steady stream of admissions for the twenty-five years after 1557, and as late as 1597 the Company unsuccessfully petitioned the Lord Mayor and Court of Aldermen to allow Ascanius de Renialme the freedom of the City so that he might be admitted to full freedom as a Stationer;[2] at his death in 1600 he bequeathed £5 for a piece of

---

[1] For examples of this, see p. 53 below. In an entry for July 17, 1576, there is the perplexing statement that Abraham Veale was both a member of the Drapers' Company and a Brother of the Stationers'. I have been unable to find any official statement about the status of Brothers outside the Company. Some, like Ascanius de Renialme (mentioned below), were free denizens, others were not; none, I think, obtained freedom of the City of London, as many aliens had been able to do earlier. The most formal reference I can find is dated April 6, 1585, and is an ordinance of the Weavers' Company which had been admitting 'foreign brothers' since April 2, 1550. This refers to the established custom of admitting aliens and foreigners, some of whom had not served as apprentices; in future none is to be admitted unless he has served an apprenticeship in the Weavers' Company and is well reported on. But why a foreigner (who might be an Englishman living outside London) should not take up full freedom by servitude, I cannot understand. From an earlier order (1564), 'foreign brothers' were allowed to take apprentices with the approval of the Wardens. (Frances Consitt, *The London Weavers' Company*, Oxford, 1933, pp. 137, 271, 309–10.)

[2] *Acts of Privy Council 1597–8*, p. 290. There is much information about Ascanius in 'Christopher Plantin's Trade-Connexions with England and Scotland', by Colin Clair, *The Library*, 5th ser., xiv, 1959.

plate 'as a token of my goodwill beinge a brother of the said companie'.[1]

One of the results of obtaining the Charter, which was formally laid before the Court of Aldermen on June 3, 1557, by 'the wardens of the fealowship of Stacyoners and their assystauntes', was the grant by the City on February 1, 1560, of the right to have a Livery.[2] From that time the Stationers have had the full status of a Liveried Company of the City of London, with precedence next after the Poulters. Liverymen were supposed to attend the Lord Mayor 'at all comen Shewes' and were entitled to vote in mayoral and parliamentary elections. The precept defines the number of Liverymen in the Company merely as 'all suche and asmeny' as can afford the Livery; how many of the senior members availed themselves of this privilege is unknown. Twelve months passed before six of the Yeomanry were formally elected to the Livery on payment of 15s each; the most senior of these were the printers Edward Sutton and John Day, who were numbers 52 and 56 in the Charter list. It seems likely that, apart from the members of the governing body, those who had prior claims (on grounds of seniority) over Sutton and Day were elderly journeymen, who were not eligible and who certainly could not afford the honour. The point is a small one; what is important is that election to the Livery created a new pattern of seniority which superseded that by date of freedom; early election was essential for anyone ambitious to hold office in the Company.

The reason for this is that the two Renter Wardens, whose main job was collecting the quarterly subscriptions from all freemen, were chosen from the Livery and that, until a man had served these two offices, he was not eligible for election to the Court of Assistants. When the crafts of the text-writers and lymners came together again in 1403 they elected a Warden each to manage the affairs of the gild. In the course of time the two Wardens were assisted in their work by senior members of the brotherhood, who may have been past-Wardens; before 1554 there is no mention of a Master. Almost exactly a month after the date of the Charter, the Wardens 'and their

[1] *Abstracts from the Wills of English Printers and Stationers from 1492 to 1630*, by H. R. Plomer, 1903, p. 35.

[2] Arber is wrong, I think, in suggesting (*Transcript*, vol. i, p. xx) that this was a regrant of an old privilege. It was the first grant under the new rule that, since the franchise was based on the Livery, applications from companies had to be approved by the Court of Aldermen. (P. E. Jones, *The Worshipful Company of Poulters*, 1939, p. 7.)

assystauntes' presented it to the Court of Aldermen; the Court of Assistants was therefore the governing body at the time of incorporation, but how long it had been in existence before cannot even be guessed. I shall discuss later the powers of, and the elections to, the Court; the points I want to make now are that from 1554 it was presided over by the Master and consisted of about a dozen and a half of the Ancients, two of whom were Wardens.

By the summer of 1562, and within five years of incorporation, the shape of the Company was clear. At its head were the Master, the Upper Warden and the Under Warden, assisted in the business of government by a group of experienced but elderly men. Immediately below them were the Senior and Junior Renter Wardens who were not members of the Court but whose work brought them into close touch with the Wardens; the experience of being a Renter must have been invaluable. The Renters were senior members of the Livery, which at this time consisted of at least six (not counting the Assistants who would rank as Liverymen for civic purposes) and which was added to at irregular intervals. Below the Livery came the Yeomanry which was fed by the admission, as freemen, of apprentices, of the sons of freemen, of (less often) those who were translated from other companies or who bought their way in. Parallel with the Yeomanry, but having no access to the normal ladder of promotion, were the Brothers. At the very bottom came the apprentices. Cutting clean across these gild categories were the distinctions between the crafts or trades followed by the members of the Company; and cutting across the largest category, the Yeomanry, was the distinction between the young master—the employer of labour who aspired to (or at least was eligible for) the highest rank in the Company—and the journeyman. It is worth remembering that printing and bookbinding bred more journeymen than did bookselling.

BY-LAWS BEFORE 1557

One of the powers given to the Stationers in their Charter was that of making ordinances for their governance. The ancient fellowship must have had a body of rules, nearly all traces of which have now disappeared; after the incorporation these were thought to be in need of 'mending' and, after considerable debate and certain law charges (which were borne by William Seres and Richard Tottell), new ordinances were approved by the Lord Treasurer and the two Chief Justices in 1562. These were written into what was known as the Red Book and were added to from time to time; though the Red Book disappeared, probably during the confusion caused by the Civil War, it is possible to piece together, from references to their being invoked, some plan of the ground the ordinances covered. To what extent the 1562 rules applied before that date would be difficult to decide, but it will be worth while trying to discover, first of all, if there were within the Company any interests which might have power enough to influence the redrafting of the ordinances.

Of the three sections of the book trade[1] which together made up the Company in the middle of the sixteenth century the oldest comprised the bookbinders; their numbers had increased since the introduction of printing but, while their work was normally completed by the binding of a single volume—as it had been a hundred years before—the operations of all printers and of some booksellers were wholesale. Bookbinders could compete with booksellers for the retail trade as long as they could buy at the same rate; when even the middle-sized bookseller put his money into having a small book printed and then stocked his shop by exchanges with other booksellers and printers, at rates between the prime cost and the wholesale price, the bookbinder, whose money had to go into the materials required for his craft, was left behind; he worked at home and could have an apprentice (unless he were a Brother), but his position in the trade and in the Company was that of a superior journeyman.

The next oldest section was composed of the booksellers, the retail side of whose business went back to the Middle Ages. But with the exchange method of stocking a shop, and still more with the development of selling by wholesale throughout England the products of London and continental presses, the man with a little capital had been able to increase it in ways impossible in the days of the hand-written book; and the bookseller with rather more capital—who was sometimes free of a company like the Drapers or the Haberdashers,

[1] Since the specialization to which I referred in Chapter I (p. 24 above) was by no means complete, there were men like Tottell and Day who were primarily printers but who owned copyrights, functioned as booksellers by wholesale and retail, and employed journeymen bookbinders. But if a man had a press I have called him a printer because, as Christopher Barker—a printer—pointed out in 1582 (Arber, i, p. 114), it was the *owners of presses* who had been losing ground to the copyright-owning booksellers since the reign of Edward VI; it was the owners of presses who were the most conscious of being a group with common interests.

39

a richer man with experience of wholesaling—was beginning, but only beginning, to exploit the conditions created by the press.

It was, however, the youngest of the groups among the Stationers—the printers—who dominated the new trade during the first century of its practice in England. Although the alien printers lost their early ascendency, they lost it not (as yet) to another branch of the trade but to English printers whom they had trained; and it was this group of men who were the prime movers in the negotiations which led to the Charter. Of the ninety-seven named in it, thirty-three were master printers; of the first fifty in the list no fewer than twenty were printers. The trades of the others are more difficult to be certain about; some, like the Master, were not engaged in the book trade; some were bookbinders; many were perhaps wage-earners in printing houses; the rest—and I can be certain of less than a score—were booksellers. The power in the Stationers' Company at the time of the incorporation lay with the printers.

The terms of the Charter confirm this. There were to be no printers in England who were not freemen of the Company, except those licensed by the Crown; the sole exceptions were likely to be the Queen's Printers. One of the main purposes of this concentration of printing in the capital was the protection of the right to copies, and the printers were the main investors in copies, whether these were protected by royal privilege or by the Stationers' private arrangement. During the first year after the grant of the Charter, only two members of the Company who were not printers brought books to be entered and, though the balance began to shift during the following years, the printers' use of the register still heavily outweighed its use by others.

DRAFT ORDINANCES OF 1559

In 1559 the Stationers tried to obtain even greater control of the book trade than they had achieved by the Charter. Certain articles were drawn up 'in forme of lawe', of which the headings have survived. The first objective was the confirmation of the grant from Philip and Mary, with the proviso that no one was to print unless he were free of the Company. The next was more ambitious; no one was 'to be a comon bokeseller in London or Westmynster' until he had given a bond to observe the rules which the Stationers made and which they were to be free to change as occasion arose. General warrants were to be given—to the Company to arrest offenders against its rules and to gaolers to accept the prisoners; and the Chancellor was to help them with greater authority if it were necessary. Finally, every piece of printing was to be authorized by the Company before work could be put to press.

The first of these objectives was achieved by Elizabeth's confirmation of the Charter, in the same terms as before, on November 10, 1559; the last, which was a private arrangement within the Company, was embodied in the ordinances as approved. The other clauses were too large to receive, as yet, official sanction, particularly since the Government issued in the same year a set of Injunctions condemning printers who 'for couetousnes cheifly regard not what they print' so long as they can make a profit, and outlining a complete licensing system for books; but, though the objectives were not all achieved, they show the ambitions of the ruling members of the Company whose attitude to the booksellers is particularly interesting. It is possible that the printers reached the peak of their power in about 1542, when we know that application was made for a charter, and that, though they were still powerful in 1557, they had lost some of their strongest champions (Thomas Berthelet died late in 1555 and Robert Toy early in 1556) and were beginning to sense a growing opposition from the booksellers. One of the results of compelling printers to be members of the Company would be the concentration of printing, as against other, interests within the ranks of the Stationers; a concentration of the bookselling or the bookbinding interests by a similar process would be bad tactics for the printers, even if the other companies to which booksellers or bookbinders might belong would agree to the necessary translations. But the right of the Stationers to lay down rules for tradesmen whatever company they belonged to would give the printers exactly what they wanted: control of the trade without an increase in the potential opposition within the Company; the printers would even allow the outsiders the benefit of their private copyright protection: one of the five booksellers who used the register in 1558–9 was John Wight, a Draper.

ORDINANCES OF 1562

The election of the Master and Wardens, a matter not mentioned in these abortive rules, was one of the keys to power within the Company, particularly if the Court of Assistants was composed of those who had once served as Warden. In the Charter, the Master, the Wardens and the *communitas* are to meet in a convenient place, yearly or more often or less often, to elect a Master and two Wardens. This can only mean that those who governed the Company were to be elected by the whole body of freemen. How this form of words found its way into the Charter cannot now be established; but it is certain that it represented neither the general practice of City companies[1] nor, from the earliest recorded evidence of their elections, the behaviour of the Stationers. There has been some debate about this important change in constitutional practice; the most convincing solution[2] is that the ordinances of 1562, in their 'mended' version, set the choice of all the officers of the Company firmly in the hands of the Court of Assistants. Since this brought the Stationers into line with other companies, it would attract attention only when there was an anti-Court party (as there was in the 1640's) which was looking for arguments against the oligarchs. If I am right in thinking that the printers were beginning, by the time they eventually achieved their Charter, to be aware of the growing economic power of the booksellers, it is easy to see this ordinance as an added protection for those who still held power in 1557; a majority party in a self-perpetuating body can, in theory, remain in power for ever.

The next ordinance—next, at least, in importance—dealt with the protection of the right in copies. 'We find proued and confessed', began the report of a royal commission in 1583,[3] 'that the nature of bokes and printing is such, as it is not meete, nor can be without their vndoeinges of all sides, that sondrie men shold print one boke. And, therefore, where her Matie graunteth not priuilege, they [the Stationers] are enforced to haue a kinde of preuileges among them selues by ordinances of the companie whereby euerie first printer of any lawefull booke, presenting it in the hall, hath the same as seuerall to him self as any man hath any boke by her Maties preuilege.' These are the words of intelligent outsiders explaining to other outsiders the principles governing a certain practice in the book trade. The two points of most interest are the equating once again of the Company's

---

[1] George Unwin, *The Gilds and Companies of London*, 1908, p. 217.

[2] Graham Pollard's in *The Library*, 4th ser., xviii, 1938, p. 247, an article which I found invaluable in writing this chapter. Appendix III gives the composition of the Court of Assistants, 1556–76, from such evidence as is available.

[3] State Papers Domestic Elizabeth, vol. 161, no. 1 (c); probably July 18th.

copyright protection with that given by royal privilege, and the necessity of presenting books for registration at the Hall.[1] The successful operation of the first assumption depended on the concentration of printing in London and the supervision of the trade throughout the kingdom by the Stationers; the Charter provided the necessary powers. The insistence on registration is more difficult to understand, since it was an individual's right which was to be protected; and it might be thought that if he were ready to risk infringement of his copyright it was none of the Company's business forcibly to protect him. But it is quite clear, from the fines imposed, that it was just as much an offence not to obtain the official licence of the Company and not to enter the record of it as it was to print another man's copy. One of the explanations is that registration cost a man a few pence and brought in revenue to the Company; another is that, under the terms of the Charter and still more by the Injunctions of 1559, the officials of the Stationers might be held responsible for the publication of books which smacked of sedition or heresy. But there was, above all, the determination of the ruling caste in the Company to consolidate its powers—whenever possible by codification; if others besides printers were going to invest in copies, control of such claims, through the licences granted by the Wardens, was essential.

Licence is a word whose use by the officials (and more particularly by the Clerk) of the Stationers' Company in the sixteenth century has produced many thousands of words of analysis in the twentieth.[2] I must confine myself to five observations which bear on an ordinance of which no copy exists. The first is that a new book had to be licensed —or 'allowed' or 'tolerated'—by at least one of the Wardens, preferably in writing, before the Clerk would make the entry in the register. The second is that the Company's fee for this complete process was at first 1d for every three sheets of the book when printed, with a minimum of 4d,[3] but that after March 26, 1582, the fee was standardized at 6d for a book and 4d for a pamphlet or a ballad. The third is that, theoretically, this Company approval was quite independent of any ecclesiastical or civil authorization which a royal

[1] In the first year of Elizabeth's reign Richard Tottell even brought his patent for law books, which he had obtained from her predecessor, to be confirmed and allowed by the Company; and he paid a fine of 4d for having his claim recorded.

[2] For a full discussion, see W. W. Greg, *Some Aspects and Problems of London Publishing between 1550 and 1650*, Oxford, 1956, particularly Chapter III.

[3] See William A. Jackson, 'Variant Entry Fees of the Stationers' Company' in *Papers of the Bibliographical Society of America*, vol. 51, 2nd quarter, 1957.

injunction or an Act of Parliament might require; except that, in order to protect themselves, the Wardens often insisted that the entry could be allowed only if such outside authority were obtained. The fourth is that from 1591 Richard Watkins began to act as a fairly regular licenser in place of the Wardens whoever they might be. The fifth is that at least a third of the books known to have been printed were not entered in the register and that only a very small proportion of these omissions was punished. No satisfactory explanation for this has been put forward[1]. It is acknowledged that books covered by royal patents were exempt and that Masters and Wardens economized, when in office, by not entering their own publications; but why did so many others dispense with the protection offered and how did they so often get away without fines? It is worth remembering that a Stationer would assess the value to himself of the Company's power to enforce its own rules (and its inability or unwillingness to enforce the rule about entering books did not bode well for its power to protect A from having his book, even if duly entered, printed by B, or to compel the payment of compensation by B to A should the worst happen) and weigh this against the general understanding in the trade that, on the whole, it did not pay to steal another Stationer's copy (though it was sporting to print the copy of a monopolist, just as today some people consider it sporting to swindle the Treasury or a nationalized undertaking). The more a man trusted his fellows the less he felt the need of protection from the Company and the more likely the officers of the Company were to avoid trouble and turn blind eyes on failure to use the register. Finally, there was a large class of books which were unlikely to be pirated.

The buying and selling of copies became a frequent practice among Stationers, certainly from 1562. As a result of the weakening of the printers' hold on the trade there was, even earlier, the recognition of two different rights in a book arising from the two main profits to be made from its exploitation; the first was the right to print it and the second was the right to earn what we call a publisher's profit from it. The selling of a copy by a printer to a bookseller on condition that the former might continue to have the printing of it, and the careful registering of this arrangement, on payment of the normal fee, became quite common in the course of Elizabeth's reign; it was probably not

[1] But see C. J. Sisson, 'The Laws of Elizabethan Copyright: the Stationers' View,' *The Library*, 5th ser., xv, 1960.

provided for in the ordinances but it does underline the importance to the printing caste of a rule designed for the protection of all members of the Company, and it does illustrate the economic swing away from the printers and towards the booksellers.

There is no evidence that any of the ordinances sought to lay down standards for the products of the printing houses, though before the end of the century there were complaints of the poor quality of paper and the shoddy appearance of the type-faces; the explanation of the omission may be that printing was not a medieval craft. But there were orders about the stitching and binding of books, which for a few years were strictly enforced; and binding was a craft in the Middle Ages. Books above a certain size could not be bound in sheep's leather and prayer books were not be be bound in parchment or thin wooden boards. There were also orders, both now and in 1586, about the stitching of books, which may have been supported by the printers since the bookbinders were losing business to the booksellers. Twenty-five years later, in December 1587, the Court passed a set of orders to control, in the interests of journeymen, the quantity rather than the quality of printing; books were not to be reprinted from standing type and impressions were not normally to be larger than 1,500.

The remaining rules, covering the main features of gild life, must have been such as would be found in any other company and are found in the Stationers' ordinances of 1678: the attendance, properly clad, in the Hall at the four Quarter Day meetings; obedience to the Master and Wardens and refraining from brawling and from the use of bad language; the regular payment of the quarterly dues and the liability of the officers for the election dinner. In addition, there were the rules of the City—about the binding of and caring for apprentices and the making free of those who are eligible, the employment of aliens and foreigners, attendance on the Lord Mayor, closing of shops on Sundays and Saints' Days—which the Master and Wardens of the Stationers had to see that their freemen kept.

The full tale of the Company's own ordinances was read over to the assembled commonalty at the Quarter Day meetings. These regular gatherings of all the members of a fellowship—these Common Halls—which began with business and finished with a dinner, had been important occasions when a gild was small and the majority of its members engaged in the same trade or craft; they fostered among the freemen the brotherly feeling of belonging to a *communitas* and they provided opportunities both for the explanation of craft policy and for the expression of craft complaints. It is likely that, in the fifteenth century and even for some years while the novelty of incorporation lasted, the Stationers felt the urge to congregate, as Stationers, every three months; the modern Convention demonstrates that the urge survives in many walks of life, and on several occasions in their history the Stationers found the meetings useful for the airing of grievances. But during the reign of Elizabeth I, increasing numbers, a growing sophistication and the tendency of the Ancients to become oligarchs, drained the original value of such frequent meetings and left little but the formality. The Stationers may, as members of a young company engaged for the most part in one or other section of a single trade, have retained a feeling of community longer than others, but some of them, early on, had to be punished for not attending. One cannot but sympathize with Edward Bollifant who was fined 6d for going away before he had listened to the reading of the ordinances, for they were almost certainly composed in pseudo-legal language and, with the passage of time, they did not grow fewer. It is impossible to trace the addition of each new clause, but we do know that in about 1578 there came into operation an ordinance to limit the number of apprentices; and the Court ruled on January 19, 1598, that the orders about the control of book prices and against the printing of books for those who were not freemen of the Company should be entered in the Red Book and treated like the other ordinances on Quarter Days.

CHAPTER III

THE COMPANY IN THE REIGN OF
ELIZABETH I

TWELVE MONTHS IN THE LIFE OF THE COMPANY

BY the fourth year of the Queen's reign the Stationers had set their house in order, literally and metaphorically. They had finished turning Peter's College into a proper focus for the life of the Company; they had obtained from the new sovereign a confirmation of their Charter; they had been accepted as one of the companies privileged by the City to have a Livery; they had bought themselves a grant of arms; they had reshaped the rules by which they governed themselves and had received official approval of them. Since their successors preserved many of the records which were begun anew at this time, it is possible to trace a large part of the history of the Company year by year. Moreover, from 1576 the Clerk began grouping together the decisions of the Court, instead of putting them under their appropriate headings here and there in the register; it therefore becomes easier, especially as the notes of debates grow fuller, to understand some of the reasons for the actions taken and even to perceive the working out of policy. Such embryonic minutes must also have made things easier both for the Clerk and for the Assistants.

I have set out in the Calendar on pages 48–50 all the information which the records of the Company (and other sources) reveal of its day-to-day activities during a single gild year in the middle of Elizabeth's reign, and I have then commented on this information. Since the first year of Court minutes produced only four entries, which were contained in little more than a single page, I have chosen the following year, 1577–8, when the minutes are both full and interesting.

CALENDAR OF THE GILD YEAR 1577–8

1577

June	29	Sat.	St Peter's Day. *Election*
	30	Sun.	Election Feast

Master: William Seres
Upper Warden: William Norton
Under Warden: Richard Watkins

July	1	Mon.	Admission of Liveryman under old Master and Wardens
	2	Tues.	*Court*
	5	Fri.	1 apprentice
	8	Mon.	2 apprentices; copies entered
	9	Tues.	Settlement of old Wardens' accounts
	21	Sun.	Copies entered with *Court* decision
	26	Thur.	Copy entered, 'neuer printed' added later
	30	Tues.	2 apprentices; copies entered
	31	Wed.	Copy entered
Aug.	2	Fri.	Copy entered.
	4	Sun.	1 apprentice; 1 Brother; copy entered
	6	Tues.	Copy entered
	23	Fri.	Copy entered
	26	Mon.	Copy entered [New grant to John and Richard Day]
	31	Sat.	Copy entered
	?		['The griefes of the printers. . . .']
Sept.	2	Mon.	4 apprentices; fine levied for keeping one of them unpresented
	17	Tues.	*Court*
	30	Mon.	[*Quarter Day*] 3 apprentices; copies entered, 1 'not printed'
Oct.	3	Thur.	Copy entered
	6	Sun.	3 fined for not appearing on Quarter Day
	7	Mon.	Copy entered, 'redeliuered to thautor' added later
	8	Tues.	1 apprentice
	14	Mon.	1 apprentice; 2 freemen; copies entered
	21	Mon.	*Court*, bookbinders present
	29	Tues.	[Dinner on Lord Mayor's oath day]
Nov.	4	Mon.	*Court*; 1 freeman
	11	Mon.	Copies entered
	15	Fri.	Copy entered
	18	Mon.	Copies entered
	20	Wed.	Copies entered
	25	Mon.	1 apprentice; copies entered
Dec.	1	Sun.	Copy entered
	2	Mon.	Copy entered
	7	Sat.	Copy entered
	9	Mon.	1 apprentice; 1 freeman

Dec. 10 Tues. Copies entered
13 Fri. Copy entered
20 Fri. Copy entered
30 Mon. [*Quarter Day*]

1578
Jan. 7 Tues. Copy entered
8 Wed. 1 apprentice
9 Thur. 1 apprentice
13 Mon. 1 freeman *per patrimonium*
16 Thur. Copies entered
20 Mon. 3 freemen
21 Tues. 1 apprentice; Lord Treasurer's letter
27 Mon. *Court*
30 Thur. Copies entered

Feb. 4 Tues. Order of Court of Aldermen
5 Wed. Copy entered
7 Fri. Copy entered
14 Fri. Copy entered; order taken at Merchant Tailors' Hall
17 Mon. *Court*; 2 apprentices; copy entered; fine for keeping 2 apprentices unpresented
20 Thur. Copies entered
22 Sat. Copies entered

Mar. 3 Mon. 5 apprentices; 3 freemen and 1 Brother; copies entered
4 Tues. Copy entered
8 Sat. 1 freeman
10 Mon. 1 Brother; copies entered
17 Mon. *Court*
25 Tues. [*Quarter Day*; Richard Greene and Ralph Newbery elected Renters] 1 apprentice; Timothy Rider appointed Beadle
27 Thur. Copy entered
28 Fri. Copy entered

Apr. 7 Mon. 1 apprentice
9 Wed. Copies entered
14 Mon. Copy entered
16 Wed. Copies entered
21 Mon. 1 apprentice
26 Sat. Copies entered

May 6 Tues. Renters' accounts delivered to Wardens by Henry Conway and Richard Greene
13 Tues. Copy entered
May 23 Fri. Copy entered
28 Wed. Copies entered, 1 'not printed'

D

1578

June	2	Mon.	Copies entered
	4	Wed.	5 freemen, including Christopher Barker translated from the Drapers
	[5	Thur.	Petition of poor printers to Privy Council]
	16	Mon.	4 apprentices, including 1 turned over
	17	Tues.	Copy entered
	18	Wed.	*Court*
	23	Mon.	Copy entered
	25	Wed.	2 freemen; C. Barker elected to Livery; copy entered
	26	Thur.	2 apprentices; copy entered
	28	Sat.	*Election Day;* copy entered
	29	Sun.	St Peter's Day
	30	Mon.	5 elected to Livery; 1 Assistant fined for not attending on Saturday
July	1	Tues.	Copies entered
	6	Sun.	Election Feast
	8	Tues.	Settlement of Wardens' accounts

The Election Feast, attended by the whole Company, marked the opening of the gild year and was always held on the Sunday after St Peter's Day, June 29th; and the formal election, by the Court of Assistants, of the Master and Wardens for the coming year always took place the day before. In 1577 the election fell on the Saint's Day, and William Seres (number 21 in the Charter) was chosen Master for the fifth time and for the third successive year. He was a printer in a big way of business, the profitable basis of which was the privilege, first granted to him by Edward VI and regranted to him and his son by Elizabeth, of printing service books; it was perhaps through him that the Company bought Peter's College where he had his presses until the accession of Mary. His was one of the biggest monopolies (those of the Queen's Printers and of John Day being the others) which were repeatedly challenged by the poorer members of the Company during the next few years. William Norton (number 79 in the Charter) was chosen Upper Warden for the second time; he had been Under Warden for the years 1569–71 and Renter Warden in 1563–5, having been one of the first six Liverymen elected in 1560; when he became Master in 1581 he was the first recognized bookseller to hold that office. Richard Watkins, the Under Warden, became a Stationer just too late to have his name in the Charter list; he was an ambitious printer, married Katherine Jugge the daughter of the Queen's Printer and, having acquired a half share in the patent for almanacks in 1571, worked his way into shares in the Seres and Day privileges well before the end of the century. I have already mentioned his being the official Company licenser. He had been elected to the Livery in 1570 and had served the usual two years as Renter Warden.

THE COMPANY'S SERVANTS

Though these three were elected on the last Saturday in June they did not begin their year of office until the first Tuesday in July (the admission to the Livery on the Monday having been conducted by the retiring officers). This first record of their activities introduces three part-time employees of the Company: the Cook, the Butler and the Lord Mayor's Officer. It was agreed, on July 2nd, that the first should be paid 26s 8d a year for dressing the four Quarter Day dinners and that the second should have 13s 4d for his presence on the same occasions. The third was a Carver, also at 13s 4d a year, but his office may have been a formal survival from the past when it was necessary for the City to keep an eye on the activities of the gilds. The Company also retained an Armourer, first at 13s 4d and, when the Spanish danger grew greater, at 20s per annum. A dozen years later the Court ruled that the Cook should be responsible for all dinners held at the Hall, even when it had been hired for a wedding or for the Wardmote Inquest. In the following century, Plasterers, Bricklayers and Carpenters were officially appointed to the Company and from the earliest records there is evidence of retaining fees paid to the official Counsel, and sometimes Counsels, to the Company.

There were three other paid servants: the Clerk, the Beadle and the Porter. It is probable that from the first the Clerk was, as he is now, a man with legal training who worked part-time. There is no record of a name until Michaelmas 1571 when George Wapull was taken on at a salary of £2 a year, with the fees he earned at the binding of apprentices, the taking up of freedoms, the calls to the Livery and the entering of copies; the only early clue to the value of these services is a note of 1619 that the Clerk be paid 16d for each pair of apprenticeship indentures. Wapull, however, decided to emigrate to America and was voted 10s towards his expenses. On May 30, 1575, Richard Collins, a freeman of the Goldsmiths' Company, was sworn in as

Clerk and was translated to the Stationers' in October. During his first months of office a new book of records—Register B—was prepared, to continue from where Wapull's book (now missing) left off. On folio 2 of the new register Collins made notes of his appointment and of the items he was to enter; in addition to the four on which he earned fees, there were fines and 'Decrees and ordonnances'—that is, the Court minutes. He then left a gap of fourteen leaves and began the enrolment of apprentices in July 1576 on folio 17; he intended, when he found time, to fill in the entries from the date when he started work, fair copied from Wapull's book, if it still existed, or from his own rough book. Unfortunately he never did this, and the detailed records are missing not only for Wapull's period of office but for the next thirteen months. In 1590 Collins was called to the Livery and elected an Assistant. His salary was augmented during the years of trouble by fees for the extra work he had to do and by a house in the Hall, reckoned as worth £2 a year. In 1599 his salary was increased by £2 and, in 1602, to £10 from the time he moved out of his free quarters. He died in 1613.

The Beadle was the first of the Company's full-time servants and has remained to this day the link between Stationers' Hall and the Stationers. John Fayreberne was Beadle at the time of incorporation, with a basic annual salary of £2, a rent allowance (from 1571) of £2 and fees due on the same occasions as the Clerk's. Until the appointment of Wapull, Fayreberne wrote up Register A each year, and when building work was going on at the Hall he earned overtime for general supervision. Timothy Rider was appointed as his successor from Lady Day 1578 and two years later the salary was raised to £6. The hazards of the office warranted this for in the spring of 1585 he was arrested while marching William Wright, one of the keenest anti-monopolists, to the Counter. In June 1587 Rider was pensioned off but allowed to go on living at the Hall; John Wolf took his place and managed to have his salary raised to £10 and to obtain a contract for supplying fuel for the Hall. On his resignation Toby Cooke was elected and almost immediately assigned, with the Court's approval, the duties of the Beadle to John Hardy (free five years before); Cooke kept the salary while Hardy lived on the perquisites for the three months of the arrangement. Hardy then succeeded to the full office. The Beadles always found some time to trade on their own account.

There are very few references to the Porter; there cannot have been much to carry except messages, and the job was almost certainly part-time. He had some work on the occasions of the dinners and he helped the Beadle in police duties.

ROUTINE

Nowadays, apprentices are bound, and men admitted to the freedom, only in the presence of the Court. It is obvious from the Calendar that this was considered unnecessary in 1577; but, since the occasions were supposed to be important in the lives of the boys beginning their training and of the young men entering into full membership of the Company, it is probable that the Master and Wardens were present in their gowns and chains of office. Whether they attended by appointment or at certain times every day, I do not know; but it is clear that the officers of the Company were expected to spend a great deal of time at the Hall. It is possible, also, that the Court had not attained the power which it later achieved and that, in Elizabeth's reign, the officers acted much more on their own; the absence of formal minutes before 1576 suggests this. Moreover, as late as January 19, 1590, two copies were entered to John Wolf 'in court— beinge present the master and Wardens'; Assistants were still, after all, assistants.

The admission of Brothers, though it may have lacked the emotional emphasis, was just as much part of the officers' duty. Three of them, servants to printers, were admitted in the course of the year 1577–8. On March 3rd Edward Chambers was presented and the fee was 5s; he was perhaps a Scotsman and therefore a foreigner in the eyes of the City. The other two were, from their names, aliens; their fees were 10s each, which were to be stopped out of their wages; one of them left the country within a week—and not unexpectedly, according to a note in the register. The apprentices provide further links with the Brothers; one of those enrolled on March 3rd was to serve the first six years of his time with Philip Cutier, a bookbinder but a Brother, and the last four with his legal master, James Gonneld. The binding on April 21st was of the same nature.

The entering of copies by the Clerk in the register could be done only with written authority. How much time a Warden spent examining the document which was brought him to license and whether he made any search of the records so that a copy should not be entered to B if it had already been allowed to A, it is impossible to say; but here was, potentially at least, another time-absorbing occupation. It would be good to know what the Warden put his signature to; it ought to have been the original manuscript, for only after approval should it be sent to press. That it sometimes was is suggested by the marginal note against the entry for October 7th. The entry for July 21st reads as if a newly completed law book was still 'to be printed', and it neatly differentiates between 'the said booke and thim-printinge thereof'—between the two rights which I discussed at the end of the last chapter; moreover, the licence was granted under conditions to three Stationers with successive life interests, a decision of the Court which the Clerk recorded not in the minute book but, according to the old practice, in the register of copies. These examples are, most likely, exceptions to the normal routine by which sets of printed sheets—or even the preliminary pages alone—were brought to the Hall for allowance.[1]

It is probable that the Assistants met on more occasions than on those for which formal Court minutes have survived, even though the pattern of regular monthly meetings had not yet become set. The fine on Gabriel Cawood for keeping an apprentice without presenting him at the Hall (September 2nd) may have been levied on the responsibility of the Master and Wardens and they clearly authorized, on November 11th, the licensing to James Robotham, who was not a Stationer, of a book licensed to John Arnold, who was; but the decision about the employment of John Moore was the Court's and was entered in the minutes for November 4th, the day he took up his freedom; he was to work for his late master, Thomas Dawson, for five years from the Feast of the Annunciation (July 2nd), at £3 per annum, with meat, drink, lodging and washing; and he was to provide his own clothes.

The settlement of such disputes between master and man was one of the most useful of the Court's functions; it often acted as a court of first instance, in attempts to prevent Stationers from taking their cases to the Queen's or the Lord Mayor's courts. There is no means of telling how often the appeals of individual journeymen, who felt

---

[1] On August 20, 1611, the Clerk entered for Francis Burton *Scala Coeli*, nineteen sermons concerning prayer, by Nathaniel Carmichael, 'under thandes of' Gabriel Powell (chaplain to the Bishop of London) and the Wardens. The manuscript title-page (S.P. Dom. Jac. I, vol. 48, no. 15), signed by Richard Field and Humphrey Lownes (Wardens 1611–12) is dated September 7, 1609, and carries this note: 'Hic tractatus Orthodoxus est et tuto Imprimi potest. Ita censeo. Gabriel Pouelus.'

themselves unfairly treated by their masters, were ignored by the Assistants; but a sprinkling of such cases reached the records and the rivalry between the printers and the booksellers may have been responsible for the hearings given to workmen printers' grievances. Disputes between master and master (and between man and wife) also came before the Court. On September 17th orders were made for the payment of a debt and for the satisfaction of a claim made against the Under Warden by Dunstan Whapland; Watkins was to pay him 30s worth of books or 26s 8d in cash. The orders of February 17th and March 17th are about another debt and the restoration of linen, borrowed or stolen. The minute of June 18th is the settlement of a copyright dispute. The *Little Catechism* was part of the privilege of John Day; Richard Jones had established his right to the Welsh version through license by the Wardens. The compromise to which Richard Day, on behalf of his father, and Jones put their names in the minutes was that Jones should have the edition in Welsh as his copy in all respects except that his name should appear on the title-page as the assign of John Day. It would have been well for the Company if it could have settled so amicably all the disputes in which Day was involved.

A TRADE COMPLAINT

On October 21st the Master, Wardens and Assistants were joined by those members of the Livery who were not on the Court to hear complaints put forward by the bookbinders. After some debate, agreement was reached on three points: firstly, that binders who were English and freemen of the City should have work before aliens and foreigners, provided their workmanship were good in quality and reasonable in price; secondly, that the binders should deliver the bound books on the day contracted or not more than three days later, unless further respite were agreed on; and thirdly, that any infringer of these rules should be punished, even to the extent of imprisonment, at the discretion of the Master and Wardens. The printers—that is, the master printers—had solved this kind of problem during the second quarter of the century; but the poor binders, who had been depressed almost to the level of journeymen by the copyright-owning printers and booksellers, were suffering—as the journeymen printers were going to suffer at the beginning of the following century—from competition with aliens, who probably lived in the suburbs and undercut the City-dwelling freemen.

These rules brought no relief, because the keeping of them was against the interests of that party to them which carried more weight in the Company.¹ Furthermore, the binders were experiencing competition from within the City itself. On February 4th the Court of Aldermen, on the strength of a letter from the Lord Treasurer, ordered that no action without the permission of that Court should be brought in the name of the Chamberlain against a Stationer for putting work out to strangers or foreigners in the liberties of the City. Burghley had written to request the Lord Mayor to take into his own court a case which certain bookbinders had begun in the Queen's Bench against a freeman of the Fishmongers' Company, and to see that Stationers were at liberty to have their work done by skilled craftsmen in spite of any City order to the contrary. The governing body of the Company had no incentive to guard the interests of bookbinders, and its members had sufficient influence with the Queen's chief minister to persuade him to intervene in a case brought by members of their own Company against a Fishmonger.

WARDENS' ACCOUNTS

Before I come to the important meeting of the Court on January 27th, I want to rough in the financial background to this year's activities. The Wardens derived the income for running the Company from the following sources in the following amounts:

	£	s	d
By balance from previous Wardens' account	42	12	10
cash from Renter Wardens	12	5	6
licensing of copies	2	19	2
presenting of apprentices*	2	8	0
admission of freemen and Brothers	3	17	4
calling of six of the Yeomanry to the Livery	6	0	0
fines for breaking ordinances		1	0†
letting of the Hall for weddings, etc	1	5	0
repayment of loans	1	6	8
assessment for equipping and training 15 soldiers	28	6	0
	£101	1	6

* Between January 9th and 21st the fee was raised from 6d to 2s 6d.

† Though fines totalling 4s 9d were imposed, only 1s was collected—a not infrequent result in this and other companies. ¹ See below, p. 64.

The expenses which the Wardens incurred this year were:

	£	s	d
To wages		10	0
retaining fees, Cook, etc.	4	6	8
repairs to property		5	3
contribution towards Election Feast	5	0	0
loans		18	0
equipping soldiers	31	11	9
taxes		5	0
legal expenses	1	11	0
balance carried forward	56	13	10
	£101	1	6

All the items on the receipts side are self-explanatory, but the balance received from the Renters is the sole evidence of another series of accounts; the income came almost entirely from rents and from the fourpences which every member of the Company was supposed to pay quarterly, and the expenditure normally went on the wages of the Company's servants and on items like fuel for the Hall. There was, during the second half of the sixteenth century, a credit balance on this account which was only once less than £7 10s and was several times over £25.[1]

The expenditure by the Wardens in the same period varied from under £10 to over £130 and requires further explanation than the bare entries give. The payment of the wages was irregular not only in time but in origin. Rider, the new Beadle, began his duties at Lady Day 1578 and received his first quarter's remuneration from the Wardens; but thereafter he was paid by the Renters. Six years later he repaid to the Renters part of a loan which he had had from the Wardens. The retaining fees—for the Counsel and for the services debated on July 2nd—were always paid by the Wardens. The repairs to the property was a negligible amount this year—mending the wainscot and a small piece of paving; but in 1569–70 over £50 and in 1571–2 nearly £90 were spent on a new staircase and on a new kitchen and buttery; detailed accounts survive for the materials used and the wages paid on these improvements.

The contribution to the annual feast was a standing charge against

[1] For a detailed analysis, see 'The Accounts of the Wardens of the Stationers' Company [1557–96]', *Studies in Bibliography*, Charlottesville, ix, 1957.

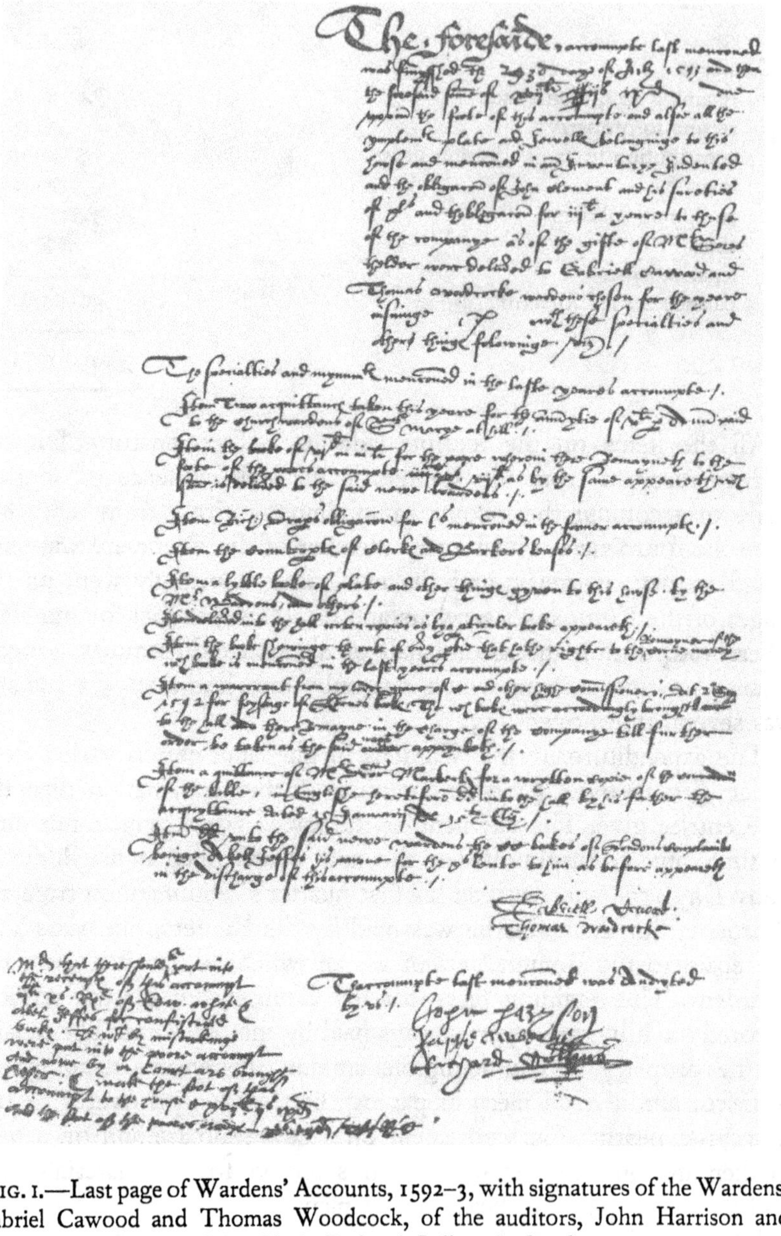

FIG. I.—Last page of Wardens' Accounts, 1592–3, with signatures of the Wardens, Gabriel Cawood and Thomas Woodcock, of the auditors, John Harrison and Ralph Newbery, and of the Clerk, Richard Collins (*reduced*).

the Company's funds and was limited to £5 as a result of one of the earliest surviving formal resolutions of the Court, probably passed and certainly entered[1] just before the accounts for 1560–1 were audited. Up to this date the whole cost of the dinner on the Sunday after St Peter's Day had come out of the 'stock' of the house; thereafter, the Company provided £5, there was a whip round among the Assistants and the Liverymen, and the balance had to be borne by the Master and Wardens for the year then ending. The growing numbers of the Company made the resolution not only a wise but a generous one; the wisdom was extended by its crystallization in the ordinances of 1562.

In March 1578 the Lord Mayor issued a precept for the provision by the companies of a certain number of men to receive training in the shooting of arquebuses. These calls on such easily accessible taxation units—not the least advantage of such a levy was the cheapness of administration—were frequently made by the City and usually on behalf of the sovereign. They might be for the provision of corn or salt against shortage in London; they might be for the equipment of ships or of land forces against the fear of invasion; on one occasion Yarmouth harbour was to be repaired and on another, aid was to be sent to Geneva. The Stationers were rated on a level with the Dyers, the Tallow-chandlers, the Saddlers and the Cordwainers and at a sixth of the assessments on the Goldsmiths and the Drapers. In other years the Stationers were compelled to contribute, along with the rest of the companies, to paving at the east end of St Paul's, to entertaining the Queen and Count Casimir of the Palatinate, to providing cresset lights; and they bought tickets in a lottery and invested money in the privateering expedition organized in 1591 by Howard and Ralegh.

The last item on the receipts side shows nearly £30 subscribed for such a particular purpose; it was not enough, as the entry on the debit side proves; but it did mean that only £3 odd had to come out of the common stock for the training of soldiers. These special subscriptions were fairly frequent and their inclusion in the accounts (along with the expenditure for which they were intended, on the other side and sometimes in the year following) gives the graph of balances carried forward each year by the Wardens (page 61) a somewhat jagged appearance. But the recessions show very clearly how dependent the Company was on special measures to meet expenditure on building

---

[1] Register A, f. 66b, reproduced on p. 60.

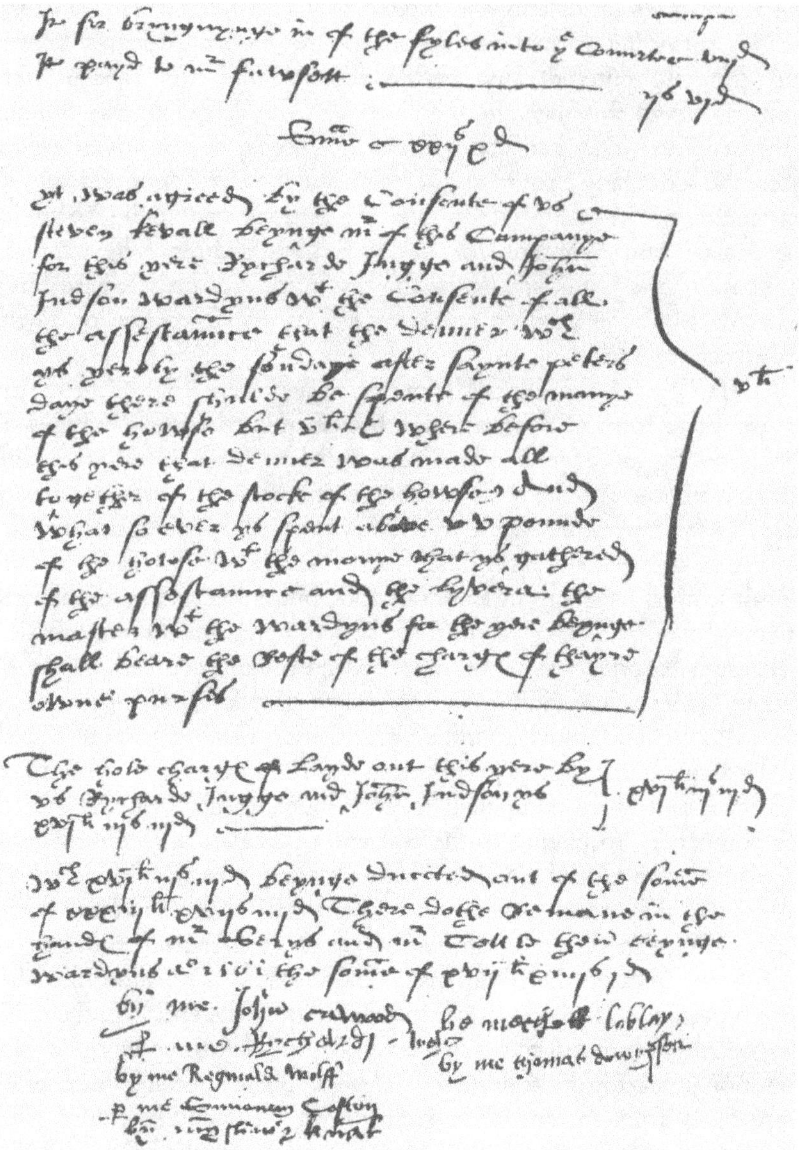

FIG. 11.—Resolution of the Master, Wardens and Assistants, 1560–1, with the signatures of John Cawood, Richard Waye, Reyner Wolfe, Simon Coston, Stephen Kevall, Michael Lobley and Thomas Duxwell (reduced).

(as in 1569, 1572 and 1592) and on the Star Chamber Decree of 1586.

In most years there was some payment by way of Poor Relief. At the Quarter Day meeting on July 2, 1565[1], the Company resolved that £2 a year out of the common stock might be spent in this way and that unspent balances might be carried forward. In a year of

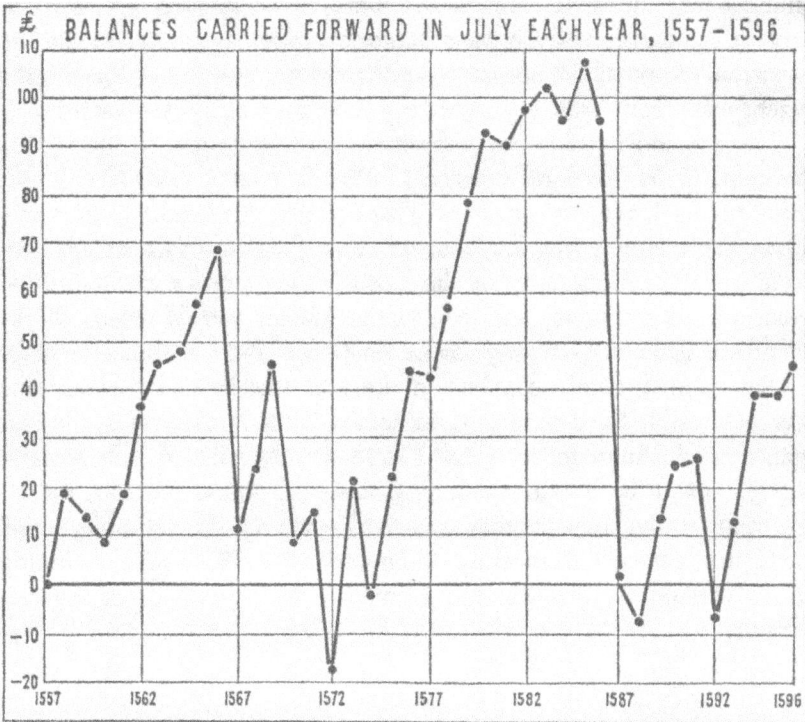

FIG. III.

trouble like 1582–3, nearly £5 was distributed by the Wardens and a further but untraceable sum by the Renters. It appears, from various Court resolutions, that the Wardens were responsible for relieving immediate distress by payments *ad hoc* and that the Renters had to find the money for pensions. From 1584–5 the latter were able to rely on a trickle of royalties from permissions to print copies over which the Company exercised control.[2] Most London gilds, after a life of a century and a half, would have attracted bequests under the wills of their wealthier members; but Stationers did not amass even

[1] Liber A, f. 8.   See below, p. 73.

small fortunes and there is no evidence of any income-bearing legacy from the days before the Charter; bequests went towards the new Hall for which Henry Smith left £6 13s 4d in 1550, or towards its maintenance for which the widow of Robert Toy left £4 in 1565. It was not until Stephen Kevall made his will in 1570 that the poor of the Company were remembered, by the legacy of property in Billingsgate, the rents from which were to be divided between the poor of the parish and the poor Stationers. Charity, therefore, had to be provided out of the common stock; money was found for about a dozen years from 1580 to help two young men at the Universities.

The last, and in some ways the most revealing, item in the 1577–8 payments is that for legal expenses. In the first forty years after incorporation the Company paid out £240 under this heading, over and above the retaining fees for Counsel. The £1 11s in this account was made up of 1s for a copy of the Lord Mayor's order about putting work out to strangers, and 10s to the Master and Wardens of the Merchant Tailors' Company for buying off Gilbert Lyllie, a member of that company and described in the accounts as an informer, who was responsible for promoting, on behalf of the bookbinders, the case against the Fishmonger to which I have already referred. The remaining £1 was a fee to the standing Counsel, Thomas Norton, for his advice in settling some trouble with the Yeomanry. This trouble, which the Court debated at its meeting on January 27, 1578, was the beginning of a great upheaval within the Company which requires a separate chapter.

CHAPTER IV

THE COMPANY AND THE MONOPOLISTS

THE MONOPOLISTS IN BOOKS

A MONOPOLIST in the book trade was the recipient from the sovereign of the right to print, or to get printed, not a single book but a whole class of books. I have already mentioned the patents granted to William Seres and his son (for service books, psalters and catechisms); to John and Richard Day (for the psalms in meter and the ABC with the little catechism); and to Richard Watkins (for almanacks) which he held jointly with James Roberts. There were also the Queen's Printers' patents, the more important of which included Bibles and testaments as well as proclamations, and the less important of which comprised certain books in Greek and Latin;[1] and patents for books of common law, for Latin books used in schools, and for books of music. Nearly all the patentees were printers and a large number of the books in their monopolies were cheap, popular and easily pirated. The monopolists were also well represented on the Court, and the official Company policy, for the first twenty years after incorporation, was to defend the privileges with every available power.

GRIEVANCES

Since there was strong and widespread feeling against all monopolies, it is not surprising that the opposition to the monopolists in the book trade was made up of different elements whose interests were by no means identical; and that the issues were often confused. There were the unprivileged master printers who were denied the regular work on cheap and easy books and who may on occasions have been genuinely short of employment. There were the ambitious booksellers who were jealous of the profits made by certain wealthy printers and

---

[1] 'The Queen's [or King's] Printer', in the singular, refers to the holder of the Office which went with the more important group of printing rights.

who supported the trade printers not only by open opposition but by secret handling of pirated printings. There were anti-monopolists in other companies who were ready to make common cause with Stationers against the general principle of monopolies. There were, fourthly, the journeymen printers who petitioned against the big masters not because they were monopolists but because their employment policy threatened the livelihood of their paid servants. There were, lastly, the bookbinders who were not harmed by the monopolies but who took every chance of putting their grievances before the Court. And the bookbinders began the formal battle.

On January 27, 1578, William Lobley and five others admitted that they had publicly complained against the Wardens and that they were sorry for not behaving as good Stationers should. On the same day the Court discussed a five-point petition from the 'poore men' and made the following answers:

1. So that the binders might have work, booksellers were to deliver sufficient sheets at the beginning of each week to such binders as would do the work well and redeliver the bound books at the end of the week, or earlier if speed were necessary. The Court promised to help those who could not get work on these terms. (It was only three months since the previous order had been made about employment for the bookbinders.)

2. The Assistants refused to forbid the giving of work to aliens and foreigners; Burghley's letter to the Lord Mayor on this subject had been written only six days before. They argued that if the orders made under the first heading were kept, 'as yt is faythfullie intended', it was not necessary to bar those who were not Stationers; furthermore, that if they did bar them, private customers would buy their books in quires and have them bound by these same strangers.

3. The Master and Wardens promised to satisfy any complaints about unfair payment for work done.

4. The Court, while admitting the reasonableness of the complaint, shrank at this stage from a sweeping reform of the excessive number of apprentices in the service of printers or others, but it agreed to look into a specific plea from a journeyman that he was kept out of a job by a supernumerary apprentice. (It immediately got its own back on John Oswald, one of Lobley's supporters, by fining him 2s for keeping two boys unpresented—a double offence—and for

employing no journeyman. Even before the meeting, the fee for enrolling an apprentice had been raised from 6d to 2s 6d, the highest allowed by the City; and shortly after the meeting, limitations were set to the numbers of apprentices which different grades in the Company could keep. In the following year half a dozen men were fined for keeping boys who had not been bound at the Hall—unpresented, presumably, because they were in excess of the newly ordained maximum.)

5. To the request that Frenchmen and other continentals who were free denizens should not have too great a number of apprentices, the Court replied that young men could not be bound to denizens but, having been indentured to freemen, were put to learn their trade from such skilled craftsmen; and, moreover, that if the Stationers' Company did not supply apprentices in this manner other companies, and particularly those of inferior standing, would do so and thereby breed a generation of bookbinders who were not Stationers. The Court promised, all the same, to keep an eye on the latent danger. (The point made here by the Assistants is an interesting one; the Stationers could offer little inducement to a Draper bookseller, and the proposed limitation of apprentices might frighten away a Cordwainer bookbinder. Control of its membership was not easy for a middling company which aimed at trade management.)

At the end of these answers the Court made, as a gesture of generosity, a further order. If any poor member of the Company applied for the right to exploit a copy to which no one else laid claim or of which the last impression was sold out, he would be favourably listened to. This is the first acknowledgment by the Ancients that the monopolies in classes of books might be causing distress;[1] previous action had been solely retaliatory. Though as early as 1560 the Court of High Commission had issued orders to the Company to stop the unlawful printing of books in the Seres privilege, and though a Decree of 1566 gave the Company additional powers of search (of which it took immediate but, apparently, not continuing advantage), the evidence for a real drive against copyright infringers does not appear until 1576. On September 3rd twelve pairs of searchers were appointed, an Assistant and a Liveryman in each pair, to inspect printing houses when called upon to do so. Searchers had been

---

[1] For a detailed study of the discontents and the remedies for them, see 'The English Stock of the Stationers' Company. An Account of its Origins'. *The Library*, 5th ser., x, 1955.

nominated before and armed with special warrants: Hugh Singleton and Thomas Purfoot had been most successful in their combing of booksellers' shops and dock-side warehouses. But in 1576 the warrants were general; returns were to be made of the number of presses, the number of journeymen (with a note of any who were not free or Brothers), the number of apprentices (with a note of any who were bound to other men), and the titles and numbers of every book being printed (with a note of the undertaker for whom the work was being done). The importance of this arrangement lies not in the achievement of the searchers (two fines for unpresented apprentices and two for disorderly printing during the whole of 1577) but in its concentration on the printing houses; since the printers were still the most powerful group among the Assistants this roster of searchers (with the threat of a 6s 8d fine for not turning out) must have been imposed on the Company from outside, possibly in connection with the activities which had produced, in the spring of 1576, a proclamation against seditious libels.

In the following year occurred signs of pressure from within the Company. In August, the month in which the Days obtained an extension of their monopoly, the Government received a joint petition from printers, glass-sellers and cutlers against the injustice of 'priuilidges granted to privatt persons'. In the printers' section nine patentees were listed, and the chief grumbles were that the books so monopolized had once been open to all printers and that their prices had been raised. The names were given of thirty-five Stationers who claimed to be 'hindered' by the privileges; over half were printers, six—including both Wardens—were Assistants and a dozen others were on the Livery. The opposition was therefore well supported by senior members of the Company; it was also supported by ten named freemen of other companies (including the future Queen's Printer) who made their living in the book trade, and by 140 (unnamed) who had been made free of the Stationers' Company since the beginning of the Queen's reign.[1]

Opposition of another kind came from the journeymen printers who sent a petition to the Privy Council on June 5, 1578.[2] They drew attention to a previous and unsuccessful petition from over sixty workmen brought up in printing and dependent on it for their living;

---

[1] Though the figure is about 50 per cent higher than the number of names in the Charter, it is probably accurate; 131 men were enrolled as freemen between July 1557 and July 1571.

[2] S.P. Dom. Elizabeth, vol. 157, no. 71; the dating is not absolutely certain.

and to certain orders which their masters were trying to get approved by the Government without the journeymen's knowledge. The Council ordered the petition to be referred to the City, with a strong suggestion that the new orders be dropped; since no more is heard of them (except for the ordinance limiting the number of apprentices) they probably were abandoned.

There is no indication of the line which William Lobley and his five confederates (one of whom was Watkins's partner in the almanack monopoly) had taken in criticizing their governing body; but it is quite clear what the main grievances were during the year 1577–8. The first was against aliens and foreigners who took work away from members of the Company; the second was against the growing numbers of apprentices who did the work of journeymen during the last year or two of their service and swelled the ranks of the journeymen when they became free. The workmen printers and the bookbinders made common cause against practices which, at the best, meant depression of wages and, at the worst, unemployment. In the third place some of their employers—both printers and booksellers—were prepared to criticize, not the Company's attitude to aliens and apprentices from which they themselves benefited but the concentration in a few hands of the rights in the most remunerative books. The creation of these monopolies could not be blamed on the Court of Assistants; but since the printing of another man's copy was against the ordinances, the Court, in trying to see that the rules were obeyed, became almost as much an object of antagonism as the individual monopolists. It was, therefore, something of an achievement for the Court to evolve in the course of the last twenty years of Elizabeth's reign a series of devices for reconciling the warring interests within the Company.

At first, however, the patentees, in order to defend their rights, took what action they could in their private capacities, either by suits in the Court of Star Chamber or by personal approach to a leader of the opposition. John Day tried the former method against Roger Ward, and Christopher Barker tried the latter with John Wolf; both failed to check the movement, chiefly because the booksellers provided speedy (and of course profitable) distribution of the books which the printers illegally produced. By 1582 the confusion had become so unmanageable that a Royal Commission was appointed and a committee of four aldermen was deputed to look into the complaints of the workmen printers. The main result of the latter interference was an appeal to Lord Burghley against Thomas Norton because he was letting his position as Counsel to the Company prejudice his advice as City Remembrancer. There were twenty-one names to this petition, five of which belonged to men of other companies, headed by that of John Wolf of the Fishmongers; among the Stationers were William Lobley, with two of his 1577 associates, and Roger Ward; both booksellers and printers were represented. The interlocking of the different grievances is clearly demonstrated by this document; although it was occasioned by an enquiry into printers' wages, it was signed by at least one bookbinder, Lobley, and it was endorsed 'The Stacioners of London against ye priviledged persons'.

ATTEMPTS AT ALLEVIATION

On March 26, 1583, the Court allowed one of the bigger printers, Henry Bynneman, to enter certain profitable copies, like Aristotle's *Works* and Homer in Greek and Latin, but only on condition that he should not confine the printing of these books to his own house but share the production with five members of the Company. It is possible that the suggestion for an arrangement of this kind had been put forward in the course of the discussions which the Royal Commission had had with the patentees and the Assistants, for six months earlier Henry Denham, the assign of William Seres, and John Day had each begun to disperse his work among seven or eight of the smaller printers, at whose presses the pirated editions might have been run off. Here is the second admission by the governing body of the Stationers that monopolies were a cause of hardship within the Company. Though the idea may have come from the Bishop of London or the Dean of St Paul's or one of the other members of the Commission and though Denham and Day may have acted rather for their own protection than out of generosity, the Assistants were careful not to allow Bynneman to establish a new monopoly. Another practical step had been taken towards peace in the trade.

A third demonstration of goodwill was the gift by the patentees of a large number of copies for the use of the poor of the Company.[1]

[1] The full list is dated January 8, 1584; but in a letter to the Commissioners of April 30, 1583, signed by nine Assistants (S.P. Dom. Elizabeth, vol. 160, no. 25) reference is made to the patentees' gift, at the Court's entreaty, of considerable parts of their property—a scheme which, it is hoped, the Commissioners will approve.

Amongst a certain amount of rubbish there were some books—the *Statutes at Large* (from Barker), Cicero's *Offices* (from Tottell), a sheet almanack (from Watkins)—which might be profitable. That the Court was ready to stand by its offer of six years earlier is shown by the grant to Timothy Rider, on April 6, 1584, of a book of home medicine which had belonged to Henry Disley (a Draper, now dead); two conditions were made: the first that Rider should not part with the copy without the Court's permission and the second that Robert Waldegrave, one of the signatories of the petition to Burghley, should have the printing of it. This directing of work towards discontented printers became more frequent in the next few years and was the fourth—and one of the most sensible—of the contributions to the solution of the lack of work problem. The death in July of John Day gave an opportunity to make other 1582 signatories happy. Richard Day was entitled to exercise his father's privilege, but he was a clerk in holy orders. He therefore formalized an arrangement, made by his father two years before, and handed over the working of his patent to John Wolf, who had been translated from the Fishmongers, and four others; the only one of these who had not signed the petition against Norton was William Wright, who would probably have done so if he had not, at the time, been in prison for handling pirated books. It is likely that the Court engineered this arrangement, for on January 18, 1585, it ordered that Thomas Purfoot, yet another who supported the appeal to Burghley, should have the printing of half the *Little Catechism* for the new exercisers of the Day privilege.

Thus in various ways the governing body of the Company had been arranging for a wider distribution of work and of opportunity for profit. William Lobley and other bookbinders were still dissatisfied and appealed to the Lord Mayor in March 1586,[1] but something had been done both for the discontented printers, masters and men, and for jealous booksellers. At the same time the Court felt that it might take advantage of the acknowledged confusion among the Stationers and the Government's desire for more stringent control of the press to strengthen the powers of the Company. In October 1584, therefore, it resolved that the Wardens might incur expenditure either on the

---

[1] An aldermanic committee visited Stationers' Hall on March 25th and, having heard all parties, made yet another agreed settlement. This laid down rules to govern methods of binding and forbade the employment, as binders, of men who were not free of the City and of women other than a binder's wife and daughters. (Liber A, f. 50; printed in S. T. Prideaux, *An Historical Sketch of Bookbinding*, 1893, pp. 239–42.)

promotion of an Act of Parliament for the confirmation of the Charter or on obtaining added authority from some other source. The result was a set of new Decrees for the control of printing which were approved by the Court of Star Chamber on June 23, 1586, and which cost the Company the best part of £80.

GOVERNMENT INTERVENTION: THE DECREES OF 1566 AND 1586

These were not the first of their kind. Almost exactly twenty years earlier the Court of High Commission, guided by the Archbishop of Canterbury and the Bishop of London, had drafted, and the Privy Council had approved, six ordinances for regulating the printing and distribution of books. The Company may not have promoted the 1566 Decree;[1] it certainly paid no special legal expenses at the time; but it was directly involved in two ways. Any books which offended against the laws of the land or against a grant or injunction issued by Her Majesty, whether they were printed here or abroad, were to be seized and brought to Stationers' Hall; half of such books were at the royal disposal and half to be delivered to the seizer or informer. More specific power of search was granted to the Wardens or their deputies than the Charter gave them, particularly the right to enter warehouses at ports and to examine any maunds or bales suspected of containing books. The last of the ordinances laid it down that any member of the book trade could be required to enter into recognizances to observe these rules and not to hinder the Wardens in the exercise of their duties.

The Decree of 1566 was a clear recognition of the Stationers' Company as an executive tool of the Government, but there is little evidence of its effect. Hugh Singleton and Thomas Purfoot were authorized to make searches and they spent £5 riding round the country; the result was a series of heavy fines on six members of the book trade—probably for copyright infringement. The Queen, however, did not receive her share and no similar fines are found for six years. The Decree was reprinted, probably in 1576 when the pairs of searchers were appointed; but though any books, printed contrary to royal letters patent, were liable to seizure, the Company had not

---

[1] See 'Book Trade Control in 1566', *The Library*, 5th ser., xiii, 1958, for an analysis of the Decree and for an account of the attempts, in 1566 and later in Elizabeth's reign, to control printing by Act of Parliament.

enough power to deal with men like Wolf and Ward who did not offend against Church or State.

The new Decree of 1586 was much more explicit and was designed as a set of published ordinances by which all members of the trade, whatever their places of business, were in future to be governed. The authority which the Wardens had been instructed to obtain emanated from the royal prerogative, but the agents for the observance of the rules were the officers of the Stationers' Company; and the nine sections of the 'orders' represent that proportion of the Company's ambitious policy of centralized control which the Government was prepared to allow; it was a considerable advance on the powers achieved by the Charter and by the Company's own ordinances of 1562.

I have shown how a combinaton of booksellers and smaller printers had already made some inroads on the empires of the monopolizing printers who had ruled the Company for forty years; the printers were still powerful, but the officers of the Company in the twelve months preceding the Star Chamber Decree did not belong to the old gang. James Gonneld and Henry Conway were not printers: there is no evidence that they were even booksellers; and Christopher Barker, who bought the office of Queen's Printer only in 1577, had always taken a broad, outsider's, point of view in dealing with Stationers' problems. It is therefore not surprising to find that the Decree began by laying down a more rigid control of printers. Those with printing houses were to make a return within ten days of all presses and materials in their possession (twenty-five did so), and no presses, except one each in the Universities of Oxford and Cambridge, were to be set up outside the City of London and its suburbs; all were to be openly displayed and accessible to the officers of the Company. No new presses were to be erected—and 'new' referred back to January 1, 1586—until the number of master printers had, by death or otherwise, been reduced to a total which the Archbishop and the Bishop of London thought large enough for the needs of the kingdom. When a new master could be allowed, the Court of Assistants was to choose a candidate, of skill and good behaviour, to present to the Court of High Commission for its approval. Only the Queen's Printer was exempt from this method of entry into the ranks of the master printers—a new élite within the Company, access to which was, as usual, by favour of the Court.

The next two clauses recalled the Injunctions of 1559 by which no books were to be printed without licence by the proper civil or ecclesiastical authority; moreover, no books were to be printed contrary to any ordinance of the Company—the ordinance about the entering of copies and the respecting of the copies of others being the one particularly referred to. A printer's punishment was the destruction of his press and type, disablement from ever printing again and six months' imprisonment without bail; that for booksellers and bookbinders was three months' imprisonment.

Clauses 6 and 7 repeated the rights of the Wardens or their deputies[1] to search the premises of any member of the book trade, to seize books which offended against the Decree and to carry away offending printing materials; the defacement of letters and destruction of presses were to be done to the order of the Assistants. Finally, official sanction was given to a decision which the Court had reached four years earlier; the number of apprentices was limited to three for those who had served as Master or Upper Warden; to two for any other Liverymen; and to one for a member of the Yeomanry provided he were not a journeyman.[2] The Queen's Printer, however, was to be allowed six apprentices; Barker was at this time Upper Warden. The printers at Oxford and Cambridge were limited to one apprentice each but were encouraged to employ as many workmen who were free of the City of London as they wanted.

The Decree does not make pleasant reading, but it does represent a theory of press control which was held in 1586 by the Ancients of the Stationers' Company and which was thought reasonable by the Queen's advisers—men like Lord Burghley, Sir Christopher Hatton, Sir Francis Walsingham and Archbishop Whitgift. Moreover, in the minds of the Assistants it was quite clear who stood to gain most from the effective operation of the Decree; on July 18th a full Court resolved that there should be a levy on the patentees or their assigns to pay for the law charges, and a week later it fixed the amounts.

How effective was the operation of the Decree? It did not prevent

[1] A roster of searchers, like that of 1576, had been appointed in January 1586, but the searchers were to work in threes rather than in pairs.

[2] The purpose of the Decree was the control of printing houses and their products, not the solution of discontent within the trade. On December 11, 1587, the Company gave official approval to a set of six orders, agreed between the master printers and their servants. These aimed to control the use of standing type, the number in an impression, the employment of apprentices, the profit from out of print copies—all in favour of the journeymen, provided they made no further complaints

the secret printing and distribution of the Martin Marprelate tracts, in spite of the trouble taken by Watkins, Denham and others to locate and destroy Waldegrave's press at Kingston in 1588. Nor did it prevent the irrepressible Roger Ward from printing privileged books—usually the *Grammar*—in spite of three separate orders to render his printing materials unusable. Nor did it prevent the sales of unauthorized editions of the psalms. But the records of action taken under the Decree during the first ten years of its existence are few enough—even with those already mentioned—to suggest that there was a period of comparative quiet in the book trade. The emphasis was naturally on a more rigid control of printers, but there is no evidence of desperation: two widows were forbidden to carry on their husbands' businesses and Thomas Orwin was prevented from working until he brought approval from the Archbishop; half a dozen printers were condemned to work as journeymen; two masters were fined for printing books without authority; Abel Jeffes, having resisted the Wardens' search, was forgiven after an apology and Valentine Symmes, though he was convicted of printing a privileged book, was punished merely by the melting of the type used.

The Company's greater power may have had a salutary effect on behaviour but it did not remove the fundamental reasons for misbehaviour. It is therefore interesting to find the Court continuing the attempts, begun before the Decree, to work out the elements of a constructive policy for the well-being of the trade. In August 1586 Robert Robinson, a printer who had been in frequent trouble, was given permission to print an impression of *The Mirror of Man's Life* (a Bynneman copy) 'for the Company'. Two conditions were made. Since Robinson wanted merely the work for his press and his men, he had to find investors to pay for the printing and the paper; such investors had to be freemen of the Company. In the second place, Robinson had to pay a royalty, calculated at 6d in the £, on the cost of paper and print, to a fund for poor Stationers.[1] This was a most ingenious arrangement, for it gave a printer legitimate work and it filled the Renters' fund for the poor. It also made it possible for any bookseller, provided he were a Stationer and had a few pounds to spare, to invest in and earn the profits on a copy, even if his interest were only a tenth; and he could become a partner in several such

[1] Ten years earlier a licence had been given to Thomas Dawson to print 1,500 copies of *The Praise of Folly* on the first of these two conditions, but this was an isolated example.

ventures. The spreading of the interest not only made people happy but lessened the likelihood of piracy, and it may have developed out of the idea of working a single privilege (for a large number of books) through several assigns.

During the second half of the sixteenth century there was a general shifting of economic power away from the craftsmen and towards the dealers in the craftsmen's products.[1] In the book trade, the early printers were also wholesale distributors; even though some specialization had occurred before the middle of the century the majority of copyright-owners in the immediate post-Charter period were still printers. Quite early, however, there is evidence that printers would sacrifice one profit from a book (the 'publisher's') provided they could keep the purely printing profit; and the trouble in the 1580s indicates how many trade printers—those who depended on the work they did for booksellers—there were. Though their number was to be limited by the Decree of 1586, the health of the trade demanded their being supplied with work in what was still a monopolistic market; hence the policy of the Court in licensing a copy to a bookseller on condition that a certain printer had the work. I have already quoted the ruling in 1584 for the benefit of Waldegrave; Robinson received in 1589 the right to print a popular school-book, Corderius's *Dialogues*, not in one impression but for as long as the monopoly lasted. In 1596 Valentine Symmes, yet another trouble-maker, was allowed to print any of Bynneman's copies (when they came to be printed) except those disposed of to other printers.

THE COMPANY'S INVOLVEMENT IN MONOPOLIES

One other element of policy, with considerable future importance, was the organization by the Court of ventures in book production which were too large for a single Stationer. This is something more than the granting of permission for the smaller men to combine in an ordinary book, and it is best illustrated by the arrangements for reprinting the *Statutes at Large*, which Barker had presented to the Company in 1583. At a Court held on June 15, 1587, it was decided first of all that cash for the Queen's share (£35) of the value of seized books should be raised through the purchase of the other half of the

---

[1] George Unwin, *Industrial Organization in the Sixteenth and Seventeenth Centuries*, Oxford, 1904, p. 103.

books by the real owners of their copyrights, and then that the *Statutes* should be printed 'for the Relief of woorkmen', provided enough Stationers could be found to put up the money. The venture went ahead; on December 4th it was agreed that the partners should pay Henry Denham, who was organizing the printing, 20s a week until the whole had been paid for, and the book was published with 1587 on the title page.

By the following winter the Court was taking the initiative in the affairs of those who were working the Day and Seres privileges. Law charges, which had been incurred by the Company in dealing with a piracy of Foxe's *Book of Martyrs*, were to be repaid by the partners in the Day patent, each in proportion to his investment, and their Treasurer was to show this amount in his next account. By August 1591 the partners in the Seres patent were similarly involved and on October 12th there is the first record of a meeting of the partners; action was to be taken against the printer at Cambridge and the expenses of John Wolf, the Beadle, were, according to an order of the Court, to be paid by Richard Watkins, the partners' Treasurer.

THE ROOTS OF THE ENGLISH STOCK

The development of the Company's control of the partners during the next twelve years will be easier to understand if I jump to 1603. On March 24th Queen Elizabeth died; three days later the Court of the Stationers' Company chose a committee of two Assistants and two others for the promotion of an Act of Parliament 'touchinge certen articles & matters here imparted to the consideration of the Company'. The result of a previous move for an Act of Parliament was the Decree of the Star Chamber in 1586; the result of the 1603 attempt was a royal grant 'to the whole Companie of Stacioners for the benefit of the poore of the same that they and none others shall ymprint the Bookes of private prayers, prymers, psalters and psalmes in English or Latin, & Almanrackes and Prognosticacõns wthin this Realme'.[1] The promise of this was obtained in May; the letters patent are dated October 29th. This was the legal basis for what soon came to be known as the English Stock, a book-producing and book-wholesaling organization run from Stationers' Hall by a paid Treasurer under the general control of the Court but under the immediate supervision of six Stock-keepers

[1] Signet Office Docquets, Index 6801, 1603–5.

elected annually and representing shareholders drawn from the three grades of the Company. These shareholders were limited to fifteen Assistants, thirty Liverymen and sixty from the Yeomanry. This brief outline of the pattern after 1603 will help to clarify what happened in the previous twelve years.

I cannot be certain whether or not the Day and Seres privileges were still, in 1591, being treated separately; but by the spring of 1594 all doubt is removed. On March 18th there was a meeting of the Court attended by the Master, the two Wardens and six Assistants; after the transaction of Company business, two of the Assistants withdrew and the rest were joined by ten members of the Company who were described as 'many' of the partners in the two privileges. They proceeded to the election, first, of a Treasurer and, out of three names proposed, re-elected Richard Watkins; and then of four Stock-keepers; one of these was an Assistant, one a Draper and the others Liverymen. In several respects the English Stock was already in existence by 1594;[1] the monopoly for almanacks was missing and the books in the two other privileges were still put out 'for the assigns of' Seres or Day; but the Treasurer was tending to become a permanent official, there was the annual election of Stock-keepers, and there was the overriding responsibility of the Court for policy. A minute of 1595 reveals that the warehouse was at Stationers' Hall.

But the Stationers were still feeling their way towards a pattern which only became clear in the years after 1603. On December 6, 1594, for example, the Clerk entered to Valentine Symmes the printing of Latimer's *Sermons*, under written authority from the Master and Wardens; but he added a note in the register that it was to be decided by a vote whether Symmes should print the book for 'the stock' or for the partners or for any members of the Company who cared to invest in it. There are no minutes to record what the decision was nor by whom, partners or Assistants, it was taken. Even individual Stationers were vague about terminology, though they were probably clear enough about what was happening. When John Judson made his will as early as 1588 he left his wife 'my stock of money which is in the handes of the Stationers for partnershippe'; but Ralph Newbery, in making his will in the last days of Queen Elizabeth's life, referred to

[1] In the Company's answer to a bill of complaints in Chancery in 1742 (Stationers' Hall document 265; see below, p. 230) there is reference to the Company's carrying on, before the grant of 1603, the business of printing and selling certain books under the direction of the Court and Stock-keepers, 'with a Stock brought in by several Members of the Company'.

his share in the Day and Seres privilege. This variation in the description of what was the same investment suggests that what we know was in existence in 1603 and what we can be fairly certain was in existence in 1594 may possibly have been in partial existence in the 1580s, when, against the background of opposition to monopolies, the Company of Stationers and the Court of High Commission induced those who held monopolies in books to share their privileges with some of those who had most bitterly opposed them.[1]

It is not surprising, therefore, to find that, when in 1598 the House of Commons made a successful attack on monopolies, the Stationers raised by assessment upwards of £20 for law charges in connection with the Company's affairs. There is no indication how the money was spent but, on May 15th, the Court decided to elect thirteen new Liverymen; the assessment was made on June 19th,[2] and on July 1st no fewer than eighteen freemen were called to the Livery at double the usual fee. This, I believe, is where the partnership pattern took its permanent form; there were fifteen Assistants in the assessment list, and the ten Liverymen added to the eighteen newcomers make all but two of the standard number of Livery partners in the English Stock.

Somehow, the Company got away with it, and there are indications that in the next five years the partners flourished. One of James's first acts, after his arrival in England, was the issue of a proclamation repeating Elizabeth's denunciation of monopolies in the hands of private individuals. The Stationers' was not the only corporation to take advantage of the opportunity to purchase a grant;[3] it is unlikely that many companies were better prepared or that any would have been thrown into worse confusion by a refusal from the King.

---

[1] A petition to Burghley (B.M. Lansdowne, 48, No. 83, unsigned and undated but c. 1583) to obtain for the Company the sole printing of the Latin *Accidence* and *Grammar* shows that the idea of the Company's sharing—as a corporation—in the monopolies was early in the minds of some Stationers. The chief argument in favour of the grant was that the Company was in dire financial straits and might be forced to dissolve.

[2] Liber A, f. 72. Note also, in Appendix I, the increase in the number of men who took up their freedoms by patrimony from 1598 and the big number of translations—of booksellers from the Drapers' Company—in 1600.

[3] George Unwin, *The Gilds and Companies of London*, 1908, p. 301.

CHAPTER V

THE LIFE OF A STATIONER

THE MASTER: JOHN HARRISON

IN Chapter III I took a year in the life of the Company in order to show the routine and some of the special problems which arose; in Chapter IV I traced the working out of solutions for a group of fundamental difficulties which had revealed their nature in the course of that year. In this chapter I want to show, through the career of a single member of the Company, the pattern of life among the Stationers as freemen of a London gild, and something of the changes which occurred in it towards the end of the sixteenth and at the beginning of the seventeenth century.

Thomas Man, whose father had been a butcher at Westbury in Gloucestershire, was bound apprentice to John Harrison for eight years from the Nativity of St John Baptist (June 24th) 1567. He was at that time about seventeen years old; we know this because the minimum age for freedom of the City was twenty-four and because, in 1582, Man stated that he was then thirty-two. The usual fee of 6d was paid to the Company when the indentures were registered at the Hall, but it is quite impossible to say whether his guardian had to pay his master a premium.[1] Harrison was a bookseller with a shop in St Paul's Churchyard and had taken up his freedom a few months too late for inclusion in the Charter list; he was not, at this stage of his career, interested in having books printed on his account—no books were licensed to him up to 1571 and no book carries his imprint before 1573. But he must already have built up a prosperous business in other branches of the book trade when Man began to work with him, for in the course of ten years he took on ten apprentices, of whom five are known to have been admitted freemen and a sixth, William Russell, to have worked as a bookseller in Exeter. Two of them, another John Harrison and Toby Cooke, were still in his service in 1567, and when

[1] For a discussion of premiums or 'considerations', see below, p. 117.

the younger Harrison took up his freedom in 1569, two more apprentices were bound to the elder. For several years, therefore, John Harrison had three young men and for some months he had four—twice as many as a Liveryman would have been allowed under the new rules. The lengths of service for which these ten were bound varied from seven to twelve years, half being for ten or more; and their backgrounds were equally varied. Three were from London, sons of a Stationer, of a joiner and of a yeoman; of the rest, one each came from Yorkshire, Worcestershire, Hampshire, Gloucestershire and Cheshire, and (apart from Man) were sons of yeomen or husbandmen; the parentage of two was not recorded; the fathers of four (out of eight) were dead before their sons were indentured. It would be reasonable to assume that boys bound to masters in the book trade would be literate, but in support of this assumption I can offer only the unique example of an exception. In 1602 James Roberts presented as his apprentice John Isham, the son of another London joiner, and his promise to put him to school until he could read and write was specially recorded. (Isham was dismissed for disobedience and for taking wages while still an apprentice, but he managed all the same to take up the freedom of the Company in 1615!)

The household into which Thomas Man was introduced in 1567 must have been like a small modern cramming establishment in which the boys and young men are aiming at different examinations but sleeping and eating together, and mixing with the growing family of the master and mistress. What form the work took in a bookselling establishment like Harrison's can only be guessed at; there would be the cleaning and minding of the shop, the collecting of stock from copyright-owning booksellers and printers, the delivering of books to customers and the calling on them for the settlement of accounts. If Harrison was, as I am sure he must have been, a wholesaler, there would be work in the warehouse, the packing and despatching of orders for the country trade and probably (after a period of instruction and in spite of the rule about stitching) the performance of the simpler operations in bookbinding. A boy of seventeen, in days when the output of books was still small, would learn enough of the business to earn the board, lodging and clothing, with which his master was obliged to provide him, several years before his time was up. This would have been true even of an apprentice in a printing house, though the period of sheer gain for the master would have been shorter.[1]

APPRENTICESHIP RULES

The value of a skilled but unpaid hand was demonstrated by Thomas Marshe's fine for the purchase from Alexander Lacey of the unexpired term of Robert Dowsing. During Man's first year, Thomas Hacket was fined 6s for a similar offence and for not reporting it, the more heinous misdemeanour being the latter. After Henry Bynneman's death in 1583 his widow was awarded by the Court £6 6s 8d for the nine unexpired years of two apprentices; and on October 4, 1586, in the presence of the Master, the Wardens and six Assistants (whose names are written in the margin of the apprentice section of the register), Robert Waldegrave assigned to William King 'all his Right and interest in the service of' Thomas Hawe, who still had two years to do; Hawe might have been a copy. The apprenticeship system, because it provided this modicum of almost free labour, was by no means an unmixed blessing, and the limitation of the number of apprentices was essential unless there could be considerable expansion in the provincial trade. There was a trickle of men like William Russell who set up as booksellers or bookbinders in Exeter or Bristol or Chester after a period of training in London (which might or might not be completed); but the concentration of printing in the capital prevented the trickle from growing into a steady stream.

The 1586 limitation of the number of printing houses to that of the Queen's Printer and twenty others, as soon as death and retirement made this possible, reduced still further the possible openings for those journeymen printers who had taken up their freedoms during the first twenty-five years of Elizabeth's reign. In the years immediately before the Charter several master printers had four apprentices (as John Harrison, the bookseller, had in 1569) and Thomas Marsh had five. Five was the number which John Wolf claimed he could have if he remained a Fishmonger; even members of the Yeomanry in the Silk-weavers were allowed to have three. It is therefore hardly surprising either that the governing body of the Stationers were unaware of the trouble which would result from a traditional attitude to the binding of

---

[1] Dr McKerrow contributed an interesting diagram, illustrating the value of an apprentice during the successive years of his service, to Sir Walter Greg's Introduction to *The Records of the Court*, p. xliii.

apprentices, in what they believed in 1557 to be an expanding industry, or that the master printers took advantage of their opportunities and built their businesses round a good supply of unpaid labour. The latter circumvented the new rule about numbers by having the indentures drawn up at a scrivener's, instead of at the Hall, or by boldly presenting an apprentice for the first time on the day he took up his freedom; even when the fine amounted to 20s, as it sometimes did, the risk was worth while.

The Court of Assistants found itself in a dilemma. It had been forced, by demonstrations from the journeymen and (probably) by pressure from the Queen's advisers, to limit the number of wage-earners. Its members, in their corporate capacity, might see the logic in this, but they felt the pinch themselves and they showed their sympathy with the small master, who could only take on a new raw youth on the day his experienced young man became a freeman of the Company, by occasionally giving permission, from 1594, for a second apprentice when the first was nearly out of his time. Moreover, there was competition from other companies whose allowance of apprentices was more generous, and the new rule tended to make this competition less manageable; limitation of apprentices was one more argument against the translation of, say, a Haberdasher bookseller to an inferior company, and every Haberdasher so lost was the source of a stream of Haberdashers, trained as booksellers, over whose quantity the Stationers had no control and over whose activities the Stationers had authority only when the City intervened on their behalf. The problem was never completely solved, but two lines of policy began to be worked out in the 1590s. The first was allowing a Stationer formally to bind a boy in excess of his allowed number but to put him to work with, for instance, Andrew Maunsell, a famous Draper bookseller; such a boy would not be lost to the Company. The second was the vague recognition that the trouble arose not from the superabundance of Stationers but from too many journeymen printers and bookbinders, and that the control of the craft a boy was taught would pose the problem at the beginning rather than at the end of his training. From 1590 there are many notes in the register that apprentices must avoid certain crafts (usually that of printing) or even 'any faculty perteyninge to the Art of Stationers'; one boy was to be employed only on the buying and selling of parchment and paper and on the binding of paper books. It was suggested that one of Wolf's apprentices might learn the art of distillation, which was Mrs Wolf's business; but it is difficult to see what value the young man would be to a Stationer except as a runner of errands and performer of similar odd jobs. At the same time there are signs of a tendency which might be expected to work in the wrong direction—the shortening of the period of service. When Arthur Pepwell made his will in 1568 he bequeathed 10s to William Browne, who had been bound to him for nine years in 1566, and remitted two years of his service.[1] The difficulty of keeping a young man unmarried and without wages until he was fully twenty-four was perhaps beginning to be generally recognized; from 1583 the Court occasionally remitted a year of the contracted apprenticeship, particularly when there was a turn-over from one master to another, and in 1596 John Harrison agreed to remit two of Clement Flement's ten years when the latter was turned over to Richard Sergier.

It is difficult to discuss the master-apprentice relationship—even that between Harrison and Man—in other than quantitative terms. In Chapter VII I shall say something of the occupations of apprentices' fathers in the 1630s as compared with the occupations of the men who put their sons to Stationers at the beginning of Elizabeth's reign; but this will reveal almost nothing of the quality of the raw material. It is possible to discover very little more of the character of the masters; some, like Cuthbert Burby, were unable to keep their boys from running away; some, like Richard Watkins, Peter Conway and Christopher Barker presented for their freedoms a very high proportion of the apprentices bound to them. The 'good' masters, according to these standards, were, as one might expect, the well-established and prosperous; the 'bad' are sometimes revealed by fines for keeping unpresented men who were long out of their time. How the widow of a butcher in Gloucestershire chose a master for the son she wanted to go into the London book trade I do not know; local associations do sometimes provide the clue but perhaps 'direction' by the Clerk or the Beadle was common. A certain amount must often have been left to chance by both parties to the indentures and there may have been an element of this which brought Thomas Man to his master; Man was not without luck at various stages of his career.

In his early years as a bookseller Harrison was occasionally in

---

[1] H. R. Plomer, *Abstracts from the Wills of English Printers and Stationers, from 1492 to 1630*, 1903, p. 17.

trouble for infringing the ordinances of the City and the Company; for keeping his shop open on Sundays or on St Luke's Day, for not waiting on the Lord Mayor at the Feast of the Purification, for selling an unlicensed publication, for breaking a rule about the binding of books. But these minor offences suggest keenness to get on rather than deliberate flouting of authority, and he was elected to the Livery only eight years after he was admitted to the freedom. In the March before he bound Thomas Man he became Junior Renter Warden and a year later, as normally happened, Senior Renter; in July 1573 he was elected Under Warden and thereby one of the Assistants. By this time Man had attained his majority and was able to take an adult's interest in the career of his master and in the official business of the Company. Stationers' Hall and the shop of William Norton, the Upper Warden, were also in St Paul's Churchyard; Man was brought up in the political and economic centre of the book trade, and when he took up his freedom, at the cost of 3s 4d and a dinner,[1] he must have known a good deal both about bookselling and about the affairs of the Company to which he belonged.

THOMAS MAN: THE YOUNG BOOKSELLER

The first ten years[2] which Man spent as an independent bookseller and paper-merchant in Paternoster Row were stormy ones in the life of the Company, and in these storms Man was heavily involved. In the first place he tried to get away with more than his proper allowance of one apprentice and in 1580 was fined 5s for keeping John Hancock, the son of a Cheshire husbandman, unpresented; two years later this apprentice was, by order of the Lord Mayor's Court, removed from his service and turned over to another Stationer. In the second place, he was mixed up in the distribution of pirated copies of cheap privileged books. His earliest entries in the register of copies show that he was interested in the marketing of ballads; he had probably been trained in the wholesale trade; it was not very difficult for the organizers of

[1] Who should pay the charges was perhaps laid down in the indentures. When John Lastlis was bound to Christopher Barker in 1579, it was agreed that, though he should serve Godfrey Isaac (probably a bookbinder and not a Stationer) for the whole of his eight years, Barker should be responsible for all charges, including that of making him free. John Reynes, however, when he made his will in 1542 (P.C.C. 23 Pynning), instructed his widow to make his apprentices free at *their* cost. By the eighteenth century the custom was for the apprentice's family to pay for binding and the master for making him free.
[2] The exact date of Man's freedom has been lost with the missing records, but one of his earliest years of independence was 1577–8, the year dealt with in Chapter III.

the guerilla warfare against the patents of Seres and Day to persuade a young bookseller that it was not only profitable (which he could see for himself) but almost a duty to break monopolies and to spread the advantages derived from them among struggling members of the trade. In June 1582 John Day brought an action in the Court of Star Chamber against Roger Ward for printing the *ABC* with the *Little Catechism*, and Ward revealed that he had bought some of the paper for this book from Thomas Man for credit. In his examination Man admitted selling paper to Ward at 2s 10d a ream for payment in three months but denied both knowledge of the purpose for which the paper was bought and lending Ward money for printing the *ABC*. Day— with some reason, at a time when so much of the trade was by barter and exchange—assumed that Man had been paid in printed sheets; but the latter denied taking copies in payment or in any other way and admitted only that he had heard of William Holmes's having taken delivery of some of the books. Nothing was proved against Man; but at least 10,000 copies were printed and distributed, and I find it difficult to believe that he was not involved. Moreover, three years later he and ten other booksellers (including John Harrison the younger) were complained of in the same court for disposing of another 10,000 copies of the *ABC* and 4,000 copies of the psalms in metre, which had been printed by or at the instigation of four of the regular pirates. The case broke down on a minor legal point before the calling of evidence, but its initiation by Richard Day and his five assigns reveals two aspects of the anti-monopoly campaign: the amount of support on which printer pirates could rely from the booksellers, and the dissatisfaction among the rank and file of the Stationers, even after the partial spreading of the interest in patents.

On three occasions during this period Man was convicted of break- ing ordinances of the Company. In May 1580 he was fined 5s for having *The Holy Fast* printed without licence. This little manual was a close imitation of one of the books in Day's privilege and Man was ordered to pay Day 10s as compensation; but he was allowed to sell out his own impression provided he did not err again. In February 1583 he was fined 3s for sending four books to press without having them licensed by the Wardens and entered in the register; one of these was a joint publication with John Harrison the younger. About two years later he was punished for a similar offence and he promised to pay the unusually heavy fine of 10s on the next Court day. In the end he paid 3s 4d and was forgiven the rest; whether such modification was due to cooling of tempers, to the production of mitigating evidence, to the appeal of a hard-luck story or to a policy of deliberate over-fining in the first place, I do not know; but I should guess not only that Man could well afford to pay 10s but that he thoroughly deserved to be heavily fined, since the book involved—*An ABC for Laymen*—was morally an infringement of a patent; and it was his second offence.

PROMOTION

The year 1586 produced not only the Star Chamber Decree but Man's first step in Company promotion. On July 4th he and a printer called John Windet, who had been free since 1579 and a master printer for two years, were elected to the Livery on payment of 20s each; the fee had gone up from 15s in 1570 and it remained at 20s until the big election of 1598.[1] In the autumn of 1589 Man and Windet were appointed to go to the Lord Mayor's Feast and on March 26, 1592, Man was elected Junior Renter Warden, the Senior Renter being Thomas Dawson,[2] a printer. Twelve months later he was fined 1s for not being present when he was chosen Senior Renter, with Windet as his Junior; but his fine was remitted, perhaps because of the services he had recently rendered in searches for hidden presses. On May 6, 1594, as was customary on the Feast of St John ante Portam Latinam, Man delivered his account to the Wardens and on May 12th he was, with Dawson, elected to the Court 'by pluralyty of voices', eight years after being called to the Livery and less than twenty from taking up his freedom. As the most junior Assistant he was appointed one of the auditors of the Wardens' accounts and the Court representative at the Lord Mayor's Feast; but unlike most of his predecessors (the first recorded election to the Court was that of Thomas Woodcock on August 3, 1590), he sat at the Table for three years before being elected Under Warden in 1597.

The career of Thomas Man to the age of thirty-five was not an unusual one for an enterprising young bookseller who had a good training and a little money behind him and who would naturally not always agree with the policy of his elders. What happened to him

---

[1] See above, p. 77. Very occasionally there were variations from the normal, as when, in 1571, Dunstan Whapland paid 40s 'when he sued' to be taken into the Livery.

[2] Free 1568 and called to the Livery 1585, the year before Man.

from the time of his election to the Livery in 1586 is quite untypical of the careers of the general run of Stationers; only forty-five men were called to the Livery in the first twenty-five years of its existence and in the same period about 350 took up their freedoms. This election was, therefore, exceedingly important both in the careers of the chosen few and in the life of the Company. From the pool of Liverymen the Renter Wardens were drawn off at the rate of one a year (each holding the offices in successive years) and created a second pool from which, in theory, a new Under Warden was drawn off each alternate year (the office being held for two, but not necessarily consecutive, years). The second pool tended to fill nearly twice as quickly as it was emptied; only the incidence of death prevented its filling exactly twice as fast. Two measures were introduced during the last ten years of the century which helped to keep the balance between the two pools by increasing the size of the Court. The first was direct election to the Table, in place of election to the office of Under Warden with *ex officio* membership of the Court; Man's was an example of this kind of promotion. The second was the payment of a fine instead of serving one or both the years required in the office of Under Warden.

Before discussing the second of these two measures, I want to make the point that though Man's career from 1586 was anything but typical of a Stationer's progress in the Company, it developed thereafter along predictable lines and was reasonably typical of what happened to those who were fortunate enough to be called to the Livery; only eleven of the first forty-five Liverymen failed to become Renter Warden and most of these were prevented by death; the number of ex-Renters who failed to make the Court was a dozen. The entrance to the governing body was through this narrow defile; the importance of early election to the Livery—within fifteen years of becoming a freeman—was therefore very great for an ambitious man. How many of the Yeomanry asked that their names should not go forward for election it is impossible to say, but in the first fifty-years of the Livery there are only two mentions of the 40s fine for refusal *after* election; the first was reduced to 20s and the second was merely a threat.

FINING FOR AVOIDING OFFICES

The 'fining' for the avoidance of office was introduced to the Stationers by Christopher Barker, the Draper who was translated to the Stationers' Company on June 4, 1578. On May 6, 1579, the Renters' accounting day, Barker paid £3 as a dispensation from ever serving as Renter. He was Queen's Printer and had been a member of one of the great companies; moreover, he did not make this gesture at the Lady Day election when refusal to serve might have been interpreted as an affront to the Ancients. It was nearly twenty years before anyone else tried to avoid this office; but in 1587 the avoidance of the Under Wardenship was posed. Henry Middleton died within a few weeks of his election, and on September 11th the Court elected Richard Greene for the remainder of the term. Barker and another Assistant, Henry Conway, went straight to Greene's house in Fleet Street to tell him the news, but they were quite unable to persuade him to serve. On their return to the Hall, Conway was elected (by the use of the Master's casting vote) and Greene was fined £5; of this half was to go to the Company and was a fine for disobedience, but the other half was to go to Conway (according, it was stated, to the ordinances) and was the payment for a substitute. On the following March 26th the Court agreed on the important ruling that Greene should rank as if he had served the Under Wardenship and sit as an Assistant. The facts that Greene, who was probably not in the book trade, never availed himself of this honour and was removed from the Board two years later are irrelevant; a principle had been established. The Court soon made it clear that, whatever the ordinances said, the fines ought to go undivided into the common stock; but as late as 1604 John Windet, having served once as Under Warden, successfully claimed the right to half the fine of his predecessor on the list of those who, one after the other, had chosen to fine rather than serve a second year.

If, however, a man were elected Renter he was still expected to serve. In 1598 James Askew utterly refused to do this, and for disobedience, obstinacy and breaking the ordinances he was ordered to prison as a warning to others and fined £5. During the summer there was a good deal of discussion of Askew's stand and it was decided in October that his fine excused him the Rentership for ever. When in the following spring the younger Harrison asked to be excused for various reasons, he was quietly and immediately fined £5. In 1602 three Liverymen were fined in succession (rather unfairly £10, £5 and £4); by 1604 the fine was evened out at £10 and as the desire to avoid the office grew so did the fines. But in 1604 the unfortunate Nicholas Ling was ordered to prison and fined £10 for refusing to serve the normal second year; acceptance meant commitment for two years.

The dispute over fining for the Rentership had been settled partly by the obstinacy of Askew and partly perhaps by the discovery in 1599 that the Court had only one member (when there should be three) with the right qualifications to stand for election as Upper Warden; all the rest were ex-Masters, ex-Upper Wardens who had served both their years, or those who had served one year at the most as Under Warden. On January 15th the Court deliberately fined two Assistants £20 apiece for their two years, the sitting Under Warden £5 for his second year and Thomas Man £3 6s 8d for the same exemption.

This was neither the first nor the last occasion on which Man was treated leniently; in December 1595 he was forgiven a fine of 10s which had been imposed on him a month before, and even when he turned up to a meeting of the Court not just late as he sometimes did but after all the business had been concluded, he was fined only 7d instead of the usual 12d. From 1597, when he was elected Under Warden, he was one of the most powerful men in the Company. Two years later he became Upper Warden and in 1602 was elected for his second year. In 1604 he became Master of the Company for the first time; he was re-elected in 1610, 1614 and 1616. His last recorded attendance at the Court was on February 7, 1619, and he died in May 1625.

MAN'S LATER CAREER: THE TRIUMPH OF THE BOOKSELLERS

In his private capacity, as his will shows,[1] he had led a successful life; he had invested wisely in copies, chiefly theological, and he had one of the original Assistants' shares in the English Stock; he had bought or inherited property in the City and in the suburbs; he had continued in the stationery business and had supplied to the Company two of the books of records which still survive—Register C and the Register of Bequests, Liber C2. Three of his sons were Stationers, two by patrimony and one by translation from the Haberdashers; one of his daughters was married to a bookseller (Humphrey Lownes, who had hired the Hall for his wedding feast and who, by his second marriage to a printer's widow and with the help of his first father-in-law, became a master printer); and he also had a cousin in the trade. But he founded no dynasty. Moreover, none of his apprentices

[1] P.C.C. 65 Clarke; made February 7 and proved June 16, 1625.

made any mark either in the Company or in the book trade; they hailed from as far north as Yorkshire and from as far west as Somerset; among them were sons of yeomen and parsons, of a miller, a chandler, a clothier, a shearman and a gentleman; if his own sons are included, three out of every four of the young men who worked in his shop took up their freedoms—a high proportion. But the impact of Man, as a bookseller, lasted little longer than that of any ordinary Stationer.

In the Company, however, his impact was exceptional. With his seniority and his practical experience he was frequently elected to committees of the Court: for looking after the property, for bargaining with the patentees, and—most important of all—for promoting an Act of Parliament or other safeguard of the Stationers' interests; as one of the four appointed for this purpose on March 27, 1603, he profoundly affected the whole of the later history of the Company by winning from James I a valuable monopoly, the foundation of the English Stock. He became Master at the first election after the royal grant and he held that position for four out of the next dozen years.

Man was also involved in an evolution which completely changed first the economic pattern in the book trade and then the political power in the Stationers' Company. His master, John Harrison, was one of the booksellers whom Barker described in 1582 as outnumbering the printers and as competing successfully with them for those copies not covered by patents. Barker, coming into the Stationers' from another company, could see as clearly as we can a change in the pattern which was perhaps hardly perceptible by those who had been part of the pattern during the previous twenty-five years. The outnumbering might have made little difference if a rift had not gradually appeared between the printers who owned enough copies, by entry in the register or by privilege, to keep their presses busy and the trade printers who worked for the copyright-owning booksellers. When young booksellers like Man joined forces with the latter to attack the strongholds of Seres and Day, and when, in order to restore some order in the affairs of the Company, the patents of the printers were farmed out among some of the malcontents and the total number of printers was limited by the Government, the dominance of the old printer was over. Nearly half of those who had printing houses at the time of the 1586 Star Chamber Decree were never called to the Livery, and three of the successful ones had to wait over twenty years. It would be interesting to know how the arguments went at meetings of the Court when calls to the Livery were being debated. Were the conflicting interests those of different trades rather than those of different personalities? Were any Assistants able to foresee the effect, on the Court of a dozen years later, of electing to the Livery a preponderance of non-printers? The rivalry between the two parties was clearly shown by the opposition which Day encountered when, in 1572, he tried to open a shop in St Paul's Churchyard, and the numerical superiority of the trading over the manufacturing interest made itself unmistakably felt in 1598 when, out of eighteen Liverymen elected on the same day, only four were printers. If, as I suspect,[1] these Liverymen were chosen to take shares in the buying out of the biggest patentees and their assigns, the economic weight of the commercial section in the Company was demonstrably in the ascendant. Thomas Man was of this party and may, as Under Warden, have had a hand in the floating of the scheme in 1598; he was certainly one of the chief planners in 1603. It was against men like him that journeymen printers protested in 1614, calling them 'the chiefe Ingrossers of these Priuiledged Copies, with some few Printers'. It was men like him whom George Wither described in 1625, the year of Man's death, as making slaves of the printer, the bookbinder and the claspmaker; and it is difficult not to see Man's hand in the Court's fierce treatment of printers during his third year as Master, when three of them were each fined the enormous sums of £6 13s 8d for binding apprentices at scriveners' and two others fined or committed for disobeying or being rude to the Master.

Man began his life in the Company ten years after the granting of the Charter and he completed his last term as Master almost exactly fifty years later. I have tried to show how his career was representative both of an apprentice's dream of success and of the new force in the book trade which gradually obtained a dominating position among the Stationers during the half-century of Man's activity. Man did not use success in his own Company as a spring-board for a leap into City politics; few Stationers did. But on all other counts he was an exemplar. As a young man with left-wing tendencies he took part in guerilla actions against the printer monopolists. When he was elected to the Livery, in what was perhaps a typical attempt—and a successful one— to win him to the side of law and order, he responded by holding all the elective offices—'into which', as George Wither wrote of 'a mere stationer', 'his very troublesomnesse sometyme helpes him the sooner'

[1] See above, p. 77

—during the period when the printers gradually lost the ruling voice in the affairs of the Company. He saw the number of the Stationers multiplied by at least three and the moving of the headquarters of the Company, in 1606, from St Paul's Churchyard to its present site. Most important of all, he was a prime mover in the foundation of the English Stock.

CHAPTER VI

THE STOCKS

THE ENGLISH STOCK

THE Charter of 1557 was in the nature of a coming-of-age; the royal grant of 1603 was in the nature of a wedding, whose importance in the life of the Company was as much greater than a twenty-first birthday party as marriage is in the life of an ordinary citizen. Though considerably altered by the passage of time, it remains undissolved to this day and is a very rare phenomenon among the companies of the City of London. Even if the English Stock had failed to dominate the Stationers' Company, it would still be worth a full description as a piece of gild history.

By letters patent of October 29th, which were 'openly Redd and published in the hall' on December 19th to the Assistants and the partners, James I formally confirmed the two privileges, which he had promised in May, to the Master, Wardens and Commonalty of the mystery or art of Stationers in the City of London, for ever. The first, for their 'helpe and releife', was the sole right to enjoy the profits from the sale of psalters and psalms, in verse or in prose, with or without music, in any format and in any English[1] version then extant or to be made in the future; and the same right for primers, which were books of private prayers for adults or children and which might contain the catechism or a simple introduction to reading. (Prayer books for use in church services, which were part of the King's Printer's privilege, were specifically excluded.) For its protection the Company was given the power to seize any books printed in contravention of these rights. The second privilege, 'for the better releife' of the Company, made

---

[1] No mention is made of Latin versions in this grant, though Latin and English are given equal weight in the Signet Office Docquet of May; see above, p. 75. For accounts of the early days of the English Stock, see William A. Jackson's Introduction to Court Book C and my article in *The Library*, 5th ser., xii, 1957. The organization set up to exploit the grant from James was called 'the English' only after the creation of 'the Latin Stock' (see below, p. 106); the earliest use of the phrase is in the Court minutes for April 13, 1617.

the same provisions for almanacks and prognostications and for any little books passing as such, provided the ecclesiastical authorities approved of them; infringing editions were likewise to be forfeited and fines of 1s imposed for every copy so seized.

The letters patent conclude with granting the Master, Wardens and Assistants the rights, firstly to make ordinances for the proper working of the privilege—provided such rules are approved by the Chief Justices and do not cut across the Star Chamber Decree of 1586—and secondly, 'for the avoiding of all confusyon', to manage the affairs of the privilege, provided always that the Master is present when an important decision is taken. Power was to remain 'wholly and fyrmelie' in the hands of the governing body of the Company.

At about the same time—and certainly before May 1605—the partners in this new privilege bought the sole right to print and distribute common-law books. Ten years earlier the Company had tried, unsuccessfully, to purchase the patent from the widow of Charles Yetsweirt, a Clerk of the Signet and the patentee. Where the Company had then failed, Bonham Norton and Thomas Wight succeeded; and it was their thirty-year patent of 1599 which was amalgamated with the grant from the King, at a roughly equal cost and after a brief attempt to keep the two investments separate.[1]

James had made his promise to the Stationers in the same month as he had followed Elizabeth's lead in denouncing monopolies; he must therefore have been convinced of the propriety of making this grant by powerful arguments. One of these was probably money and another was certainly the emotional appeal of provision for the indigent. The second is mentioned directly in the promise given in May but only vaguely and indirectly in the letters patent; it was an undertaking to pay £200 a year out of the profits of the privilege to the poor of the Company. The precedent for this was the poor fund started in 1585,[2] into which were paid royalties of 6d in the £, or 2½ per cent, on the cost of paper and print, for permissions to produce books over which the Company claimed control: £200 is 2½ per cent of £8,000, which is £1,000 less than the capital raised in 1603–5. The only pieces of evidence for the spending of this money are an order of September 1605 that Adam Islip, the chief law printer, should buy for £131 the printing equipment taken over, with the stock, from Thomas Wight; a note of July 1606 that £1,140 entrusted to Cuthbert

---

[1] See below, p. 105, for other additions. [2] See above, p. 73.

Burby, the most senior of the Stock-keepers elected in 1600 for the management of the Seres and Day privileges, had been duly and truly disbursed by him; and a statement, made fifty years later to Cromwell, that the right to print almanacks cost about £1,000. How much went into the royal privy purse and how much into the pockets of the partners in the private privileges (for stock as well as for rights) cannot now be calculated; I am sure that a good deal of the investment must have been a series of book entries by which partners' holdings were transferred from one 'company' to another; even so a considerable sum of money was involved.

CAPITAL AND SHAREHOLDING

The nominal capital of £9,000 was divided into three equal portions, with fifteen shares for Assistants, thirty shares for Liverymen and sixty shares for members of the Yeomanry. I have found nothing to support the allegation, made thirty years later,[1] that members of the Court collected the cash for shares from Liverymen and others but omitted to pay up the full value of their own holdings; they did, however, allot shares to themselves in all three grades and thus limit the benefit to fewer even than the agreed 105 partners, notwithstanding—as the allegation continues—that the Company consisted of several hundreds more.

The earliest record book devoted solely to the accounts of the new privilege is a Dividend Book of 1644; from 1650 there is a Journal for recording items of expenditure; and from 1663 there is a Stock Book which gives the whole economic picture. Fortunately, the ruling in the letters patent that the management should be firmly in the hands of the Masters, Wardens and Assistants led to the recording in the Court Book of certain decisions affecting the privilege. From this source we know that the original capital was £9,000; that the payment in 1611 for Abergavenny House[2] out of the profits increased the value of the shares by 50 per cent as they came to change hands; and that, three years later, the contribution of £520 made, on behalf of the

---

[1] In a document among the University Archives at Cambridge (33.2.93), called 'Woods information' and dated May 8, 1635. I do not know who was responsible for the final compilation of the document, but I am certain from letters in the Archives of about the same date that Henry Fetherstone and Michael Sparke supplied much of the information, which is—in the main—accurate.

[2] The site of the present Hall. See Chapter XI for a discussion of the Company's property.

Company, to the City fund for the Plantation of Londonderry increased the share value by a further 6⅔ per cent.[1] From 1614 until minor modifications in 1729, the nominal capital was therefore £14,400, an Assistant's share being worth £320, a Livery share £160 and a Yeomanry share £80; and it was at these prices that the shares changed hands.

The Court managed the allocation of shares for which, as they fell vacant, there were always plenty of applicants—of senior holders of Livery shares (who had to be Assistants) for the highest grade of holding and of senior holders of Yeomanry shares (who had to be Liverymen) when a Livery shareholder died or resigned that grade on election to an Assistant's share. From at least as early as 1609 some of the Yeomanry parts were divided into two, so great was the waiting list. A widow's right to enjoy her husband's investment so long as she did not remarry, while it saved some possible calls on the Company's pension fund, meant that still fewer of the 110 or so shareholders were active members of the Company. Moreover, shares were available for Stationers, whether or not they were engaged in the book trade; the gradual increase from 1598 in the number of men taking up their freedom in the Company by patrimony gives colour to the grumble that, in the early years, printers and bookbinders—and even booksellers—were deprived of shares by outsiders. John Jaggard, having been defeated in election for an Assistant's share by Thomas Adams, one of these outsiders, enlisted the help of a still more powerful outsider; as a result of his petition Francis Bacon wrote in general but strong terms to the Company about the advisability of keeping its own rules, and Jaggard eventually got his share. Sir John Banks's specific interference in 1634 on behalf of Matthew Walbank brought instantaneous favour for his client.

It was quickly discovered that, though partners could not normally assign their shares (because this might cut across the pattern of seniority to which the Court adhered), they could use them as securities for loans. But it was the Dividend, paid quarterly at first and, later, annually which was the drawing power of the investment; and the influence of the Dividend, for good and for ill, was of immense importance in the history of the Company after 1603. In the second

[1] The £125 contributed by the Stationers' Company towards Sir Thomas Smith's 'adventure into Virginia' was made up of subscriptions—varying from £2 to £10—from thirty-four individual members of the Company.

half of the century there were grumbles if the Dividend fell below 12½ per cent, but it is difficult to find what was paid in the prosperous early years. It is a curious comment on seventeenth-century business methods that, although Stock affairs occupy an enormous amount of space in the records of the Court proceedings, and although the Assistants jealously guarded their right to control Stock policy, there is no minute giving the amount of the Dividend or the time of payment before 1644. We know only that Dividends were still being paid quarterly in 1615, that 10 per cent was paid on July 4, 1606, and that 6¼ per cent was paid in December 1619. I would hesitate to make the logical deductions from these pieces of evidence—that the Dividends amounted to 20 per cent or even to 25 per cent—if 'Woods information' (quoted above) did not say that more than £3,000 a year had, on occasions, been paid out.

There is, however, plenty of evidence that the shares were in demand, and the acquisition of them created a variation in the pattern of the Stationers' lives. The career of Robert Mead will illustrate the progress of a stock-holder in relation to his progress in the Company. Mead was made free by servitude in October 1608 and was one of the younger men in a bunch of twenty-one (of whom only three were printers) elected to the Livery in June 1616. It was not until over two years later that he was in election, with two other Liverymen, for a Yeomanry share. On this occasion the most senior of them, Richard Moore, was chosen; but on November 11, 1618, Mead, by now the most senior of the candidates, was elected to the share which the widow of Thomas Man the younger relinquished at her death. Moore achieved a Livery share in May 1623 but Mead succeeded, three months earlier, in doing a deal with John Bolton, whereby they exchanged shares. Bolton needed most of the £80 difference in the value of the shares for repaying money borrowed from the Company, and the Court sanctioned the arrangement partly, I expect, for this reason and partly because Mead was about due for a Livery share.

On February 4, 1635, he was chosen an Assistant and almost exactly a year later was allowed by his colleagues to take over Thomas Purfoot's Assistant's in exchange for his own Livery share. Since Purfoot had, by permission, mortgaged this share for £216, the Court ordered him to repay half the loan and mortgage the newly-acquired Livery share for the balance; but it ruled that he should never again be eligible for an Assistant's share. Purfoot was a printer, but Mead

2 *An early almanack. On the left-hand page, the top line,*
Sundays and Saints' Days are rubricated

was a copyright-owning bookseller who had profited from the financial difficulties of his less prosperous fellows to pass through the two shareholding stages—in a matter of eighteen years—at a shade more than the normal speed; but his progress was only a *little* quicker than the average. Samuel Man waited eleven years for a Livery but only a further nine before he was chosen, at the second attempt, into an Assistant's share; and an analysis of the shareholders in 1644 confirms that the normal wait between elections was ten years.

It was as usual the first step that counted—the ability to raise £80 as soon as the opportunity of election occurred. Thereafter, careful management of the Dividends would provide the further capital sums required. One of the immediate results, therefore, of the creation of the English Stock was a widening of the gap between the wage-earner and the man with capital, however small; of the forty-five holders of Assistant's and Livery shares in the first complete list (1644) only five were printers working in London, one was a Printer to the University of Cambridge and three were the widows of printers. There is, on the other hand, little evidence in the same list for the criticism that many of the best shares were still in the hands of those who did not work in the book trade; the widow of George Cole, a Proctor in the Court of Arches, held an Assistant's share and three holders of Livery shares have left no traces of their trade. It is worth mentioning that over a quarter of the 1644 Dividends were drawn by widows.

MANAGEMENT

The business of the English Stock was so important that the Court decided early in 1607 to meet once a fortnight instead of once a month; but a more compact committee, like the one which operated before 1603, was necessary for day-to-day supervision. To the Master and Wardens were added two Stock-keepers representing the interests of the partners who held Assistant's shares and two representing holders of Livery shares. These were chosen by the Court on March 1st each year for the twelve months beginning at Lady Day; only in 1608 were two Stock-keepers allowed to represent the holders of Yeomanry shares. On this occasion the partners were called over by name before the 'elections' took place and before the newly-approved ordinances for the Stock[1] were read to them; then there was a debate which ended

---

[1] The earliest to survive are those of 1681, when they had been revised along with the Ordinances of the Company.

in the carrying of a resolution that the Under Warden should not be one of the elected Stock-keepers—i.e. that if a Stock-keeper, elected on March 1st, were chosen Warden in July, his Stock-keeper's place should be taken by another. (In 1617 this rule was made to apply to *both* Wardens.) By this means the Court ensured that five (two Stock-keepers and the three officers of the Company) out of the committee of nine would always be Assistants. The oligarchic governing body, having made a tentative democratic gesture with one hand by permitting Stock-keepers for Yeomanry shareholders, promptly negatived it with the other hand by making certain of its own control of the committee. Democratic representation faded out altogether twenty years later when Liverymen were regularly chosen to represent the Yeomanry interest; by 1644 thirty-one Yeomanry shares were held by Liverymen or their widows.

The 'manager' of the Stock, under the immediate direction of the Stock-keepers, was still the Treasurer, the official who had acted for the pre-1603 partners. His annual election on March 1st was largely a formality, Edmund Weaver and George Sawbridge holding the office between them for over sixty of the first hundred years; there was therefore some continuity in management to offset the yearly changes of Stock-keepers. The Treasurer normally lived at Stationers' Hall and had some assistance from the Clerk, the Beadle and the Porter; he drew books from the Stock-keepers for his current stock and filled from it the orders he received from booksellers; he was responsible for money received on the Stock's account from all sources and, under instruction, for all payments incurred in the production of the books; he submitted his accounts—at first every six months and later annually or at even longer intervals—to the scrutiny of six auditors[1] elected, with the Stock-keepers, each year. He received a salary of £40 (raised to £50 in 1615), besides free quarters, and he was not debarred from trading on his own account.

The Stock-keepers were, primarily, what their name implies, guardians of the warehouses; and each elected pair had a key to one of the three locks on each of the doors. The full committee was responsible for deciding what books to send to which presses, for approving estimates and paper samples, for delivering paper from and receiving printed sheets into the warehouses, for supplying the current stock

---

[1] At first, two of these were, like the Stock-keepers, real members of the Yeomanry and not just holders of Yeomanry shares; in 1632 one was a Liveryman; from 1638 both were.

of the Treasurer, for authorizing all payments. The burden on those who took their committee work seriously was considerable; Robert Mead was a Livery Stock-keeper in 1619, 1626 and 1634, an Assistants' representative in 1636 and 1640, Warden in 1638 and 1642 and Master four times between 1644 and 1657; he was also an auditor in 1632. How meticulously he and the other Stock-keepers in the first half of the century carried out their duties it is impossible to say; the only evidence comes, as it so often does, from a quarrel and reveals a concern rather for personal interests than for the welfare of the organization.

In 1628 the Clerk did not, as usual, enter the names of the Stock-keepers chosen on March 1st, though there was a meeting of the Court that day. But on March 3rd the Court made an important order about the bad workmanship and the nefarious practices of the printers who worked for the Stock, and laid it down firstly that the Stock-keepers should be allowed to see the documents relating to the Stock property, and secondly that an inventory of them be made for their use. Trouble was obviously brewing. On August 5th the Court summarily dis- :nissed William Aspley and John Parker, the two Stock-keepers for the Livery, sequestered their Dividends and arbitrarily nominated two Liverymen, neither of whom had Livery shares, to fill the vacant places. The reasons given for this action were that Aspley and Parker had, on their own initiative, put out work to the very printers complained of on March 3rd and had refused to deliver paper to Humphrey Lownes,[1] although the Court had ordered on May 5th that he should continue to have the printing of the psalter. Supported by a faction among the partners Aspley and Parker had refused to hand over their paper-warehouse key and had spoken jeeringly to the Master and Wardens in the presence of others with, so the Court was persuaded, 'a purpose to make a tumult or Combustion amongst the whole Corporacõn'. Parker had even threatened the Master, George Cole, with physical violence and would have 'borne him down backewardes' if Cole had not received support from bystanders. Aspley gave in immediately and was fined 20s, but Parker declared that he would be hanged at the gate of the Hall before he would submit. When called to a Court and asked why the Assistants should not discharge him from the Livery, he answered that they could do so if they had the

---

[1] He had married, as his second wife, the widow of Peter Short and had thereby succeeded to a master printer's place. His first wife was the daughter of Thomas Man; see above, p. 88.

power. Parker eventually submitted and was restored to the Livery, but only after Cole's death and on the strength of a restitution order from the Court of King's Bench. When, in 1641, he and some of his friends were Assistants, he succeeded in having the offending orders erased from the Court minutes on the ground that Cole and *his* friends had abused their position to bring about a miscarriage of justice. I am inclined to think that Cole, who was not in the book trade, and some of the richer men had used their gild power in their own interests; but it is fairly certain that Parker had tried to use his position as a Stock-keeper to pay off a score which he owed as a shareholder in one of the other stocks[1] and it is quite certain that, when he became an Assistant, he set his face against any diminution in the power of the Court.[2]

Three points emerge from the Parker episode. The first is that there existed in the 1620s an opposition party which had somewhat different grounds of complaint from those of the 1580s. The second is that the business of the English Stock and the business of the Company were difficult if not impossible to keep separate. Sometimes it seems as if the confusion were deliberate; in 1614 Melchisidec Bradwood's fine of £4 for not serving as a Stock-keeper (because he was then working at Eton) was paid to the Wardens; and in 1629 the Dividends payable to the widows of Masters of the Company were to be stayed until the Court was satisfied that the silver gifts due from their late husbands had been presented. The third point, which grew out of the second, is that the power of the Court was increased by its ability, after 1603, to employ economic sanctions by withholding the Dividend of a disobedient member of the Company.

But in spite of its capacity to deal with direct opposition, the Court was unable to keep the Stock free from less organized forms of trouble within the Company. The most persistent of these was the difficulty —amounting sometimes to the impossibility—of collecting the debts. Booksellers took such advantage of buying from the Treasurer on credit that it was at times difficult to find the cash for the Dividend; in April 1608 £30 had to be borrowed for paying it. Threats to withhold a man's Dividend towards the payment of his account or to charge him interest at 10 per cent were seldom carried out, and there developed a casual attitude to this kind of obligation which only the destruction wrought by the Fire was able to cure.

[1] See below, p. 106.   [2] See Chapter VIII.

Problems of a different kind arose at the production end of the business. I have already mentioned the 1628 order about the printers' bad workmanship; a much more dangerous offence was the over-printing of the Stock books and the selling of the results under the counter. As early as 1606 Humphrey Lownes (the favoured one twenty years later) and Felix Kingston, who were in partnership, were convicted of running off many more copies of the primer than had been ordered; but they were fined only the cost of the paper. As some check on this practice, the printing of a single book was often divided between two or more printers. A greater offence was the secret printing of Stock books. In 1611 Nathaniel Butter, who had four years earlier lost the post of Treasurer, was found to have had an impression of the primer printed for him at Dort and was deprived of his Yeomanry share; in 1632, because his unauthorized printing of the psalms was a first offence, Thomas Harper was let off with a fine.

But the most dangerous and expensive troubles arose from the claims by individuals, or by organizations outside the Company, to part of the monopoly which the Stationers had bought. The liability to pay James Roberts, one of the partners in the old almanack privilege, an annuity of £50 was acknowledged from the beginning, though the paying of it out of the poor fund for the fifteen years of his survival seems somewhat mean; but the successful claim in 1604 from the administrator of the other partner, Richard Watkins, was an unexpected shock which cost the Stock £160. A much greater blow was the discovery ten years later that in 1591 Elizabeth had granted Verney Alley[1] the reversion of the Day patent from the death of Richard Day. Alley received little benefit from it but his executors settled for £600 in November 1614.

COMPETITION FROM THE UNIVERSITIES

Time tended to obliterate the traces of these misfortunes but time, to balance the account, tended to aggravate the claims of two corporations, persistent and undying: the Universities of Cambridge and Oxford. By a charter of 1534, the Chancellor, masters and scholars of Cambridge[2] obtained the right to appoint three stationers and

[1] Possibly some relation of William Alley, Bishop of Exeter 1560–70, who had a royal patent for printing *The Peacemaker* and whose book *The Poor Mans Library* was printed by John Day.

[2] See 'Early Cambridge Printers and the Stationers' Company', *Transactions of the Cambridge Bibliographical Society*, vol. ii, pt. iv, 1957, pp. 275 ff.

printers, aliens or natives, to print any kind of book approved by the Chancellor. No immediate advantage was taken of this privilege and, when the Stationers of London obtained their Charter in 1557, no book had been produced at Cambridge for nearly forty years, and the University's right to a press—a remote danger, it must have seemed— was referred to in the letters patent only by a general 'notwithstanding' clause. For the next twenty-five years it was taken for granted in London that it was the policy of the Government, as it had been the ambition of the Company, to allow no printing outside the City and its suburbs. Lord Burghley's interference in 1576 to stop the University's plan of printing, under the guidance of John Kingston, books belonging to the privileges of the Queen's Printers and others must have allayed the fears which Kingston's appointment as printer had raised.

When, therefore, Thomas Thomas, on his appointment in 1583, went to the expense of buying a press, the Stationers' Company seized it and, on behalf of the patentees, confidently pulled all the strings it could and used every kind of argument against both the man and his proposed practice: that he was untrained and would in his ignorance attract the wrong kind of journeymen; that he would be ruined by retaliation; that supervision by the Company, which was difficult enough in London, would be impossible elsewhere; and that, anyhow, there were enough printers already for the needs of the kingdom. Since the University could not be prevented from doing what it had a right to do, the Company put on pressures of a different kind. In the Star Chamber Decree, Cambridge was allowed only one press and its printer was allowed only one apprentice but as many journeymen free of the Company as he could afford to pay; books sent to London for sale were seized and the University printer was prosecuted for printing other men's copies, particularly those controlled by the partners in the Day patent.

Thomas was succeeded in 1588 by a young professional printer, John Legate, who had been trained in the Queen's Printing House; he quickly realized that, if he was to stay in business, he had to print some books which were profitable, even though these were nearly all in the hands of London Stationers and guarded by royal patents. For the next thirty-five years Legate and his successor, Cantrell Legge, battled for a place in this particular sun. In their struggle they were supported, naturally, by the University. In 1591 it petitioned Burghley to use his influence with the patentees so that 'our poore Printar may, with there good patience, now and then Deale with some fewe of the most salable Copies for his necessary maintenance in honest sort'. The result was the first of a series of concessions to which the Company unwillingly agreed; it allowed the Cambridge printers a month's option on any books brought from the Frankfurt Fair, provided their choices were entered in the register and 'orderlie allowed'.

The formation of the English Stock in 1603 shifted the burden of opposition to the Cambridge printers' encroachment more firmly on to the shoulders of the Court, but it gave no greater legal or moral power to avoid a second and more important concession. By a Privy Council decree of December 10, 1623, the University printers obtained the right of comprinting with the London patentees, up to the capacity of one press; that is, of printing certain privileged books, including such almanacks as were first offered to them, even though the same books were being printed in London. It was clearly laid down by the same decree that London booksellers were not to discriminate against books printed at Cambridge. Since there were members of the Company who felt aggrieved by the limitation in the number of master printers or by their inability to participate in the printing and selling of privileged books or at the way in which the affairs of the Company were mismanaged (the Parkers and their friends), and since Cambridge books sold more cheaply than those printed in London, it is not surprising that the Company, acting on behalf of the English Stock and the King's Printers, was unable to resist a third concession. Another Privy Council decree, of April 16, 1629, allowed the University printers to print certain sizes of Bible in any quantities, some versions of the psalms, and Lily's *Grammar* up to 3,000 copies a year.

A little over two years later Cambridge had lost some of the ground which the printers with London experience had won for it; instead of replacing them, when they died, by other professionals, the University put in academics, and by the autumn of 1630 the three printers' places were held by the three Buck brothers. Early in the following year a committee of Stationers went to Cambridge and negotiated an agreement, which was signed by Thomas Buck and by Edmund Weaver, the Treasurer of the English Stock, on July 22, 1631. By this the printing of privileged books at Cambridge (which could not be avoided) was in future to be done at the charges and to the orders of the English Stock on paper supplied from London; the finished sheets were to be delivered at Stationers' Hall, except those needed for the Cambridge market. The Company had seized the opportunity afforded by the Bucks' lack of interest in and understanding of a printer's economic problems to introduce complete control of the privileged books printed at Cambridge; the price paid for this arrangement was an agreed printing rate well above that paid in London.

About a year after this compact was signed Roger Daniel, a professional printer, took the place of Francis Buck. He found the arrangement with the Company irksome and complained to the Vice-Chancellor that 'the University Presse is servant to the . . . Stationers'; but he was probably party to an agreement with London in 1636 and he was certainly party to one in 1639, a few days after he had taken over, for ten years, all John Buck's interest in the University privilege. By this agreement the English Stock and the farmers of the King's Printers' Offices jointly guaranteed to sell Cambridge booksellers sufficient privileged books for their needs and to pay Thomas Buck £75 and Daniel £125 a year for ten years to refrain from printing such books except under written instructions from London, when the work would be done on paper supplied and at London rates. At a cost of £200 a year, competition from Cambridge had been bought off.

The story of printing at Oxford, so far as it affected the Stationers' Company, can be told in a few words. It begins only in 1632 with Archbishop Laud's determination firstly that his own University should not lag behind Cambridge either in the printing of learned works or in the right to print all sorts of approved books, and secondly that Oxford should avoid the expensive and time-wasting business of quarrelling with the London monopolists. The threat of printing the Bible and almanacks was therefore used to force the King's Printers and the Company to pay the University £200 a year to refrain from printing them. A 'covenant of forbearance' on these terms was signed on March 12, 1637, and set the pattern not only for the Oxford arrangement during the next twenty-five years, but for the Cambridge arrangement in 1639.

Though the London parties to these agreements could combine against dangers from outside they found agreement on the proportion each should pay much more difficult. When the farmers of the two King's Printing Offices refused to abide by the Court's decision that their contributions should be £110, the Court ordered the purchase of new founts of type for the printing of the Bible, the most valuable part of the King's Printer's privilege, which the Universities were being paid not to print. This reaction was typical both of the Court acting as the Board of the English Stock and of the capitalists among the Stationers combining, under the umbrella of the Company, to 'engross' another section of the book trade. I have already mentioned[1] the early purchase of the patent for common-law books by the partners in the 1603 privilege. This was only the balance of a thirty-year grant which, on its termination, was lost in 1629, regained in 1662 and finally abandoned, as the result of a prolonged lawsuit, shortly after the Fire. By 1607 the Stock had also arranged for the assignment of Henry Stringer's privilege for school-books, a valuable addition for which new patents were issued in 1613 and 1631;[2] the Stock managed to retain the rights in these books, at the cost of payments to rival claimants who had reached a King's ear first, and the *Gradus ad Parnassum*—the only Stock publication to survive to the present— was added to this section of the privilege early in the eighteenth century. In addition to these two classes of books, the Stock acquired profitable and well-established single books, like Speed's *Genealogies* which, with stock and rights, cost £700 in 1638.

The climax of the monopolistic wave came a dozen years after the first grant and lasted at its highest intensity for just over three years. On May 9, 1615, the Assistants and the master printers agreed that, in addition to the King's Printers, there should be only nineteen printing houses, of which fourteen were to have two presses each and the rest one. On January 3, 1616, the Latin Stock was floated (the working of which I shall deal with on page 106), and two months later the second grant for the English Stock, clearing up the Alley confusion, was obtained, on surrender of the first. In June the Court elected twenty-one new Liverymen in order to strengthen the 'establishment'. There was then a lull for over a year. On September 4, 1617, Thomas Jones, the Common Serjeant, was appointed Counsel to the Company at the enhanced fee of 44s per annum, and in March of the following year the third of the Company's trading concerns—the Irish Stock—was launched. In October the Court began a long battle to keep the printing and marketing of ballads out of the hands of

---

[1] See above, p. 93.
[2] See below, pp. 193–6, for an account of this section of the business.

Thomas Symcock, acting as an assign for a protégé of the King, and in the hands of a small group of Stationers. The officers of the Company for the four gild years involved were Thomas Man, William Leake, Thomas Adams, Thomas Dawson, Humphrey Lownes, George Swinhowe, Matthew Lownes and Simon Waterson. All were heavily involved in the Latin and Irish Stocks or in lending money to the Company.

THE LATIN STOCK

The primary purpose of the Latin Stock[1] was the purchase, through factors and agents on the Continent, of books printed abroad; these were to be distributed to the trade in this country from a shop built on part of the garden of the new Hall in Ave Maria Lane; the rent was £40 a year, payable to the English Stock.[2] It was perhaps hoped that successful distribution of such books might take the sting out of the concession made to Cambridge in 1591. The shareholders, as in the English Stock, were divided into three classes, the sixteen in the first class having between them, at £100 a share, the same stake as the sixty-four in the third class. About 75 per cent of the nominal capital of £4,800 was paid up, and the English Stock type of organization —annually elected Stock-keepers working with the officers of the Company under the general direction of the Court—was set up; but the manager worked only part-time.

On June 27, 1627, the partners decided to wind up the affairs of this Stock and, although the Company was heavily involved, there is no mention of this decision in the Court minutes. What exactly went wrong, I do not know; the pointers are the failure to declare a dividend, except in 1619 when it was paid out of capital; the determination of many of the partners, after about two years, to dispose of their holdings while they could still get cash for them (an ambitious bookseller named John Parker bought up a number and attributed his loss on them to George Cole); and a disastrous reliance, with the official backing of the Company, on loans. In 1624 £2,000 was borrowed at 6 per cent from the Countess of Nottingham, when at least £700 of earlier loans remained outstanding, besides printers' bills for the books which the Stock had decided to print in London.

---

[1] An article by H. R. Plomer in *The Library*, 2nd ser., viii, 1907, throws a certain amount of light on both the Latin and Irish Stocks from two sets of Chancery proceedings.

[2] The later locations of this warehouse are dealt with in Chapter XI.

It is difficult to resist the conclusion that a group of rich and power-ful Stationers attempted to 'engross' a specialized part of the book trade and to use their standing in the Company for their own rather than for the general advantage. The clue to this lies in the names of the ten partners who bound themselves jointly, in the sum of £4,000, to repay the Countess of Nottingham within two years. These ten were:

George Swinhowe*	Thomas Pavier†
George Cole	Bonham Norton†
Simon Waterson*†	Richard Field*
Matthew Lownes*	Humphrey Lownes*
Clement Knight†	Adam Islip

Four of them (marked with †) were the special committee appointed by the Court, a month before, to look into the affairs of the Stock; five of them (marked with *) were already standing as sureties for a £600 loan negotiated in 1620; the first six in the list were the original Stock-keepers who were accused of refusing either to give up office or to submit accounts or to call meetings of the partners; most of them were engaged in the wholesale trade and all of them, except the favoured law-printer Islip, were ex-Masters or ex-Wardens and among the biggest capitalists in the Company.

I cannot believe that the demand for books from the Continent suddenly dried up; the activities of booksellers like Henry Fetherstone, Humphrey Robinson and George Thomason prove that, at a slightly later date, it was still strong. The kindest explanation is that men who were extremely competent in their own businesses made, during a period of general economic depression, a complete mess of an organiza-tion from which, as booksellers, they might expect direct competition if it were well enough managed to pay dividends to the partners. The importance of the Latin Stock in the history of the Stationers lies in the Company's having officially sanctioned the undertaking and allowed its seal to be used for the raising of money. In the spring of 1638 the Assistants were compelled, by the threat of legal action, to authorize the repayment of the balance of the last outstanding £300 loan; not until the end of August in the same year was the Company finally clear of all liabilities.

THE STOCKS

THE IRISH STOCK

The Irish Stock was created about two years after the Latin and
brought about as much credit to the Company. In March 1618, at the
instigation of Felix Kingston, the Court approached the Privy Council
which obtained from the King a grant of the rights of the King's
Printer in Ireland for the Company. This was for twenty-one years
and in the names of three of its members; Kingston, originally a Grocer
and the son of a printer to the University of Cambridge, was one of
these. It was probably thought that Ireland, as a result of recent
Government policy, would become a profitable colonial market; the
Privy Council, in its letter to the Lord Deputy in Ireland, referred to
the Company's promise 'to settle a factory of booksellers and booke-
binders'.[1] This hope quickly proved illusory and the Stock, instead of
selling large quantities of London-printed books through its Dublin
warehouse, was forced to use its press there to print books for selling
in England; the 1621 edition of Sidney's *Arcadia* was one of these.
How many partners there were and what the share arrangement was
are not known, but about 90 per cent of the nominal capital was
subscribed; a good deal of this must have been spent on the letters
patent and on buying out the rights, the stock and the printing equipment of John Frankton, the previous holder of the office. There were
Stock-keepers, though there is no record of their election, and there
was a warehouse—at first in the Hall and, from 1630, in the new
building on the bowling alley; the Treasurer of the English Stock
acted as part-time manager. There was a succession of Dublin agents
or factors, one of whom had a salary of £100 a year with a further £10
for an apprentice; their accounts had to be checked by delegations
from London. The usual series of committees was appointed to look
into and advise on the Irish affairs, and the financial interdependence
of the various Stocks became almost inextricable; on November 7,
1631, the deed by which William Bladon, the Dublin agent, covenanted
to pay his Dividend from the English Stock into a fund for paying
interest on Latin Stock loans was handed to the Irish Stock-keepers
for locking up with their letters patent.

In 1635 the Court intervened to prevent Thomas Weaver, the son
of the Treasurer, from suing certain Irish Stock partners in the Court
of Star Chamber for debts which, as late as 1638, he put at £50; and

---

[1] *Acts of the Privy Council 1618–1619*, 1929, pp. 65–6.

in October 1639 the Company accepted from Bladon an offer of £2,600 for the stock and rights in Dublin. The Civil War prevented a neat conclusion of this arrangement; by 1642 Bladon had paid only £974 and in 1648 there occurs, in the Court minutes, a last but irrelevant reference to the partners. At some later, but unknown, date, the Company was finally rid of its responsibility for a second mismanaged venture into monopoly trading. The mismanagement, but continued survival, of the English Stock I shall deal with in Chapter X.

CHAPTER VII

GROWTH, 1603 TO 1641

NORMAL GILD ACTIVITIES

THE attempts—both by wealthy, powerful Stationers operating with the backing of their Company and also by the Company itself—to build exclusive trading empires form one part of their history. The Government's employment of the Company as its agent for press control forms another part. In the reigns of James I and Charles I the Company also lived the life of an ordinary middle-sized gild, which was exceptional only in the close association of that life with the trades followed by the great majority of its freemen.

It might be expected that this association would lead to a good deal of interference by the governing body in the lives of Stationers; but the evidence of this is meagre. In 1607 a man was fined for binding books in a manner forbidden by the ordinances. Booksellers were occasionally ordered to pay 1s each for opening their shops on Saints' Days, and on two or three occasions they were punished for buying from apprentices or journeymen printers; in 1617 Richard Meighan was fined for enticing a chapman from another bookseller's shop. Very occasionally notice was taken of faulty printing. There were, of course, infringements of the rules about the licensing and entering of books in the register,[1] and frequent references to decrees and proclamations on the subject; but cases involving punishment were fewer than one a year. There were disputes between individuals over the ownership of copyrights, and there was continual watchfulness, on the part of the Court, over the affairs of the English Stock. But the records of the exercise of discipline might, in the main, be those of any other company. Freemen failed to attend a quarterly meeting or went and played

---

[1] On December 7, 1607, the Court repeated an order of January 19, 1598, that the Wardens were not to allow the entrance in the register of any book except for a member of the Company resident in or near London; and no member was to act as a cover for a stranger. These orders were, perhaps, aimed at booksellers and printers in the Universities and were, certainly, moves in the fight to keep the control of copyright in the hands of the Company.

bowls instead of hearing the ordinances read; Liverymen came with-out gowns to the election of Stock-keepers or went to a funeral in 'falling bands'—or didn't go; Liverymen cut the mayoral election or the Ash Wednesday sermon, and freemen cut a train-bands parade. More serious were the breaking of apprenticeship rules—by not bind-ing boys at Stationers' Hall, by not bringing an apprentice to be formally 'turned over' or by trying to make him free before his time (a rare fault). There are the usual examples of ill-temper—striking an apprentice in front of the Court, 'undecent speeches' to the Master or even to the whole board of Assistants; Bonham Norton was fined £20 for maliciously 'and often' striking Warden John Bill; John Harrison, the eldest, and Michael Sparke were punished for arresting fellow Stationers without permission.

Along with a company's attempt to maintain a reasonable degree of good behaviour went rather pleasanter functions. One of the increasingly important of these was the dispensation of charity. That of the Stationers had been limited in the reign of Elizabeth by lack of funds; but the Court, with the aid from 1580 of the Kevall bequest, had made small grants to relieve a wide variety of distress: 5s towards the cost of burying the wife of Giles Hooke, the Porter; 2s to release Dowsing from prison and 10s to Roger Ward's wife when he was in prison at the Company's suit; 3s to Edward Couek, a claspmaker, to make good his mistress's debt to him; 10s to enable Edward Day to get his tools out of pawn; 6s 8d to Thomas Settles when he was hurt, and various grants to those sick of the plague or other diseases. From 1583 a few pensions were paid by the Renters to those who, like Peter French, were too old or too ill to work, and to widows; Mistress Crowley was granted 26s 8d in 1592. It is unlikely that before 1600 the Company spent more than £10 a year on charity, but the establishment of the trading monopoly by the grant of 1603 settled at £200 the annual amount to be laid out on pensions[1] and enabled the money available from the normal revenue to be devoted solely to miscellaneous calls for relief.

I have already mentioned[2] the bursaries paid out of the Company's stock to young men at Cambridge and Oxford. In 1593 William Nor-ton made provision in his will for financial support of a different kind;

---

[1] This was laid down in the renewed grant of 1616 and was implied in that of 1603. A book for recording the quarterly payment of pensions was opened early in 1608 but the payments may have begun four years earlier. The full £200 was not paid to proper pensioners until after the death of James Roberts in 1618. See above, p. 101.   [2] See above, p. 62.

he left £6 a year to create a fund from which young Stationers could borrow money, interest free for three years, to help them over the early stages of independent business.[1] Ten years later Robert Dexter left £20 to be lent and re-lent to four young men. This aiding of the enterprising but penniless freeman was a common practice in the London companies, and in the difficult days of the 1580s the Stationers had occasionally made small loans—usually to printers who were in trouble. By the 1630s, however, when there was over £200[2] at the disposal of the Court each year, the booksellers were getting more than their fair share; moreover, they were making excuses to retain their loans for years after the date for repayment and were thereby depriving others of the benefit. Later on, the abuses grew even worse; in 1644 John Clarke, a bookseller of about forty-five in a fair way of business, received a loan of £50 and when he repaid it nearly seven years later his son, also a bookseller, took it over and had it renewed. In 1653 a committee was appointed to report on the misuse of loan money, and particularly on the £100 still owed by the executors of Thomas Whittaker who had died three years before and who had had one of the best bookselling businesses in London. The committee's report (if it was ever made) was not recorded, nor did the abuse cease. Printers were not blameless, but they were given far fewer opportunities to be blameworthy and they stored up resentment at this discrimination against them.

In all companies there were groups of men who complained to their governing bodies—against harsh treatment at the hands of other groups or against the unfair operation of the ordinances. In the Stationers' Company the journeymen printers frequently appealed to the Court against their masters;[3] less frequently the master bookbinders drew attention to their troubles. On May 19, 1612, the Assistants made a sensible order that if a bookbinder reported when his single apprentice had served four years (bookbinders seldom had a Liveryman's entitlement to more than one), the Master and Wardens were empowered to allow him a second, so that at no time would he be without some skilled help. (The same concession was to be permitted to other tradesmen when their apprentices had served all

---

[1] Arthur Pepwell, when he made his will in 1568, left £100 for this purpose, but only on condition that neither of his sons survived to the age of twenty-one. (H. R. Plomer, *Abstracts*, 1903, p. 16.)

[2] Largely through the bequest of John Norton in 1612; see below, p. 210.

[3] See below, p. 151.

but one year of their time.) Eight years later this privilege was taken away from the binders because it was contrary to the Star Chamber Decree of 1586; but at about the same time (1619) a schedule of rates for binding over 100 of the commonest sizes and kinds of books was negotiated with the booksellers and received official approval. It is difficult to see how any other group among the Stationers could have been hurt by the apprenticeship concession to the binders; but since the Decree was the basis of copyright control an appeal to any of its provisions—from perhaps a jealous printer—would almost certainly be successful. In 1629 a compromise was reached whereby the Court could allow *any* Stationer a second apprentice when his first had served to within two years of his term.

In November 1635 a committee of Assistants was appointed to discuss with six representatives of the bookbinders a petition which the latter had submitted. The outcome cannot have satisfied the binders, for eighteen months later they appealed (without success) to Archbishop Laud[1] to prevent any books being despatched unbound from London, except to the Universities, because binders in the provinces were subject to no authority; to decide what books should be bound in sheepskin; and to make the Company agree to a new scale of prices. In addition, they prayed that the number of apprentices be limited (had the concession of 1612 produced too many binders for the work available?); that freemen be compelled to serve as journeymen for two years before setting up as masters; and that binders who were free of other companies should obey the rules of the Stationers'.

Forty years before, an Aldermanic committee had reported[2] that the trade of bookbinding should 'not be dispersed into more Companyes then allready it is' and that the Star Chamber rules 'for the stinting of Apprentices to such free men as Do vse that trade of booke binding printinge or booke sellinge' be embodied in an Act of Common Council. The Act never came, and the mere suggestion that the exercise of a particular craft should not be open to all freemen of the City was contrary to custom. It was the ambition of those companies which maintained lively associations with their trades[3] to gain direct control

---

[1] August 2, 1637, S.P. Dom. Car. I, vol. 365, no. 15.
[2] October 6, 1597, Rep. 24, ff. 132–3.
[3] As the Weavers and the Brewers who, in 1622 and 1631 respectively, made successful bids to control those engaged in weaving and brewing, in spite of protests from the City and, in the latter case, a petition to the King from the Stationers', the Grocers', the Drapers' and other companies. The Aldermen described the action of the Brewers as a bad example to other

of all who practised their crafts, and there was a big translation of Drapers to the Stationers' Company in 1600 'by Consent of bothe Companies, Accordinge to the Constitutions of the Citie' (which may have been brought about as much by the attractions of English Stock investment as by official pressure). But the Stationers, though they had a large measure of success towards the end of the seventeenth century, had earlier to be content with individual bargains. Richard Jones was permitted on August 15, 1597, to enter two ballads in the register of copies provided he did not print them for a Draper; on May 30, 1603, the Court, in allowing Robert Triplet (translated *to* the Brewers in 1631) the sole right to a kind of Ready Reckoner, stipulated that he should sell the books to free Stationers only; and in 1605 Edward Venge was forbidden to sell *A Weeks Work* to Haberdashers. Since it was not possible to force all those in the book trade to become Stationers, it was essential to prevent (where possible) the loss of Stationers to other companies; in 1618 the Weavers agreed that Thomas Howard and such others as were weavers should remain Stationers, even though they bound their apprentices at Weavers' Hall.

The Stationers were at least lucky in this, that in the control of their trades they were not challenged by another company, as the Leathersellers were challenged by the Glovers. Moreover, their strength increased with their growth in numbers. The average intake during the first forty years of the seventeenth century was more than twice that of the previous years for which the evidence survives, and a measure of the growth is the occasional rewarding of the Senior Renter Warden for the additional trouble he had had in collecting quarterage; in 1625 John Smethwick received £3 4s for what must have been the record sum of £63 6s 2d,[1] and seven years later Thomas Downes £3 6s 8d for 'a greater Sume then euer'. The number of Liverymen also increased, to such an extent that in 1631 the obligation of the Master and Wardens to entertain them at home on election day was discontinued and the allowance of £5 towards the expense of the quarterly dinner was raised to £13 6s 8d. Exact numbers are difficult to find; but in 1620 the Company reported to the Lord Mayor that

companies and as 'a great breach of the whole frame of the City's government'. (*C.S.P. Dom. Car. I, 1629–31,* p. 440; and *Remembrancia,* pp. 103 and 108.) The 'whole frame' was, anyhow, feeling the strain from the housing development outside the City boundaries; craftsmen and shop-keepers were attracted both by the cheapness and by the freedom from interference which living in the new areas offered.

[1] Five hundred quarterages at 1s 4d produces about £33; some of the total came from arrears and some from rents.

the total of its Livery was forty (including the Master and Wardens), and that the length of their standing for the welcome of the King at St Paul's on March 26th should be at least eighty feet; and in 1638 nearly ninety were recorded in the assessment for the renewal of the City's charter.

Along with the increase in the number of those clothed went a stiff increase in the cost of the privilege. Up to 1606 the fine was not more than £2; from 1607 it was £10; by 1611 (when Francis Archer was made to pay £5 for *refusing*) it had risen to £20 where it remained until the nineteenth century. At a slightly later date the fine for the next step in the ladder of seniority—the fine to avoid serving the office of Renter Warden—was similarly fixed; in 1606 it became £20 and from 1632 it remained at £24. Over the same period the fines to avoid serving as Wardens were being scaled *down*, on the understanding (perhaps) that a man usually served his first year. Whereas fines had been as high as £20, from 1632 that for second time Under Warden became £5 and, from 1637, that for Upper Warden £6 13s 4d. Since the three candidates necessary could sometimes be provided only by compelling men to fine, and since the Renter Wardenship was a barrier through which only the ambitious need pass, it is understandable why the fines for the former went down and for the latter rose as high as the market would stand.

There is no doubt about the increase in the size of the Company nor about the crystallization of certain patterns of gild behaviour during the years before the Civil War; but it is impossible to be dogmatic about the quality of the men who were part of this increase and helped to shape the patterns. A comparison, however, of the antecedents of the 700 boys bound apprentice in the gild years 1630 to 1639 with the 350 bound during the years 1576 to 1585 (the earliest for which details are available) reveals two general differences: proportionately, many more boys, in the later period, came from the London area and far fewer were fatherless. These changes indicate, I believe, an improvement in the Company's standing in the capital and (even when allowance has been made for an increase in the expectation of life) a widespread tendency to regard the Company as one worthy of a parent's choice rather than as the orphan's last chance. The change in the trades of apprentices' fathers[1] confirms this

---

[1] See *The Library*, 5th ser., xiii, 1958, pp. 2 and 292–9, for details. See also D. F. McKenzie's 'A List of Printers' Apprentices, 1605–40', in *Studies in Bibliography*, Charlottesville, xiii, 1960.

improvement in the Company's social reputation. In the later period the proportion of husbandmen was half that in the earlier, but the proportions of gentlemen[1] and country parsons increased fourfold. The association of the Church and the Stationers reached its peak towards the end of the century when the clergy were also the most prolific authors; but even in the 1630s a yearly average of seven and a half clerical families were putting sons to work in the book trade and five and a half of these were doing so with the eyes of the head of the family still open, so to speak. Freemen of the twelve Great Companies, with an average of six a year, were looking to the Stationers twice as much as in the earlier period and, in both, the Merchant Tailors were the most heavily represented.

Unfortunately, very little can be found about the premiums which parents paid at the binding of their sons. Thomas Lawrence, gentleman of Lambeth, put down 30s in 1595 when his son John was bound for eight years to Ralph Blower, a printer; 15s of this and the boy's apparel were returned when the father decided, seven months later, to set the boy to work elsewhere. In 1613 John Garrett, a Clothworker, paid £10 (again for eight years) with the promise of £3 6s 8d at a later date if Richard Redmer, a bookseller, treated his son fairly. In the same year George Vincent, a bookseller and also perhaps a dealer in paper, received £20 with John Bainbridge, son of a London tailor, and when Mrs Vincent gave up business in 1618 she was ordered to pay back £4 for John's two unexpired years. Two disputes, brought to the notice of the Court in 1618 and 1619, refer to premiums of £10 and £20. These figures would have caused no comment, either way, a hundred years later, but it is impossible to tell how typical they were of the early seventeenth-century practice in the Company. One practice, which was fairly common later in the century but strictly forbidden at the beginning, was the employment, as apprentices or otherwise, of girls, unless they were members of a bookbinder's family.[2]

THE STAR CHAMBER DECREE OF 1637

Though it is difficult to find evidence, during the first eighty years of its chartered life, for changes in the standing of the Stationers' Company in the City of London (except that its size increased

---

[1] See below, p. 126, for the intake of the sons of gentlemen by John Beale, who nearly always went to the provinces for his apprentices.   [2] See above, p. 69, n.

threefold or even more), it is easy to trace the steps by which its status in a national context was strengthened. The ordinances which were drafted in the year after the granting of the Charter were too ambitious at that early stage; but the Decree of the Star Chamber in 1586 gave the ruling element in the Company a large part of the power it wanted, particularly for the protection of copyright. Such protection was of the utmost importance to the Company itself after the English Stock grant of 1603, and the Decree was invoked over and over again in the early part of the seventeenth century and reaffirmed by royal proclamations—in that of September 25, 1623, for instance. But the powers it gave were still not great enough for dealing successfully either with infringers of the Company's rights (cheap and popular books being particularly vulnerable) or with those who printed (or imported) and distributed criticisms of Charles I's government of Church and State; and on July 11, 1637, the Privy Council approved in Star Chamber a Decree 'Concerning Printing' which the Attorney-General had drawn up with the advice of the Lord Keeper, Archbishop Laud and others. 'For his Loue & kindnes to the Company', the Assistants voted the Attorney-General £20, and the Clerk was awarded £15 for all the extra work which had fallen on him. There is no doubt that the 1637 Decree, like that of 1586 and like the grant of the Charter in 1557, was promoted by the Company for the benefit of Stationers and obtained the sanction of the Government because it promised more effective safeguards than those already in existence, against the printing and distribution of schismatical publications which were, as on previous occasions, becoming sources of extreme embarrassment. But the decision of no fewer than four Assistants to fine for Under Warden in July 1637, rather than serve the office during the first twelve months of the operation of the Decree, is a clear comment, by those who knew, on the difficulty of controlling an expanding and ebullient book trade by Tudor methods, even though those methods may have seemed, to the promoters, the best means of curbing invasions of copyright.

The Company was so deeply involved in the provisions of the Decree[1] that I must treat them in some detail. The clauses fall into

---

[1] This contains thirty-three clauses as printed. There is a draft (S.P. Dom. Car. I, vol. 376, no. 15) in eighteen clauses which omitted much of what the Stationers particularly wanted. In what follows an asterisk indicates the absence, in the draft, of a clause which appeared in the final version. Clause iii (the licensers) was envisaged but not included in the draft. Arber reprinted the Decree in vol. iv of his *Transcript*, pp. 528–36.

three groups: those of a general nature, those aimed at booksellers, those aimed at printers and letter-founders; and between them they cover, as I shall show, many of the book trade problems which the Court and the Government had had to face during the previous fifty years. Naturally clause i forbade the production and selling of books and pamphlets which incited to sedition or heresy; though offences under this heading were matters for His Majesty's courts, the Assistants had decided on May 10, 1634, that the condemnation of Michael Sparke to stand by Prynne in the pillory with a paper on his hat (for publishing *Histrio-mastix*) reflected on the good name of the Company and they had suspended him from the Livery. Clauses ii and iii* attempted to reduce the chances of such 'offensive' printing by ordering all books to be licensed (law books by one of the Chief Justices and nearly everything else by the nominees of the Archbishop of Canterbury) and entered in the register at Stationers' Hall. This was an old idea, and as recently as August 15, 1624, a proclamation had been issued on much the same lines. On September 27, 1622, the Court had ordered that no printer was to start work on a book unless the Clerk signified in writing on the copy that it had been entered in the register, and a year later the ancient ordinance that printers deposit at the Hall a copy of every book printed had been reaffirmed. Two copies of each manuscript (clause iv) were to be provided for licensers (a clause of great annoyance to authors) and one approved copy was to be kept for reference; additions and other alterations had, on occasions, been made between licensing and printing. Even reprints (clause xviii) were to be licensed afresh; what had been proper reading in the reign of Elizabeth might be dangerous in that of Charles I. The names of authors, printers and undertakers (the booksellers responsible for the publication) were to be printed (clause viii), and the mark of the Stationers' Company and the name of anyone lawfully entitled to a copy were not to be forged (clause ix); in November 1630 the Archbishop had issued instructions, through the Company, that every piece of printing was to bear the printer's name and that the name must belong to a master allowed under the provisions of the 1586 Decree. It is odd that there was no insistence on the printing, in the book, of the licence itself, since George Cole, as Master, had ordered the printers, when they appeared for the quarterly meeting in January 1632, to observe this rule—at any rate so far as concerned books licensed by the Bishop of London.

The right to search—nominally for seditious or heretical books but really for infringements of copyright—had been one of the earliest achievements of the Company, and at times of crisis rosters of searchers had been appointed.[1] In November 1631 the Court had instructed the Wardens to organize searches, in London or the country, of any premises suspected of housing 'Counterfeit books & all other things disorderly printed'. Clauses xxv* and xxvi* ordered searches, particularly of printing houses, for unlicensed printing and for books suspected of criticizing Church or State. The Stationers saw no reason to draw attention to *their* reasons for entering premises since clause vii forbade the printing or importing of any copy which the Company or an individual had the right to print through letters patent or entrance in the register; in the previous thirty years there had been a steady stream of attempts to break the Company's monopoly, either by printing 'in Corners' or by selling the products of Dutch presses.

Searches might have had a fair measure of success, even against importations, if books had been sold to the public only by freemen of the Stationers' Company. Clause x aimed at stopping the distributive holes by forbidding haberdashers of small wares, ironmongers, chandlers (the worst groups of offenders) or anyone who had not served a seven-year apprenticeship to the trade of bookselling, printing or bookbinding, from selling books by retail. There was little chance that this order could be successfully carried out either in the provinces where adequate supervision was impossible[2] or in London where it cut across the custom of the City. Though early in 1615 the Archbishop had written quite sharply to the Lord Mayor about the right of the Commissioners in Causes Ecclesiastical to invade the jurisdiction of the City and had asked what business it was of his 'to iudge of matters concerning bookes', to the City authorities books were commodities like soap or haberdashery in which all freemen were at liberty to deal and in which they continued to deal. But City support was readily forthcoming for the provision of clause xii* which made it an offence for any stranger or foreigner to sell in this country books printed abroad; such trade was to be confined to Stationers of London

---

[1] See above, pp. 65–6 and 72, n. 1.

[2] A few months after the Decree, complaint was made to Sir John Lambe on behalf of five booksellers in Exeter against four ironmongers and a haberdasher there who had no intention of giving up selling books. (*The Library*, 3rd ser., x, 1919, pp. 135–6.) See also *C.S.P. Dom. Car. I, 1637–8*, p. 73, for an appeal to Laud that certain mercers in Coventry be allowed to go on selling books, particularly to the grammar school.

who had been bred to the book trade and who earned their living in it. A joint committee of aldermen and common councilmen had been appointed in 1615 to survey the problem of alien competition on the strength of reports from the companies; the letter from the Stationers suggests that they were unable to support their wives and children owing to the increase in house rent and the cost of food, but it does not mention the impact of aliens on the book trade.

RULES FOR BOOKSELLERS

The next group of clauses applies mainly to the booksellers. Even though imports of books could not completely be denied to the small but successful group of Stationers who specialized in that trade, some books printed on the Continent might be dangerous to the State and might compete with local editions. It was therefore laid down in clause xi that no books wholly or mainly in English were to be printed abroad for importation and, in clause xxxii, that all books from over-seas must be landed at the Port of London. Moreover, no bales or packets of books were to be opened, even by Custom House officers, unless representatives both of the ecclesiastical authorities and of the Stationers' Company were present (clause vi); and no imported books were to be put on sale before a list of each consignment had been sent to the Archbishop or the Bishop of London (clause v).[1] Thirty years earlier the Assistants had forbidden the importation of certain school-books (which were part of the English Stock) except in small quan-tities of the least popular sizes, and had borne witness to the importance of the decision by signing their names in the Court Book. In 1625 a royal proclamation—more limited in scope than a Bill which the Company had tried to persuade Parliament to pass a year or two before—had forbidden the sale of imported Latin books which had been first printed at Oxford or Cambridge. The Farmers of the Cus-toms had, however, been prevailed upon, late in 1627, to write to nine of the outports and warn them against 'the secrett & private wayes of bringing in' books which infringed the patent of the King's Printers

[1] On September 13, 1628, Adam Islip, Edmund Weaver and Humphrey Crosse (the two Wardens and a messenger) compiled a list of thirty-eight booksellers who dealt in old libraries (i.e. second-hand books) and 'Mart Bookes' (i.e. importations from the continental book fairs) and who had been told not to sell any future purchases until they had supplied lists of them to the newly appointed Archbishop, Laud. Out of the thirty-eight, twenty-five were Stationers; half of them had shops in Duck Lane or Little Britain. (S.P. Dom. Car. I, vol. 117, no. 9.)

or the Company of Stationers—ways in which the shipmasters were so adept that they were able to 'cozen the devil';[1] and in 1630 the Privy Council had issued an order to mayors and sheriffs to assist Robert Barker, the King's Printer, in his search for imported Bibles. In 1635, when the Clerk was suing David van Hoogenhosen for importing Latin books, the Court had decided to approach the King's Advocate and the Attorney-General for relief against the importation by strangers of great quantities of books which infringed royal patents and other copyrights; twelve months later another proclamation had been issued.

RULES FOR PRINTERS AND LETTER-FOUNDERS

But the real matter of the Decree was 'Concerning Printing' and a dozen of its clauses were aimed directly at printers and letter-founders. Moreover, the punishment of offending printers was to be much more severe than that of others; while the latter would suffer the con-fiscation of unlicensed books and such other penalties as the Courts of Star Chamber or High Commission might impose, a printer, in addition, might have his types defaced or even suffer the loss of his printing house; his livelihood was at stake. The number of masters allowed (clause xv*)[2] was set—unrealistically—at the 1586 figure: twenty in London (excluding the King's Printers) and those allowed at the Universities; the names of the London masters were given. In addition, clause xvii* limited each master to two machines unless he had been Upper Warden or Master when he was allowed three. The fears which dictated these repressive measures were no longer, I think, those of the booksellers, who were by 1637 all-powerful in their Company and who could only gain from competition between printers for work. The fears were in the minds of the King's advisers, who believed that repression was capable of frightening any but the twenty from setting up, and in the minds of the few privileged printers who thought they might lose business. On half a dozen occasions during the reigns of James I and Charles I the Court had taken action about supernumerary presses and printing houses; on May 9, 1615, this had been at the instigation of the master printers and on November 10, 1635, at the request of Laud.

[1] *C.S.P. Dom. Car. I, 1629-31*, p. 306.
[2] The draft obviously intended the limitation in the number but omitted the names—as clause iii omitted those of the licensers.

The privileged twenty were ordered (clause xvi) to bind themselves within ten days in sureties of £300 not to print unlicensed books,[1] while anyone setting up or working at an unauthorized press was to be pilloried and whipped (clause xxiv). These general orders were far more severe than any earlier measure except when an individual had been convicted of printing a particularly offensive book. Many unlicensed printers had been discovered: John Hamon had had six different presses seized by 1632; but there had been no violent retaliation on the part of the Court, and a printer was nearly always able to find money for a new press. As some check on the acquiring of premises in which to set up an unlicensed press, no one was to allow (clause xiii) even so much as a room to be used for printing without giving notice to the Company.

The rules governing employees were much the same as those of 1586. By clause xix apprentices were limited to the number of machines allowed; this limitation was not to be circumvented either by the introduction of sleeping partners or by binding boys at scriveners', and a runaway apprentice must not be replaced until his name had been erased in the register at the Hall. No master printer was to employ, in addition to his apprentices, anyone who was not a freeman bred to the trade (clause xxiii*), and because secret printing was partly the result of unemployment among free journeymen the Company was to take special care to find them work (clause xx*), trying first a man's original master. Moreover, every printing house must provide work for at least one journeyman, even though it could be run without. Clause xxi* laid penalties on officers of the Company who refused to go job-hunting with a journeyman at his genuine request and on journeymen who refused genuine offers. Petitions are to be treated as warily as lapidary inscriptions, but it is possible to find evidence for the main grievances as they are detailed in petition after petition— to the Court of Assistants, to Parliament, to Sir John Lambe (for Laud). That of May 16, 1613, was addressed to the Lord Chancellor by fifty-four journeymen, whose names are given, and made three points. The first was that some masters kept twice, or even three times, as many apprentices as they should. The Court had, three years before, foolishly given Melchisidec Bradwood permission to take on six apprentices for the special purpose of printing the *Works* of St John

---

[1] Clause xxxi laid it down that bonds for good behaviour could be demanded from others than printers, *after* conviction.

Chrysostom in Greek; it is impossible to say how many printers sheltered behind this precedent, but in 1627 Augustine Matthews was found to have three boys more than his allowance, and in 1629 the practice of binding boys at scriveners' had grown so common in the City that the Lord Mayor banned the enrolment of an apprentice in the Chamber of London unless he could produce indentures drawn by the clerk of his company. The second grievance was that by making and breaking partnerships it was possible for one printing house to accumulate as many as ten apprentices. The truth of this is difficult to establish; but the Court was aware of the danger for in March 1613 it made a general order about the excessive number of apprentices and ruled that John Beale and John Pindley might jointly work a printing house as 'one printer'. The third complaint was that the printers at Oxford and Cambridge were employing apprentices only and throwing their journeymen on the London market. (Clause xxii* in the 1637 Decree allowed the University printers as many apprentices as they wanted, provided they found work for their own freemen.) It is curious that no complaint was made on this occasion against the practice of binding at scriveners', since several printers had been fined for this offence before 1613 and at least two dozen were punished (some of them several times) for this evasion in the thirty years before the Decree. Early in 1635, however, the journeymen had appealed once again to the Court on the old grounds, with the addition, this time, of a grumble about binding boys at scriveners'; they also complained about the keeping of formes of type standing. The sub-committee appointed, under the chairmanship of Felix Kingston, to deal with the problem made its report on November 16th;[1] though the most general of its nineteen recommendations were eventually embodied in the Decree, the printers were so dissatisfied with the absence of immediate action that they petitioned again in 1636 and yet again early in 1637.

Clauses xiv and xxvii* to xxx* aimed to control the raw materials of printing. No joiners or smiths were to make any part of a press without informing the Company, nor was any type to be cast here or imported without similar notification. Master type-founders were limited to four (who were named) and were bound to observe the same rules as the printers in the employment of apprentices and

---

[1] There are strong echoes in this report of the orders made on December 11, 1587; see above, p. 72, n. 2.

journeymen, except that each might have a boy to pull off the knots of metal from newly cast letters. Forty years earlier the Company had demonstrated its awareness that supervision of native type-founding was one of the essentials in the control of London printing by coming to an agreement with Benjamin Simpson, who was not a Stationer, that he should enter into a bond of £40 not to deliver any type without notifying the Master and Wardens in writing. In addition, Simpson's apprentices in 1599 and 1605 were bound to printers, as extras to the number allowed, so that they might be free as Stationers. On May 11, 1622, the order about bonds was repeated.

The last clause of all (xxxiii*) introduced an element which was to be a feature of all subsequent measures of copyright control: a copy of every new book must be provided free to the University library at Oxford. Early in 1611 the Company had agreed with the University that such copies were to be delivered to Sir Thomas Bodley, and on January 28, 1612, had issued a printed order[1] to that effect; but by 1635 the Stationers had already begun to evade their obligations and and the librarian had noted that only Henry Fetherstone was sending books regularly.[2]

THE CAREER OF A PRINTER

During the first forty years of the seventeenth century the economic subservience of the printers to the booksellers, who were dominant in the Company, had not grown less; and the printers, according to the records, were the breakers of rules and disturbers of the peace. In order to illustrate the difficulties under which printers worked during this period and to provide clues for one of the major developments in the Company during, and immediately after, the Civil War, I give below brief notes of the career of John Beale, one of the two printers who were Assistants in 1641.

1608. Nov.   7   Free as the servant of Mrs Waldegrave, the widow of Robert Waldegrave, one of the most enterprising and courageous of the Elizabethan printers. J. B. was fined 4s 2d for not having been presented as an apprentice; Mrs W. was at this time receiving a pension from the Company.

1611. July   6   Presented Nathaniel Gosse (bound to John Read on June 17, 1604) for his freedom.

[1] No. 126 in the collection of broadsides belonging to the Society of Antiquaries.
[2] *C.S.P. Dom. Car. I, 1635–6*, p. 65.

1612. March 9   Bound his first apprentice—William Beale, son of John, gentle-man of Coventry, deceased, for seven years from Lady Day next. (William took up his freedom on April 5, 1619.)

Oct. 12   Entered, with William Hall (with whom he was perhaps working) Bacon's *Essays*—his first entry.[1]

1613. March 1   J. B. and John Pindley allowed, in partnership, to take William Hall's place as a master printer on the condition already mentioned.

1614. April 4   Fined 1s for absence on quarter day.

April 7   Entered six copies which had been Hall's, including certain printed forms in which J. B. specialized.

July 15   Fined £6 13s 4d and ordered to be committed to prison for binding at a scrivener's an apprentice above his allowance of one. (The threat of prison was probably an attempt to frighten him; the fine was reduced to £5 and paid on October 27, 1615.)

1615. May 9   In the survey of printing houses, J. B. is shown as having two presses.

Oct. 23   Bound his second apprentice, Edward Winslowe, son of Edward, gentleman of Clifton, Worcestershire, for eight years from August 19, 1613. (Winslowe was the boy for whom he paid the £5 fine a month after formal presentation; he was probably well worth the money, particularly since he was not free until 1635.)

1616. June 21   Clothed at £20, one of twenty-one, only three of whom were printers.

1617. Aug. 2   Elected to half Yeomanry share in the English Stock.

1618. March 16   Bound his third apprentice (the first being a year from his time), Henry Adshead, son of Reynold, yeoman of Chester, deceased, for seven years from Lady Day. (Adshead was never free but it is impossible to say how long he survived as J. B.'s apprentice.)

Nov. 27   Elected to Mrs Vincent's Livery share in the English Stock (unusually rapid promotion).

1619. Feb. 18   Entered, with the Attorney-General's warrant, H.M.'s commission to J.P.s for assessing horse-meat prices.

1620. April 3   Fined (and paid) 2s 6d for keeping an apprentice unpresented.

May 29   Having presented Richard Smith (bound for nine years on March 23, 1612, to William Hall) for his freedom, J. B. bound his brother as his fourth apprentice—Samuel Smith, son of Henry, gentleman of Baydon, Wiltshire, for eight years from midsummer. (Samuel was never free.)

1621. April 9   Bound his fifth apprentice, Benjamin Greene, son of William, yeoman of Reading, for seven years from May 1st. (Greene was free on June 9, 1628.)

[1] Only a few examples are given of his copyright entries.

1621. July 9 Elected Stock-keeper representing Livery shareholders.

1622. Oct. 19 Fined 1s (with Fetherstone and Haviland, among others) for absence on quarter day.

Oct. 29 Chosen to go to the Lord Mayor's dinner.

1623. March 1 Fined 1s for coming late on quarter day.

Aug. 20 Ordered to make good badly printed sheets of Speed's *Chronicle* and to restore certain printing materials used for the *Genealogies*, for which Speed had the sole right.

1625. Dec. 20 Bound his sixth apprentice, Thomas Ginne, son of Edward, clothworker of Lavenham, for eight years from that day. (Ginne was never free.)

1626. Dec. 5 J. B. ordered to appear at the house of Bonham Norton, the Master, at 1 p.m. the following Wednesday in connection with the printing of Gouge's *Domesticall Duties*, the copyright of which was in dispute.

1628. March 3 Fined 40s for unfitting words and 'Contemptable Behaviour' to George Cole, the Master, in Court. The occasion of this may have been Cole's handling of the Latin Stock business. On the same day he bound his seventh apprentice, Henry Holden, son of Henry, husbandman of Warwick, for seven years from that day. (Holden was free on June 5, 1635.)

May 5 The 40s fine, which he refused to pay, to be stopped out of his Dividend.

June 9 Court decided to find some other way to make him pay.

Nov. 3 Bound his eighth and ninth apprentices: John Dennys, son of John, husbandman of Thrapston, deceased, for eight years, and William Hewer, son of John, glover of Penrith, deceased, for seven years, both from that day, when J. B. must have had at least four apprentices in his house. (Dennys was never free. Hewer was free on November 10, 1635.)

1629. July 6 Dispute, in which J. B. was involved against two Stationers and the widow of a third, referred to arbitration.

1630. April 19 Thomas Brudenell's petition against J. B. for recovery of £140 paid for partnership, referred by Lord Keeper to Court; J. B. to have a copy and give his answer by Friday. (As so often happens there is no further information.)

Nov. 12 J. B. subscribed £6 towards the repair of St Paul's, along with other master printers. No one gave less; William Jones gave £40. (S.P. Dom. Car. I, vol. 175, no. 45.)

1631. March 1 Court approved the assignment of Dr Jackson's *Justifying Faith*, which J. B. had entered on December 2, 1614, to John Clarke for 50s. (The price in such a deal is seldom mentioned.)

1632. March 26 Elected, and chose to serve as, Renter Warden.

1635. Feb. 4 Elected Assistant, with Robert Mead, and fined twice, soon afterwards, for coming late to Court.

1635. Nov. 10   Fined £4 (paid January 13, 1636) for binding Robert Hughes (free on August 7, 1637) at a scrivener's. (The fine was a nuisance but, as before, worth while when a journeyman's weekly wage might be 8s for working at the press; see Court decision of January 12, 1631. If Hughes had been a compositor he would have earned the fine even more quickly.) On the same day J. B. bound his tenth (lawful) apprentice, Thomas Elie, son of Robert, carpenter of Moulton, Lincs, for seven years from July 1st, when he had been first presented but deferred owing to the discovery of Hughes's existence. (Elie was free in 1647, after J. B.'s death.)

Dec. 7   John Legate assigned to J. B. his right in a portion (three sheets—twelve pages) of vol. 1 of Samuel Hieron's *Works*; since on the same day J. B. had taken over from another printer the rights in vol. 2, he had gained control of this popular publication.

1636. March 1   Auditor of English Stock Treasurer's accounts.

1637. July 11   Star Chamber Decree. J. B. no. 6 of the twenty printers listed as allowed. About this time Sir John Lambe described him as blind and 'of great estate but a very contentious person; he took 50 li to furnish ye pore with bread and doth not do it'. (This was in one of Lambe's numerous notes on printers, made for Laud; the logic here is difficult to follow.)

Aug. 7   Bound eleventh apprentice, Ambrose Turner, son of Edward, hosier of Abingdon, for seven years, from that day. (Turner was never free.)

Dec. 4   Bound twelfth apprentice, Thomas Roycroft, son of Thomas, clothier of Coddington, Cheshire, for eight years, from that day. (Roycroft was made free by John Parker in 1647.)

1638. June 21   Bound thirteenth apprentice, Walter Phillips, son of John, husbandman of Dingeston, Monmouthshire, for seven years, from June 24th. (Phillips was rebound to John Dawson on September 3rd—perhaps because J. B. already had his full quota.)

Dec. 3   Bound fourteenth apprentice, Thomas Harding, son of Richard, ploughwright of Elsworth, Cambridgeshire, for seven years, from that day. (Harding was free in 1647.)

1639. May 6   Paid 3s, with Nathaniel Butter, for coming late to Court on three occasions.

June 27   Court ordered J. B. to pay for paper—forty reams at 3s 6d each—used in an English Stock book which he had printed so badly that the copies were unsaleable.

July 18   Paid £5 fine for first time Under Warden.

Aug. 12   Ordered not to proceed in reprinting Bacon's *Essays*, since the right to the copy was in dispute.

1639. Oct. 3   Suspended from Court and ordered to pay £6 13s 4d to the poor for disobeying order of August 12th, which had been repeated on September 2nd.

1640. July 4   Fine reduced to £3 (paid July 14th) and J. B. reinstated.

Sept. 7   Court referred letter from Lord Privy Seal about Bacon's *Essays* to arbitration.

1641. June 22   J. B. not to be 'warned' to Court, for 'indirectly' printing *A Protestation* and other pamphlets which an Assistant ought not to have printed.

Nov. 18   Co-opted to Committee of twelve, with Flesher and Kingston (see below, p. 132).

1642. July 4   Readmitted to Court and fined for second time Under Warden.

Oct. 3   Bound fifteenth apprentice, Thomas Stacey, son of William of 'ffosell', Warwickshire, gentleman, deceased, for eight years, from that day. (Stacey was never free.)

1643. April 8   Elected to an Assistant's share in the English Stock.

July 1   Fined for first time Upper Warden.

Aug. 7   Bound sixteenth apprentice, Robert Beale, son of Bartholomew, gentleman of St Andrew's, Holborn, for seven years, from that day. (This Beale was never free.)

Sept. 17   Died.

The good that men do is too often buried with them and Stationers, like other men, are more likely to be remembered, if not by their evil actions, at least by those which brought them into conflict with authority. Fines and disputes are recorded; the keeping of rules and living at peace with one's neighbour leave few traces. Petitions and lawsuits draw attention to maladjustment or ill-treatment, not to contentment and fair conditions. Even if we forget, in concentrating on the manuscript evidence, that the majority of Stationers lived quiet, orderly and reasonably prosperous lives and that their Company was not (as this chapter in their history tends to suggest) continually in a state of crisis, printed books exist to provide entries on the credit side. Stationers were in business to make money, but in the course of their business they printed and sold the Authorized Version of the Bible, the plays of Shakespeare and Ben Jonson, *Comus* and the poems and sermons of Donne, the works of Francis Bacon and Sir Walter Ralegh, Speed's *Theatre* and Mandeville's *Voyages*, and the earliest English newspapers. The 'midwives of literature' were kept busy in the reigns of the first two Stuarts, and they have their memorial.

CHAPTER VIII

CIVIL WAR

THE BREAKDOWN OF ROYAL AUTHORITY

TWENTY-FIVE years elapsed between the signing of the 1637 Decree and the passing of the Act for the Regulation of Printing—a careful attempt, by its sponsors, to give the authority of King in Parliament for what had previously derived first from the royal prerogative and later from the House of Commons. This momentous quarter of a century seemed to begin quietly, and even prosperously for the Stationers. The Company made agreements with the University of Oxford and with the University printers at Cambridge for the protection of the English Stock books; it bought, for £700 from John Speed, his sole right to print the *Genealogies* which, by royal command, had to be sold with Bibles; six Liverymen were co-opted to the Court and twenty-four of the Yeomanry called to the Livery; indiscipline punished by the Company was limited to a few fines for printing without entrance in the register and for binding boys at scriveners', and to the seizure of an unlicensed press; the three printers caught printing the psalms at Henley were eventually discharged by the Court of Star Chamber on entering into recognizances. But in the autumn of 1640 the Long Parliament met and on July 5, 1641, the King gave his consent to the abolition of the Courts of Star Chamber and High Commission.

The removal of the threat which these Courts had exercised, coupled with the powerful psychological effect of such a successful attack on royal and High Church power, created conditions in which the Company was challenged from within on two sides and in which the Company not only struggled to replace the lost basis for its authority (particularly as the guardian of copyright) but even made inroads, in the interests of the English Stock, on other monopolistic empires. The challenges came first from a group of disgruntled booksellers and then from a body of master printers; the struggle for new authority led to a series of ordinances and Acts of Parliament, and the empire-building affected not only the patents for Bibles, for law books and for the *Grammars*, but also the ownership of the King's Printing Houses in London and Edinburgh and the press of the University Printer at Cambridge. These attacks and counter-attacks were spread over many years and the Company was frequently fighting on two fronts at the same time; but for the sake of clarity I must treat the campaigns separately.

MICHAEL SPARKE AND THE FIRST CHALLENGE
TO THE ASSISTANTS

In the summer of 1641 the most vulnerable points in the defences of the Company were its presence among, and its support of, monopolists. Prynne, acting as its standing counsel, pleaded unsuccessfully before the Committee for Printing that certain patents—notably those for Bibles and law books—should suffer the same fate as other monopolies and be 'put into the whole Companyes hands for the Common good of the Realm'.[1] The weakness of his case was demonstrated in August when Michael Sparke, his bookseller, published *Scintilla, or a light broken into darke warehouses*, a pamphlet in which he attacked the principle of monopolies in books, with particular reference to those of the King's Printers and to the Scotch, Irish and Law Patents. When he reached the English Stock, a corporate rather than a private monopoly, he said: 'Here I could open another window, but I see many poore stand within to keep it shut, and I will not adde misery to their affliction.' But he called on Parliament, to which *Scintilla* was addressed, to correct abuses in the Society of Stationers by allowing the printing of copies entered to the Company yet kept out of print, and by raising the number of Assistants to twenty or twenty-four, none of whom was to be Master more than twice, 'for now six or 8 of the Eldest Combining, carry all to their own mark'. Under cover of an assault on what a rhymster called

> ... those Drones, that fly about in mists
> Divelish *Projectors*, damn'd *Monopolists*,

Sparke was attacking the oligarchic nature of the Court—a body of sixteen, with an average age of sixty and an average attendance of ten.

---

[1] B.M. Harl. MSS., 5909. For a more detailed study of the events described in this chapter, see 'The Stationers' Company in the Civil War Period', *The Library*, 5th ser., xiii, 1958.

On Monday, October 4, 1641, at the usual quarterly Common Hall, a paper of complaints was presented to the Court. Though 'differences & distractions' were mentioned, the chief worry was that, in *Scintilla*, 'all the secretts & misteries of this profession were laid open tending much to the Ruine of the English Stock & Corporation'.[1] Sparke had moved too fast and the first reaction was a closing of the ranks. The Assistants promised to hold a special Court on Thursday which the nominees of the complainants should attend. A committee of twelve—all Liverymen, with Sparke among them—was elected and began its meetings with apparently the full co-operation of the Court; but having co-opted, at different times, two wholesale booksellers, two book-binders and three printers (in that order)[2] it became so unwieldy that, apart from suggesting additions to the ordinances, it made no recommendation until May, when it proposed an increase in the number of Assistants. This suggestion was debated by the Table on May 16, 1642, and the Master, Henry Fetherstone, following the accepted practice, put forward three choices to vote on: that the Assistants should number thirty or thirty-two or thirty-four in addition to the Master. Even Sparke had not proposed so large a Court and the majority refused to vote on these numbers until they had voted that these were proper numbers for them to vote on—which Fetherstone refused to allow. In reply the Wardens and a majority of the Assistants proposed twenty, twenty-four and thirty, and chose twenty-four. But since the Master would not assent to the three numbers last put forward and since the Wardens and the majority would not assent to the first, 'nothing could this Court be further done herein'. And nothing further was done before the committee was voted away nearly a year later—not by a Common Hall but by a meeting of the partners in the English Stock.

About a year later still, when the Court felt itself under no immediate pressure, it elected seven new Assistants, three of whom were members of the old committee. Six of these took their places and, in their gratitude, clubbed together to buy a new green carpet for the Council Room.[3] But Michael Sparke, being called in and asked whether or

[1] The Ancients did not at first take the trouble seriously, for the account of this incident (and of some immediately following it) was only added to the Court minutes at a later date.

[2] Humphrey Robinson and George Thomason; Rapha Harford and William Tyton; Felix Kingston, John Beale and Miles Flesher.

[3] The seventh was Henry Walley, the Clerk, who asked not to sit at the Table but to count otherwise as an Assistant, i.e. when his turn came to be elected to an Assistant's share in the Stocks.

not he would serve, said 'that he reioyced to see so full a Table' but
that he intended to retire to the country as soon as the war was over
and desired to be passed by. Since he promised to pay his Renter
Warden fine, the Court accepted his answer.

After the announcement of the new Master and Wardens in July
1644, and when the news of Marston Moor had just reached London,
fourteen members of the Company, of whom only three were Liverymen and nearly all of whom were booksellers, demanded admittance
and complained that the Commonalty ought to be present at elections.
A joint committee was appointed, but it did—or was allowed to do
—nothing. The incident is important only as showing a new trade
element in the opposition and the first indication of a democratic
demand, such as the Yeomanry in the Pewterers' Company had made
four years earlier, and such as certain 'inferior citizens' had made at
Guildhall on September 21, 1644, for a say in the choosing of Sheriffs.[1]

At this stage personalities begin to appear with more clarity and
eight of them are important. The first is Henry Fetherstone a past-
Master; he was the son of a gentleman in Chancery Lane—a lawyer,
probably—and was free in 1607; he was elected to the Court in 1630
and must have been something over sixty in 1645; he may have been
the unnamed Assistant who, in 1635, was divulging what took place
at meetings of the Court; he was certainly a bookseller in a big way
of business (particularly in importations) and he died a rich man. The
second, Michael Sparke, was the son of a husbandman at Eynsham in
Oxfordshire and had been free since 1610; he had reacted strongly
against his first master, who dealt in popish books, and he remained
to the end a sturdy Puritan. The third is George Thomason; he was
the son of a husbandman in Cheshire and had, as one of Fetherstone's
apprentices, acquired a knowledge of and an interest in the Latin trade.
The next two, John Bellamy and Luke Fawne, were officers in the
Parliamentary army and staunch Presbyterians. Fawne was the son
of a schoolmaster at Leicester; Bellamy's antecedents I have been
unable to discover but he was a City politician and fought vigorously
for the rights of the Common Council. The sixth is John Partridge,
the son of a Merchant Tailor and a close friend of Fawne. The next,
the only printer among the eight, is George Miller, the son of another
schoolmaster in the Midlands, this time from Kettering. The last is
Thomas Underhill, the son of a nailer at Sutton Coldfield; he com-

[1] Cal. Letter Book K, pp. 286-7.

pleted his nine years' service with Robert Bird (like Sparke, a wholesale bookseller) on March 1, 1641, and cannot have been more than
twenty-seven or twenty-eight in 1645; he had already shown himself
to be a young man of character by appearing as one of the fourteen
who had demonstrated in 1644 and, at a later date, he came forward
strongly, with Luke Fawne, as a Presbyterian against the Independents.

THOMAS UNDERHILL AND THE SECOND CHALLENGE
TO THE ASSISTANTS

The final crisis blew up early in 1645 and we have two sources for
the story during the next few months: the official version in the Court
Book and a printed account which was put together by Sparke.[1] The
Committee of Examinations had threatened the Master and Wardens
with revoking 'the orders of Parliament made in favour of the Company' unless they took more care to stop disorderly printing; and the
Court had summoned a Common Hall for January 23rd, less than a
fortnight after the execution of Laud. In the middle of investigations
into the printers and publishers of a Lilburne pamphlet, 'one Thomas
Vnderhill', according to the Clerk

'a young man of the yeomanry of the Company, craved leaue to speake
to the Court & those of the Comunalty then present, intimating that
he had things of speciall moment to acquaint them with for the pub-
like good of the Company, which, though very vnseasonable at
that tyme, was condiscended vnto, and haueing a paper in his hand,
after some expressions of his well wishes to the Company, read a
charge devided into seuerall Articles against the said Mr. & wardens &
some others of the Assistants, taxing them with sundry misdemeanors,
as he conceiued of a very high nature, insomuch that they were not
fitt to sitt at that Table. Wherevpon the Mr. & wardens and those of
the Assistants thus publikely charged desired to haue a copie thereof,
which the said Vnderhill utterly refused—saying that if the Comunalty
then present would choose a Comittee he would giue them a Copie
of the said charge & vndertake to make good his said Articles. . . .
Upon a motion then by Mr Sparkes that the said differences might be
heard by some of the Company, The said Mr. & wardens & the rest

---

[1] Reprinted by Arber, vol. i, pp. 589–92.

thus charged, being willing by any meanes to vindicate themselues . . .
consented therevnto.'

Underhill chose Sparke, Miller, Bellamy, Partridge, Thomason and
Fawne as his six representatives; but although the committee was
ordered to meet on the following Monday, nothing further is heard of
its activities. On April 1st, however, another Common Hall elected
yet another committee of twelve. Its function was not only to redraft
the ordinances, which would settle both the number of the Assistants
and the method of electing them, but also—a most astute move on
the part of the Court—to settle the way in which the Bible should be
printed for the Company.[1] The committee had the power to co-opt
and the right to examine the records; its quorum was fixed at seven
and it was to present its report to a Common Hall on May 1st. The
interesting members were Fetherstone, who had expressed his dissatisfaction with the Court by attending only two meetings since the
end of his mastership in July 1642, and Underhill with four of his
January choices: Sparke, Miller, Bellamy and Thomason. The committee had many meetings and even took counsel's opinion; but the
Wardens, 'in a jeering manner' according to Sparke, denied access
to the books, and at a special Common Hall on April 21st Fetherstone, Bellamy and Underhill made speeches which caused such
opposition that no business could be done.

That was on Monday. On Thursday the Court was asked to choose
three of its members to meet Bellamy and two others of the committee
at 7 a.m. on Friday and to reach agreement. By Saturday evening these
six had been able to get the agreement of the Master and Wardens and
of all but four of the committee to a scheme which was, in Fetherstone's
absence, unanimously accepted by the Court on the following Monday,
even though it was 'conceived to be contrary to the constant practice
of this Court in many things'. The four who had stood out were
Fetherstone, Sparke, Thomason and Robert Dawlman, Fawne's
partner and the leader of the 1644 protest; Underhill was being wooed
by the Ancients. The Court sat again on Tuesday with the majority
of the committee to choose twenty-eight Assistants to the existing
Master and Wardens; the candidates were the twenty-six reputed
Assistants, sixteen of whom (according to Sparke) had voluntarily
resigned, and the sixteen most senior Liverymen. In the end,

---

[1] For the manner in which this opportunity occurred, see below, p. 141.)

thirty-one were chosen, and that 'was the end of that day's work'. On May 5th, another Monday, the Court, ignoring this selection, called in five new Assistants and noted that Sparke and Partridge 'came not'; this was because no one, in their view, could be an Assistant until he had been confirmed by a Common Hall. And so the battle went on, partly over the status of the Assistants and partly, at last, over the printing of the Bible; Underhill was nominated to one committee on May 16th to act for the Bible partners and to another on June 2nd for petitioning the House of Commons about the psalms. Though the Court had consented, under pressure, to an increase in its number, it refused to countenance any delegation of power to the Yeomanry. It therefore ordered Sparke and Partridge, on June 4th, to enter into bonds to pay their Renter Wardens fines. On Tuesday, June 10th, the election committee held its last meeting, in the course of which Sparke, Partridge, Underhill (with the opposition again) and Benjamin Allen (another of the 1644 protesters) walked out because they could not persuade the majority that it would prejudice his case in the eyes of the Commonalty if anyone seemed ready to buy his way on to the Court through paying his fine before his election had been publicly approved.

On Saturday, the day on which the battle of Naseby was fought, the Court sat again and, having formally accepted once more the recommendation of the committee, set it aside and admitted just two new Assistants. It also agreed on a petition to the Lord Mayor against Sparke and others who, 'out of private humour and designe (perhapps) of profitt to themselues', were trying to upset the manner of choosing the governing body of their Company—a method which had worked well for 240 years (that is, since 1403)! The petition suggested that this might lead to similar revolutions in other companies and that, in the Stationers', control by the Commonalty would lead 'to the utter ruinating of a joynt stock of great valew'—an argument which had appeared in a petition to the House of Commons two years earlier, when monopolies were a major grievance, as 'the benefit of Printing a few small Bookes'. But the Court showed its shrewdness in pinning its faith to the English Stock, and it ordered that all partners should be called to the Hall on Monday to sign the petition to the Lord Mayor and, almost as an afterthought, that 'all other Members of the Company who approue thereof be desired to subscribe the same'.

With Monday came a fine turnout of partners, the further refusal of Sparke to appear before the Table because there was still no Court of Assistants, and the appointment of Mr Bradshaw and Mr Steele as additional counsel to the Company; Prynne might be on Sparke's side. On Thursday Fetherstone handed the Beadle 500 tickets for distribution to all freemen, summoning them, on behalf of their committee, to a Common Hall the following Monday. The Beadle asked the Court, at its Saturday meeting, what he should do with the tickets; he was told to leave them with the Wardens and to deliver instead the usual summons to a Common Hall on the last day of June. Sparke's final gesture was the distribution of a small printed sheet (which may have been the agenda for his meeting of the freemen) asking the committee to answer specific questions about the government of the Company and the disposal of its funds. This reached Thomason on the last Saturday in June; on July 1st, Thomason, along with Fetherstone, Sparke, Partridge and Underhill, were summoned before the Court of Aldermen and reprimanded. This civil war in the Company was over; the Assistants had defeated the Yeomanry and, though different forces were already at work behind it, the façade of *gild* authority had been repaired.

The list of signatories of the petition to the Lord Mayor is interesting. All male holders of Livery shares—even Miller and Bellamy—signed as required, and all but three holders of Assistants' shares. Fetherstone was, of course, one of the three; Butter was in prison as a royalist spy and Rothwell had not attended a Court since July 1642. Of the sixty-seven holders of Yeomanry or half-Yeomanry shares only twenty did not sign; among these were Partridge and Thomason and the Company's agents in Scotland and Ireland, and nine of the rest did not sign even for their Dividends the previous Christmas. The support, therefore, from partners was firm; but it made up only about a third of the 224 signatures. What is remarkable about the other two-thirds is the high proportion of printers who rallied to the support of the establishment. The leaders of the opposition were booksellers, whose importing and wholesaling businesses had been hit by the war; only four of the 1644 protesters signed the 1645 petition. But the printers were flourishing as they had not flourished for a hundred years.

I have described the climax of this struggle in some detail for three reasons. It shows, firstly, the great strength of the conservative element in the Company. By limited concessions to democratic demands, by

offers to individual members of the opposition, and by reliance on
the ordinary man's respect for authority, the Court was able to ride
out the storm and remain almost as oligarchic as at the beginning. The
same tactics had been successfully employed in the 1580s. Secondly,
the story shows the value of the English Stock as a stabilizer. In addition to the emotional appeal from its support of widows, there was
the hard fact that well over a hundred shareholders had £14,400 locked
up in a trading organization controlled by the governing body of
their Company, and there was a queue waiting to take up shares as
they fell vacant. Thirdly, the failure of Sparke and his supporters is
typical of failures in other companies, and in the City, at about the
same time. Unwin has pointed out that 'the revived activity of the
yeomanry, which seemed for a time to be about to make the companies fully representative of all the classes engaged in each industry,
proved in most cases to be the final flicker that precedes extinction'.[1]

MILES FLESHER AND THE MONOPOLIES

By an odd twist, the general unpopularity of monopolies in 1641,
which Sparke had used as a stalking horse, turned temporarily to
the advantage of the English Stock. The chief argument against
monopolies in books was the old one that they inevitably led, as
Sparke showed with a wealth of illustration, to increases in price. He
also pointed out that one section of monopolists—like the University
printers and the King's Printers in Scotland and Ireland—whose
competition had tended to keep London prices down, was apt to
compound with the biggest patentees, the King's Printers and the
Stationers' Company, 'so that *Scotland* and *Ireland* must grind at their
Mill'; and he referred to the agreements with Oxford and Cambridge.
In the years immediately following the publication of *Scintilla* the
monopolizing of monopolies in books was carried further than ever
before; for a short period the Stationers' Company, through the
English Stock, controlled the printing of the Bible and the *Grammars*
(the most profitable elements in the privileges of the King's Printers),
regained control of the Law Patent and owned the printing houses
of the King's Printers in London and Edinburgh and the printing
materials at Cambridge.

The central figure in the story of the Company's manœuvres to

[1] *The Gilds and Companies of London*, 1908, p. 343.

obtain possession of most of these concerns is Miles Flesher, the son of a wheelwright at Otley in Yorkshire. After a seven-year apprenticeship to Thomas East he obtained his freedom in 1611 and worked for some years as a journeyman printer, being one of the signatories of the 1613 petition to the Lord Chancellor. In 1617 he bought, with the Company's approval, a half-share in George Eld's two-press printing house, which he took over, with Archiepiscopal approval, on Eld's death seven years later. With capital behind him, he developed his business along three lines: he bought copyrights, a field of activity dominated by booksellers; in partnership with John Haviland and Robert Young he took over three other printing houses for the sake of the additional presses; and the three partners secured the benefit of four profitable privileges. They leased from John More in 1629 the working of the patent for books of common law; they obtained in 1632 both the office of Royal Printer for Scotland (in the name of Young) and a lease of the Grammar Patent from Roger Norton; and in 1634 they leased from Robert Barker his share of the King's Printing Office. Sir John Lambe's note that Haviland had presses at Oxford and Cambridge is probably mistaken, but the making of such a note, by a man whose duty it was to be conversant with the activities of printers, is a measure of the dominance of the three partners at the time of the 1637 Decree.

Haviland died in 1638 (Flesher succeeding to his Livery share in the English Stock) and Young died in 1643. But Flesher, having been chosen an Assistant in 1642 and having fined in 1645 for both terms as Under Warden, became Upper Warden for two years in 1649 and Master for two years in 1652; he was Master, again for two years, in 1662. He was therefore able to add a position of authority within the Company to his pre-eminence in the book trade; and since he became one of the most regular attenders of Court meetings (he missed only eight out of fifty in 1644–5 and was never absent during his second year as Upper Warden) his influence on Company policy, from shortly after Sparke's attack until well into the Restoration period, was probably considerable—with, I suspect, a strong bias in favour of measures from which he himself would benefit. But first he had to live down ten years of opposition. Although as a newly-elected Liveryman he was appointed in 1629 to the committee for negotiating the termination of the Symcock patent for ballads, he was in trouble three years later for printing an abridgment of Foxe's *Book of Martyrs*, which belonged to the English Stock. In 1634 his Dividend and those of his partners were suspended as a punishment for printing the psalms at their printing house in Scotland, and in 1635 there was an argument over the rights in a law book. In 1638 the Company prepared to invade the Flesher territory by ordering type for the printing of the Bible.[1] It had thus come about that in all four branches of their business—as general printers, as Scotch and Law Patentees and as farmers of half the King's Printer's Patent—Flesher and his partners had been at odds with their Company; they had even discovered that the interests of one part of their own empire might clash with those of another.

The compounding of the Scotch Patentees (Flesher and Young) with the King's Printer (for whom Flesher and Young worked), which Sparke condemned as a move 'most cunningly' to maintain the prices of Bibles, had been preceded by a similar arrangement with the Stationers' Company over the printing of psalms; eighteen months after the suspension of their Dividends Flesher & Co. were forgiven on payment of a fine and were allowed £40 towards their costs 'by reason of some passages' since their offence. What the 'passages' were is not recorded; but there is no doubt about Flesher's prosperity, for he was able in 1639 to lend Nathaniel Butter £600 on the security of his copyrights and Assistant's share, and in 1640 to lend the Company £500 as a mortgage on the Feathers Tavern in St Paul's Church-yard, and to pay—with Young—£930 to the executors of John More for the rights in, and the printing materials belonging to, the Law Patent.[2]

The abolition of the Court of Star Chamber was as severe a blow to Flesher as it was to the Company and the departure of the King from London in January 1642 even more severe since it jeopardized both the monopoly in Bible printing and the right to print for the Government. But Flesher was clever and resilient, and his ability, during the next half-dozen years, to lend cash to his less affluent fellows suggests that he continued to prosper. Moreover, it seems likely that he used his position as an Assistant and his knowledge of the empire-building ambitions of the English Stock to unload his monopolistic interests on to the only shoulders capable, or likely to take the risk, of bearing them—the Stationers' Company.

[1] See above, p. 105.   [2] A rent of £60 a year was also agreed to.

THE BIBLE, SCOTCH, GRAMMAR, LAW AND IRISH PATENTS

After abortive attempts by a group of patentees and by the Company to obtain parliamentary sanction for Bible printing, the Court set up a committee early in 1644 to advise about treating with the royally appointed patentees for Bibles and law books. Since nothing came of this, a committee of slightly different composition was directed on July 1st to devise means for obtaining the office of King's Printer and suppressing, or compounding for, the Scotch Patent which was 'of very evill consequence to the Company'. The Law Patent negotiations were for the time being dropped, but those for obtaining the King's Printer's rights were—largely in order to win over those likely to support Sparke and Underhill—vigorously conducted. Two factors favoured the Company. The first was that John Bill, who owned half the patent, was a royalist and his property forfeited; in March 1645 his presses and letters were acquired by the English Stock for £173. The second was that the Barker family was in deep financial trouble and also of royalist sympathies; it was not difficult to persuade Robert Barker, shortly before his death, to accept a pension of 10s a month for his half-interest and for the use of his printing materials. At the quarterly meeting in January 1646 the Court was able to report the printing of Bibles and Testaments, in two formats each, and to ask for a decision about the control of such printing in future. It was voted that a stock, separate from the English Stock, should be raised and nine Stock-keepers (Underhill among them) were appointed to collect the money and to manage the business.

Flesher probably salvaged nothing from the once profitable arrangement with the Barkers except his share as an Assistant in the new partnership for producing Bibles; but this may not have worried him, for there was a boom in printing and the new Stock was soon faced with competition from three sides. In the first place the Dutch had taken advantage of the disturbed conditions of 1642 to print again for the English market and it was difficult to stop importations from Holland. In the next place, William Bentley, with the support first of the Westminster Assembly of Divines and then of Parliament, and with financial backing from a small group of City merchants, set up a printing house at Finsbury in 1646 and began printing Bibles; it was not until July 1649 that the Company could make an agreement whereby it purchased Bentley's stock and printing materials.

In the third place, John Field and Henry Hills (the most successful in a long line of 'official' printers who shared one side of the King's Printer's business) persuaded Cromwell to grant them a patent for the sole printing of the Bible; the rumour of this reached the Company in March 1655 and almost exactly a year later the Court reluctantly allowed them to enter in the register their right to the Bible. The partners in the new Stock had had a short run for their money.

The second of Flesher's big interests was in the patent for King's Printer in Scotland which had, in June 1641, been regranted jointly to his partner Robert Young and Evan Tyler. So long as the Civil War lasted the Company could do little, except protest, about the threat of cheaply printed Scottish books; but with the fall of Oxford in June 1646 and the return to more normal trading conditions the need arose for an arrangement similar to those made with other privileged printers outside London. In October a new committee was given full power to come to terms with Flesher, Tyler and John Parker,[1] and the partners in the English Stock approved the terms at their annual meeting on March 1, 1647: £430 was to be paid—by instalments up to December 1649—for all rights and materials, and Thomas Pape was appointed to manage the printing house. It is possible that, as a prevention of further competition, the investment was justified; but the meagre records suggest that the distant commitment was a cause of worry and expense. An octavo Bible had to be printed there to keep the workmen busy; Pape died before the end of 1647 and John Twyn,[2] his successor, was young and inexperienced; imports of books from Scotland were forbidden and it was decided to ship the type to London; then Christopher Higgins was appointed agent and, having in 1652 moved the remainder of the materials to Leith, asked for further equipment; in 1659 the Stock-keepers were deploring the losses but at the Restoration the Company approached the Earl of Lauderdale about a renewal of the patent. Higgins stayed on in Leith and, at his death in 1668, over £350 belonging to the English Stock was found in the printing house. The matter dragged uncomfortably on until Andrew Anderson obtained a new patent in

---

[1] He may have bought the Young interest on the latter's death in 1643; he had been a considerable buyer of Latin Stock shares, see above, p. 106.

[2] This unfortunate man ended his life at Tyburn in 1664 for his part in the production of the pamphlet, *A Treatise of the Execution of Justice*, which was held to be an incitement to rebellion.

1671 and, out of the wreckage, the Company received £150 towards the rebuilding of the Hall after the Fire.

The third of Flesher's investments in monopolies derived from an agreement of February 22, 1632, whereby Roger Norton conveyed all his rights in the office of King's Printer in Latin, Greek and Hebrew to Flesher, Young and Haviland for twenty-one years at an annual rent of £240.[1] When Haviland died in 1638 his share passed to John Wright, a bookseller whom Flesher and Young tried to get rid of by persuading Norton to bring a collusive action against all three partners for non-payment of rent. Wright saw through the trick and entered bills of complaint against the other three in the Court of Common Pleas, where it was ordered, early in 1640, that Norton's action be stayed and that Wright was to share in every way equally with the others. All might have been well if, in the summer of the following year, Felix Kingston, John Beale and other printers had not taken advantage of the abolition of the Court of Star Chamber to print grammars—very likely on the English Stock account. Flesher & Co. again held back the rent with the excuse that Norton had leased an exclusive right which he was unable to maintain; but Norton's reply was to enter the grammars in the register as if they were ordinary copies rather than parts of a monopoly derived from royal letters patent and to reopen the earlier case as a real threat instead of a means to dispose of Wright. This in turn led to a bill of complaint in Chancery against Norton; but the only result was the Company's taking over of the books in the Norton privilege, on the grounds that it ought to have been the original grantee.[2] The claim was underlined by the payment, from English Stock funds, of the Norton share of the money due to Oxford under the 1638 agreement. For nearly a dozen not very prosperous years the Stock 'enjoyed' the profits from the grammars; Norton was persuaded to drop a case in Chancery against the Company and, in March 1653, he induced his colleagues on the Court to reinstate his 1641 entry in the register which had been deleted at the height

[1] This had been granted to Roger's father, Bonham, in 1613 for thirty years and in 1615 to John Willis, the stenographer, for forty-one years after the end of the first; Roger had secured both the original and the reversion. The office carried an annual stipend of 26s 8d and gave the right to print the Bible in Latin, all Greek and Latin grammars, certain books in the classical languages, and all charters, maps, etc., which the King might think necessary. The details of the Norton–Flesher arrangement come from Chancery documents of November and December 1641, C 2 Charles I, F 3/60; I am grateful to Miss Handover for this reference.

[2] At the height of the troubles in Elizabeth's reign—probably about 1583—the Company had appealed to Burghley for the sole right to print the *Accidence* and the *Grammar*, the basic text-books for the study of Latin. See above, p. 77, n. 1.

of the Sparke trouble in 1645. That this was allowed within a few days of the expiry of his agreement with Flesher suggests that the latter was able, with his usual flair, to salvage some benefit to himself from an arrangement which had been so profitable in the 1630s that Norton's efforts to buy it back had, according to his account, been steadily refused.

Flesher judged that the fourth of his monopolies—for books of common law—was much less vulnerable than the others, and he resisted the overtures made to him in 1644. For a further seventeen years he enjoyed the profits, with only minor interference from a small group of law booksellers. But in September 1661 he quietly sold to the Company for £200 the remaining six years of the More patent, having got wind that More's daughter and her husband, Richard Atkins, were about to reopen an action (stopped by the Civil War) to prove that Flesher had forfeited his rights because he had failed to pay the rent agreed on in 1640. At the end of nine years—in the course of which Flesher had twice been Master of the Company and had refused to put his name to a formal assignment and had died; in the course of which another Master, Andrew Crooke, had been accused of trying to obtain the assignment for himself under cover of acting for the Company; in the course of which Chancery lawyers had collected fees from the Stationers, from the Flesher family and from the Atkins family—on October 12, 1670, the Company set its seal to a document renouncing any claim to a new privilege (which had been granted to Edward Atkins in trust for Richard in 1660) and promising, in the interest of the assigns,[1] to add a by-law against infringement of these rights. Almost five years later the new ordinance came into force.

It is now necessary to go back and clear up the Company's monopolizing activities in the two directions in which Flesher was not personally concerned. The Irish business, such as it was, continued to be conducted by William Bladon acting, in spite of the sale agreement of October 1639, as the representative of the partners. The Court instructed him in July 1648 to subscribe £6 13s 4d for the relief of Trinity College, Dublin, and agreed that the Company would find the money if the partners refused—because there might be no money.

---

[1] Who were John Streater, Henry Twyford and—of all people—James Flesher, the son of Miles. The details of this arrangement and of much of the previous history (including the action brought to a successful conclusion in June 1664, by Atkins and his wife against Miles Flesher and the Company) are to be found in a Chancery bill of complaint brought by the Company against the Fleshers in October 1664, and in their demurrer to it; C 9, 31, 126.

The lack of mention in Court minutes and the half-heartedness of the attempt to prevent the appointment of John Crooke, the brother of Andrew, as King's Printer in Ireland after the Restoration suggest that official interest in the Irish Stock had died—perhaps in 1639.

THE COMPANY'S PRINTING AT CAMBRIDGE

Affairs at Cambridge, the other field of Company expansion, went for a time much better. The arrangements made in 1639 to eliminate competition from the University press worked smoothly for ten years—so smoothly that Roger Daniel spent most of his time in London and had his appointment cancelled by the Vice-Chancellor for neglect. His successor, John Legate, held the office for five years and was even more complaisant towards the Stationers' ambitions than Daniel had been. By an agreement in 1653 the English Stock bought from the two non-professional printers their shares of the printing equipment at Cambridge and guaranteed them an annual income of £25 each (£20 for leaving the printing house vacant and £5 for not resigning without consulting Legate). So long as Legate continued to co-operate with the Company and retained the confidence of the University authorities, the press at Cambridge worked to the orders of London. But in spite of warnings from the Company's agent that the printer was not spending enough time at Cambridge, Legate in 1655 lost his appointment. This was another opportunity for John Field, who obtained the office through Cromwell's influence at his old University. Field was determined to make use of the additional printing facilities and, having bought the presses and types from the Company, he forced the English Stock to guarantee him £500 a year for printing almanacks and school books. This arrangement, which was on the lines of the 1631 agreement with the Bucks, lasted until Field's death in 1668.

CONTROL OF PRINTING BY ORDINANCE AND ACT OF PARLIAMENT

All these complicated and only partially successful manoeuvres, aimed at adding, in the name of the Company, to the empire of the English Stock, had taken place against a series of attempts to work out, with successive Governments, a set of rules to replace those thrown over-

board with the Court of Star Chamber. If it were not for these negotiations we would scarcely be able to deduce from the Company's records
the form of the national upheaval. There are brief notes about the
handing in of arms, the stock of gunpowder, the provision of a soldier,
the selling of plate, the cancellation of a dinner 'in respect of the sadnes
of the Tymes'; but there is no direct indication why the times were
sad nor where personal and gild sympathies lay. This is true of the
records of other companies and the writer of a newsletter in 1647
provided the answer when he wrote that 'the citty is subject still to
be ridden by every party and wilbe so rather than endanger trade and
stock'. The Stationers, because of the unique commodity from which
they made their living, could behave in no other way; copyright
could not be protected without Government support.

The Long Parliament set up in 1641 a Committee of Printing to
deal with specific complaints of disorderly publications; but this
provided no constitutional backing for the Company. In the spring
of 1643 Henry Parker, Secretary first to the Parliamentary Army and
then to the House of Commons, drafted on behalf of the Stationers a
'Humble Remonstrance' in which he argued at length the necessity of
filling the void by an Act of Parliament. On June 14th an Ordinance
for the Regulating of Printing was passed. All books were to be
officially licensed and entered in the register; no book belonging to
the English Stock was to be printed without the Company's consent;
powers of search and seizure were provided. The Government and
the Stationers were once more in partnership on much the same terms
as in 1637.

As power seeped away from the Long Parliament, so the Ordinances
became less and less effective either to control the publication of news-
books and pamphlets which criticized the Government or to protect
copyright-owners—from the competition of imports, for instance. On
the petition of the Company in January 1649, the month of the King's
execution, the Marshall-General of the army was ordered to see that
the Ordinances were observed; but the new masters could not operate
the decrees of the old and on September 20th the army-controlled
Parliament passed an Act for the 'better regulating of Printing'. The
same old regulations occur with the same old prohibitions and punish-
ments. In two points only was there any attempt to adapt the Act to
conditions in the book trade: firstly, a press was permitted to operate
at York and the press at Finsbury was allowed to continue the print-

ing of Bibles and psalms; secondly, there was no limit set to the number of master printers, and thirty-six of them entered bonds for good behaviour within the next few weeks.

With continued disagreements between Parliament and the army it was unlikely that the Act would have sufficient authority completely to prevent either the printing of criticism or the distribution of books which infringed copyright—pirated copies of the *Primer*, for instance. In the summer of 1652, therefore, yet another Bill was drafted and just before it became law on January 7, 1653, all the Assistants were urged to go down to Westminster and 'improve their severall interests to promote it'. The only significant addition to the Act of 1649 was the placing of the final responsibility for printing and the behaviour of printers on the Council of State—an attempt to give, behind the façade of an Act of Parliament, the administrative bite which Laud, briefed by Sir John Lambe, had provided. But it was an unsuccessful attempt for, a few months after Cromwell became Protector, the Court voted Marchamont Needham £20 in gold for putting before the Council the Company's case for further power. Nothing came of this, and the Act of 1653 remained the basis for control in the book trade until after the Restoration—control which was just about as successful as it had been after the Act of 1649 and the Ordinance of 1643.

THE 'COMPANY' OF PRINTERS: A CHALLENGE
TO THE STATIONERS

The desire of a majority of the Long Parliament that there should be freedom for the printed criticism of the King's civil and ecclesiastical government matched a public ready to pay for such literature and printers ready to provide it; moreover, once the ancient filter had been removed and the tap had been allowed to pour forth the clear water of criticism, the refixing of the filter when the water ran muddy was almost impossible. One of the immediate results of the removal of the Court of Star Chamber was the increase in the number, the courage and the power of the printers. The main opposition parties were able to provide money to replace types and presses which had been confiscated and rooms to serve as printing houses; and there were hawkers willing to earn a quick penny by selling direct to eager purchasers in house and street. This by-passing of the booksellers' shops, the normal channels of distribution, not only deprived the booksellers of business but gave the printers a welcome sense of independence. They felt strong enough to break, more blatantly than before and often with impunity, the rules of their Company—particularly by binding, at scriveners', apprentices in excess of their permitted number and by employing, as journeymen, those not free of the City. That the printers made no attempt in 1645 to exploit the Sparke-led revolution shows, not the weakness of their old subservience, but confidence in a new strength; and in the course of 1651 they petitioned the Committee for the Regulating of Printing that they might be made a Fraternity or Company distinct from the Stationers. Here is the second of the opposition movements within the Company. Nothing more is known of this manifestation of it than that it was unsuccessful and that William Ball, in *A Brief Treatise Concerning the Regulating of Printing* which he published in November 1651, devoted a section to condemning the printers' 'not only unsound, but even dangerous Petition, and desires' and to refuting their argument that, since the Apothecaries had successfully broken away from the Grocers, the printers could exist apart from the Stationers.

With the return of Charles II in May 1660 the Assistants looked to see 'their wonted power confirmed', the absence of which they had admitted to Thomason in February 1655; and the printers, reacting against a return to pre-1641 conditions, made another bid for separate incorporation. The first Bill for the regulation of printing was dropped in July 1661, but early in 1662 a new Bill was introduced and, after representations to the Lords from certain printers and a counter-petition from the Company, 'An Act for preventing the frequent Abuses in printing seditious . . . Books . . . and for regulating of Printing and Printing Presses' received the royal assent on May 19th. The clock was put firmly back to 1637.[1] On June 20th the printers were summoned to the Hall to hear the new Act read and to learn that, as occasion occurred, the number permitted to keep a printing house was to be reduced to twenty. This triumph of conservatism was probably achieved by two letters from the King to the Commons —letters which Secretary Nicholas wrote and for which he was rewarded by a fee representing, in equal proportions, the gratitude of the Company, of the English Stock partners and of the restored King's Printers.

[1] For a discussion of the Act, see below, p. 153.

On May 11, 1663, the printers were ordered to present themselves and their journeymen at the Hall the following morning, so that a count of printing houses and operatives could be made: '59 Mr Printers were acknowledged; some of ym seemed to be angry at their sum̃ons'. But the increase from thirty-six in 1649 to fifty-nine in 1663 gave them courage and within the next few months eleven of them petitioned the King to grant them independence. The 'reasons' with which they supported their petition[1] can be divided into those which might carry weight with the King's advisers and those which were important to the printers. The former were, first, that only printers had enough technical knowledge to be effective searchers of printers' premises; second, that only incorporation would sufficiently encourage printers to expose dangerous publications and that twelve months' good management would show results; third, that the Stationers' Company had grown so large that a man reached a place of responsibility only when he was too old for active searching; fourth, that searches were usually conducted for the discovery rather of copyright infringement than of heretical or seditious printing; fifth, that such printing disturbs the mind and takes it 'off from solid reading of Divinity, History or Romance'; sixth, that there were good precedents for relieving one mystery from control by another—the Feltmakers from that of the Haberdashers, for instance; and seventh, that the printers were ready to forfeit their new privileges if they did not discover all illegal printing! The real reasons were that the booksellers dominated the Company and contrived 'daily the hurt and detriment of the Printers'; that the latter hardly ever reached the highest offices, and that the former, who stood to gain most from the sale of illegal books, encouraged a superfluity of printers whose need would compel them to undertake dangerous work. (As on previous occasions, it was Government rather than Company policy to limit the number of printing houses.)

These reasons were elaborated in *A Brief Discourse Concerning Printing and Printers*, which was published for 'a Society of Printers' in 1663. The charter of 1557 was 'without doubt made in favour of Printers and for their encouragement and security . . . [and] might conduce to their well-being then, when the Book-sellers were very few, and as inconsiderable, and so the Printers sufficient to hold the balance even'. But in 1663 the booksellers 'are grown so bulkie and numerous

---

[1] For a more detailed discussion, see 'The "Company" of Printers', *Studies in Bibliography*, Charlottesville, xiii, 1960.

(together with many of several other Trades that they have taken in) and so considerable withal (being much enriched by Printers impoverishment . . .) that there is hardly one Printer to ten others that have a share in the Government of the Company'. Moreover, few young master printers had in recent years been able to make a bid for the copies of an old printer (as Flesher had so successfully done) and 'the Booksellers having engros'd almost all, it is become a question among them, whether a Printer ought to have a copy or no. . . .' The only solution was that the printers be independent, for 'as reasonably', the writer concluded, 'may the Buyer have the Rule of the Seller, as the Book-seller govern the Printer'.

Why were these appeals to the King and the public unsuccessful? There was, of course, the understandable opposition of a corporation to the loss of about a third of its membership. Secondly, the booksellers were able not only to muster an overwhelming majority on the Court but to make direct approaches to men like Nicholas and Lauderdale who were close to the King. Thirdly, there would be a strong temptation for the Government rather to pin its faith to an arrangement which, but for the Civil War, might have worked satisfactorily, than to sponsor a quite untried method. The Decree of 1637 may have seemed to the King's advisers, as it did to the author of *The London Printer his Lamentation*,[1] 'the best and most exquisite Form and Constitution for the good Government and regulation of the Press'; and the Decree had been sponsored by, and could only be worked with the aid of, the Stationers' Company.

Fourthly, Sir Roger L'Estrange was not in favour of a Printers' Company, and he had enough influence at court to create and to obtain for himself the post of Surveyor of the Press. Early in the summer of 1663 he published a pamphlet setting out his views on press control and he said some hard and interesting things about the booksellers and the need 'to Disengage the *Printers* from that Servile and Mercenary *Dependence* upon the Stationers, unto which they are at present subjected'. But the solution was not by a separate incorporation of the printers for 'it were a hard matter to Pick out *Twenty Master-Printers*, who are both *Free of the Trade*, of *Ability* to *Menage* it, and of *Integrity* to be *Entrusted* with it'. Fifthly, the printers themselves were not united. Why did only eleven out of about sixty master printers sign the petition to the King? Even if the eleven were acting

[1] September 1660.

on behalf of a majority of their fellow employers, how far were the
journeymen, for whom they claimed to be speaking, in favour of
the break? Between 1650 and 1658 there were seven complaints to the
Court by workmen printers against various malpractices of their
masters, and in 1660 the London Printer in his *Lamentation* bewailed
the excessive number of printing houses and the complete lack of
training and experience in some of those who ran them. It is possible
that the grumblers were no more representative of the general body of
workmen than the eleven who spoke for the masters; but the existence
among the printers of a small element which was inclined to seek
support from the booksellers on the Court would provide a further
argument—to anyone looking for such—against giving the masters
even more power over their employees. Support from higher authority
than the Court was aimed at in 1660. The journeymen, in a petition
to the Archbishop of Canterbury, harked back nostalgically to the
1637 Decree, with its limitation in the number of apprentices, and
drew attention to the increase, in the last twenty years, both of presses
and of Dutch and other unfree workmen; the foreigners were said to
outnumber the free workmen Stationers and to be preferred for secret
printing because they had sworn no oath to obey the rules of the
Company.

The idea of a Printers' Company did not die with the failure in
1663, but L'Estrange was mainly responsible for keeping it alive. On
Tuesday, June 10, 1679, the day on which the Printing Act (in spite
of the efforts of the Stationers) was allowed to lapse, he wrote to
Henry Coventry, Principal Secretary of State, and enclosed 'The
Printers Reasons' for separate incorporation. The previous Friday,
according to L'Estrange, over a score of printers had voluntarily
offered to serve the King in return for a charter, with the normal
powers of a company and their proper share of the English Stock.
L'Estrange urged Coventry to give the printers some encouragement,
since such an opportunity might never recur; 'ffor ye Booksellers
(especially ye ffactious Part) fall foul upon ye Printers allready, and
upon my self too; and ye Printers are utterly ruin'd for their Loyalty,
if they be not protected in it'. This time the precedent quoted is that
of the Tinmen, who had succeeded in breaking away from the Ironmongers. The printers' reasons included the statement that they were
less tempted than the booksellers by profit (the ratio of temptation
being £5 to £50) not to suppress libels, and an assurance to justify,

on oath, that the booksellers gave private warning of impending searches, refused licensed work to those printers who refused to print unlicensed, and denied informers their promised rewards for discoveries.

Two days later L'Estrange again wrote to Coventry. Both parties had been ordered to attend the Attorney-General on Thursday with their proposals for press control; the printers had appeared but the booksellers had been allowed till Tuesday to prepare their case. Meanwhile the printers were beginning to weaken. 'There has been great Art and Industry used by fair words and by menaces, to corrupt ye Printers', and one of them, a 'prating' fellow, had reported to L'Estrange, with evident satisfaction, the dictum of the Attorney-General that 'he would neither meddle nor make in ye matter'. And there the story of the printers' bids for independence comes to a whimpering end—or disappears for want of evidence.

CHAPTER IX

THE COMPANY IN THE REIGNS OF THE LATER STUARTS

THE PRINTING ACT OF 1662

THE period which stretches from Charles II's return in 1660 to Queen Anne's death in 1714 covers the last attempts at rigid control of printing and the passing of the first Copyright Act in 1710. The change of thinking on these related subjects was of profound importance to the Stationers' Company, as the guardian of rights to copies and as a corporate copyright-owner; and the most powerful group among its members, the booksellers, was largely responsible for promoting the new concept and the statutory machinery by which it was to be operated.

Though the author of *The Case of the Booksellers and Printers Stated* could assert in 1666 that 'the Author of every *Manuscript* or Copy hath (in all reason) as good right thereunto, as any Man hath to the Estate wherein he has the most absolute property', the Court of Assistants, the London Printer in his *Lamentation* and the King's ministers were still thinking in terms of the 1637 Decree which was, in its turn, an amplification of the 1586 Decree. Even if we did not know that the drafters of the 1662 Bill had been referred back to the wording of 1637, it would have been possible to deduce the reference from similarity in phraseology and from the fact that two dozen of the clauses in the Decree found places in the Act. Of the clauses which were dropped, four dealt with type-founders who, in the Act, were still limited to four but covered by the provisions about printers; four others related to the giving of bonds for good behaviour (which had proved worthless even in 1649), the finding of work for journeymen and the interference with printers at the Universities (one of the clauses in the Act making it clear that the privileges of Oxford and Cambridge were not affected). The attempts to license reprints and to make authors produce two copies of a manuscript were given up as unworkable, and the control of imports was made considerably lighter; the Act specifically allowed Stationers freely to import books published ten years previously and not formerly prohibited, and the Latin Stock—had it survived—might have flourished again. One major change was the dropping of quite unrealistic penalties.[1]

In other ways, those responsible for the Bill took notice of what had happened in the book trade during the previous twenty-five years. One clause made provision for those shop-keepers who had been licensed by a bishop to sell books and another clause for those stall-holders in Westminster Hall who were in business on November 20, 1661. The press at York was to continue, under the eye of the Arch-bishop, but it was not to print Bibles or English Stock books. The King's Library and the Library at Cambridge were joined with the Bodleian in the right to receive a free copy of every new book; this 'tax' on publishers was no more popular then than it is now and it was dodged with considerable success.[2] An important addition was the order that the licence, which was no new idea, must be printed *verbatim* at the beginning of each book; and for this reason the statute of 1662 is often called 'The Licensing Act'. The House of Lords, after throwing out the first Bill on the issue of searches, successfully included a clause in the second to ensure that the houses of peers—and of tradesmen not cited in the Act—could not be searched by the officers of the Company without a special warrant. Finally, no pro-vision of the Act was to apply to holders of royal grants or to Col. John Streater who was negotiating with the Atkins family for the working of the Law Patent.

The difficulties in which the Stationers were involved over this patent necessitated reference to their Charter; but the Company's copy could not be found. The Court therefore resolved in March 1665 to ask William Prynne, who was then keeper of the records in the Tower, to have a copy made from the enrolment. On the strength of this the Company obtained from the King on August 10, 1667, a new Charter in exactly the same words as those of the original—which might so easily have been destroyed in the Great Fire! This *inspex-imus* version still exists. In August 1670, however, legal proceedings, which had been threatened in 1664, were begun, by order in council, to compel the Company to show by what authority—*quo warranto*—

---

[1] Document 184 at Stationers' Hall is the draft of a grant from the King, for the poor of the Company, of all the fines exacted under the Act; but it remained a draft.

[2] See 'The Deposit of Books at Cambridge . . . 1662–79, 1685–95', by J. C. T. Oates in the *Trans. Cambridge Bib. Soc.*, II, part iv, 1957.

it acted, or failed to act, in suppressing libels and in clearing up the Law Patent quarrel with Atkins and Streater. If it had not been for the intervention of Sir Roger L'Estrange, who assured the Government that the Company would provide more effective by-laws, the Charter would have been forfeit. Rather more than seven years later the new Ordinances came into operation.

THE NEW ORDINANCES OF 1678

The by-laws of 1678 were, presumably, based on those which had been drawn up in 1562 and which had been added to from time to time. But this can be no more than a presumption because the Company, having mislaid its own Book of Ordinances as well as its Charter, applied for a copy—with unrecorded result—to the Master of the Rolls in 1668. Since therefore it is possible only to deduce the earlier Ordinances from resolutions of the Court and from the records of their operation, and since, with the Charter and the Printing Act, the by-laws dictated the Company's pattern of behaviour, I must devote some space to them. In what follows, my glosses are set within brackets.

At meetings of the *Court*, Assistants were to appear punctually (i.e. at 10 a.m.) 'in their Gowns and other decent Apparel', and not to leave without the permission of the Master or a Warden, on pain of 1s fine. (In the hot weather of 1691 it was agreed that gowns need not be worn in the summer; but unpunctuality had to be punished five years later with forfeiture to the Poor Box of the half-crown dinner money, by those who appeared after 11 o'clock.) The business of the Court was the 'better Ordering' of the Company, the correction of abuses and the admission of apprentices and freemen. (One of the more unusual 'corrections' was the attempt in 1673 to reconcile Peter Lilliecrap and his wife.) The *Rules for Debate* were that there should be only one speaker at a time, who must address the chair and speak bareheaded (all the Assistants bared their heads when a letter from the King was read); that all must keep silent at the order of the Master or Wardens; that 'all Debates [must] be serious' and that, in the Master's absence, election to the chair was to be by simple majority. ('According to the antient Custome of this Corporacõn' the Court met on the first Monday in the month, unless that was a holy day; between December 1666 and March 1669 Tuesday was substituted—probably because of accommodation difficulty after the Fire. In March 1676 the quorum was fixed at Master, one Warden and ten Assistants out of a maximum muster of two dozen; there had been only fifteen in 1665. The minutes of the previous Court were normally read first; in December 1696 it was decided that no Court should rise until the minutes of that meeting had been read, but there is no evidence that this difficult practice was ever tried out. On April 7, 1701, it was made a standing rule that the Master should have but a single vote in elections and the passing of orders—an alteration in the terms of the Charter which the Assistants had no power to make.)

There were also to be four Quarterly Courts to which all freemen might be summoned and at which orders might be read and quarterage paid—8d for Assistants, 6d for Liverymen and 4d for the rest. (In spite of the threat of double fees for those who did not pay regularly, many freemen were perpetually in arrears. In December 1669 the Renters were ordered to attend on Dividend Day and collect arrears from partners in the English Stock. But only the more prosperous freemen were lucky enough to draw Dividends and when, in November 1698, Benjamin Harris[1] came to bind an apprentice he was found to owe 24s—i.e. for eighteen years; he was let off with 12s. Early in the eighteenth century the Company made a determined effort to collect arrears, and some freemen were brought before the Court of Conscience.)

Every *Nomination and Election*—for officers, Assistants, Liverymen and servants of the Company—was to be by a majority of the Court 'as usually heretofore hath been'. (These decisions of the Assistants were no business of the Yeomanry, nor even of the Livery.) The fines for refusing to serve were, at the Court's discretion, £10 to £20 for Master, £12 to £24 for first time Upper Warden and £6 for second time, £10 to £20 for first time Under Warden and £5 for second time. (An order of June 1659 made it imperative that anyone who, having been nominated by 'scoring', wanted to fine for either of the Wardenships must declare his intention before going to the ballot box; some men had been waiting until the result showed whether the spending of money was necessary.) The Wardens were responsible for the Election Dinner to the Livery, with the customary allowance from the Company. (A tradition had grown up that the Master provided a buck or £5 for this dinner, and the tradition was crystallized

---

[1] He had returned three years earlier from New England where he had published the first newspaper.

in an order of November 6, 1676; but there is no mention of this in the Ordinances two years later.) Wardens' *Accounts* were to be rendered within two months, and the fine for failure could be £100. (I will deal with the details of these in Chapter X; here I will merely say that Richard Royston, Under Warden 1666–8, submitted his accounts for auditing only on January 17, 1673, and that the temptation to put off the day of reckoning was not confined to him.) The *Chest*, containing the common seal, the Charter (when there was one) and the plate was to have three keys, one each for the Master and Wardens; and any of these who did not make proper provision of a key-holding substitute in his absence could be fined £5. The *Seal* was not to be set to any document without the consent of a majority of the Court, and anyone committing the Company on his own authority could be fined £100, disfranchised and be liable for any financial loss to the corporation.

The *Assistants* were to be elected by the Court and only from those who had fined or served as Renter Warden, and on election they were to pay 10s to the Clerk and 5s to the Beadle. (The Court's sole right of election was, however, challenged from two sides. On May 11, 1663, Richard Royston, the King's Bookseller, was elected by royal *mandamus*, and five years later Roger Norton—the holder, in place of his father, of the smaller of the King's Printers' Patents, and translated from the Merchant Tailors in 1663—Samuel Mearne, the King's Bookbinder, and Thomas Roycroft, recently appointed King's Printer in Oriental Languages, were also elected on the strength of a letter from Charles II praising their part in suppressing licentious practices in the trade. In July 1678 Henry Twyford was chosen as a result of a petition to the King in which he had strongly criticized his Company; finally, in June 1681 Charles ordered the election of no fewer than six Stationers—among them John Playford and Robert Scott—who had been zealous in the discovery of unlicensed pamphlets. These royal nominations were part of the King's policy to ensure loyalty in the corporations, and their immediate effect was resentment among senior members of the Company. On October 3, 1681, about three months after the election of the six royal nominees, the Court resolved, in answer to the petition of six Liverymen, that 'noe Members of this Company have any absolute right or priviledge to be of the Assistants . . . by seniority, but only by & at the Election of' the governing body. The leader of the movement, which—unlike that of forty years before—did not ostensibly involve the Yeomanry, was John Starkey, an enterprising bookseller who had ten years earlier warned the Court about 'privat contrivances' against the government of the Company.[1] The unsuccessful action, which he and his five colleagues brought, cost the Company about £50, and in 1683 one of the five, Thomas Bassett, obtained a Livery share in the English Stock by apologizing for his conduct and by paying a sixth of the Company's law charges. During the reign of James II the Liverymen wisely lay low, but soon after the accession of William III another group, led by Daniel Blague, an auctioneer, put forward its claims. The complaint this time was not entirely a manifestation of personal grievances but a reaction, perhaps, against the Court's resolution of March 1st—English Stock election day—1688 that no one should be an Assistant who, at the time of his election, was not a printer, a bookseller or a bookbinder. Early in 1690 Starkey renewed his application and was elected; but when he found that he had to sit as the most junior Assistant he threw in his lot with Blague and petitioned the Lord Mayor, who ordered the Master and others to appear before him with the names of the fifty most senior Liverymen. The Company's answer, based on counsel's opinion that the elections had been conducted in accordance with the by-laws, was for the moment accepted; and on July 15th the Beadle reported that Starkey, having read his summons to attend the Court, 'toare [it] to peeces in greate wroth & indignation'. A year later the Assistants twice refused, *nem. con.*, to obey an order of the Court of Aldermen to elect Giles Sussex, another supporter of Blague. On July 28th the Master, Edward Brewster, and the two Wardens were, as a formality, committed to Newgate for contempt of the Court of Aldermen and on August 1st they received the thanks of their colleagues at the Table for asserting the franchises of the Company. What they had really done, I think, was to reassert the old policy of 'The Stationers' Company for members of the book trade', at a time when the tide in most companies was running the other way.)

The 1678 by-laws dealing with the *Livery* placed the election firmly in the hands of the Court and fixed the fine on acceptance at £20 and

[1] On July 1, 1671, Roger Norton, Thomas Roycroft and Samuel Gellibrand had 'gone to the box' for Younger Warden and Gellibrand had been elected. On July 3rd Norton, Roycroft and Samuel Mearne, having uttered 'severall menaces', withdrew from the meeting while Gellibrand was allowed to fine and heartily thanked for doing so. Norton was then elected in his place. On August 3rd it was ordered that all references to the recent disagreements be expunged; they were crossed out in the 'waste' Court Book and were not fair-copied.

the fees to the Clerk and Beadle at 10s and 5s. After the election 'the Master . . . shall cause the Beadle . . . to put upon him so elected a Livery Gown . . .; and then the said Master shall put upon his shoulder a party-coloured Hood made after the usual manner; after which the said Master and Wardens, each in their order, shall give to such person . . . his and their hands, saying these words, (*Videlicet*) *Brother, you are Admitted to the Cloathing of this Company*; or words to that effect'. The fine for refusal without reasonable excuse was £40 and that for failing to attend a summons or for leaving a meeting without permission was 1s. There must, however, have been some grumbling about calls to the Livery when Starkey was protesting about the election of Assistants, for in a Supplement to the Ordinances, approved by the Lord Chancellor and the Lord Chief Justices on October 7, 1681, the rule about the Livery was repeated in much the same words. (The practice from 1656, apart from a few 'Speciall Calls', was to open a call to the Livery and to let it run for three or four or even seven years; all those elected during the period would rank for seniority not according to their dates of election, but according to their dates of freedom, 'without anie respect had to ffreedome by Patrimony'. The only reason I can suggest for this unpopular arrangement was that it gave the poorer Stationers a year or two in which to put together £20 for the fine—which had to be paid within nine months of election—without loss of seniority. In November 1700 the Court decided that no call should run for more than two years; the next was allowed to run for four years, but it was the last. In spite of the understandable reluctance of those Stationers not engaged in the book trade to go on the Livery and a tendency in the 1690s even for others to postpone acceptance of clothing, the size of the Livery steadily increased until in 1699 the 226 Stationers stood seventh among the London companies.)[1]

The *Renter Warden*, having been elected by the Court from the Livery, was to collect quarterage and rents, and to account to his successor within a month, with a fine of £5 for every month's delay. Fines of £50 for refusing election (or of not less than £24) and for refusing to provide a dinner for the Livery on Lord Mayor's Day could be levied. An *Assistant Renter Warden*, chosen in the same way,

[1] I shall discuss the possible reasons for this increase on p. 184 below. The order of the Court of Aldermen on July 27, 1697—that no one with an estate of less than £500 be elected to the Livery of an inferior company—did not affect the intake.

was normally to become Renter the following year. These two clauses do not make sense and did not represent the practice of the Company; one, therefore, of the Supplementary Ordinances of 1681 made the two Renters of equal standing and reduced the service to one year; at the same time the maximum fines (which were never asked) were reduced from £50 to £40. (It was in June 1671 that the Court put in hand a general revision of the by-laws and appointed a committee to meet every Thursday until the work was done. By November a large measure of agreement had been reached—even with L'Estrange; but in March 1672 Thomas Vere, the Assistant Renter, was allowed to fine for the main office. Thereafter, two new men were elected each year, though it was not until July 7, 1679, that the Court passed the resolution which contradicted the by-law. At about this time the growing number of Liverymen began to pose two new problems: the effect of serving or fining as Renter on seniority and the financial burden on Renters in the entertainment of their fellow Liverymen. On October 4, 1686, the Court laid it down that, in the roll of the Livery, those who had passed through the Renter turnstile should have precedence over those who had not; and on June 18, 1689, Thomas Burrow prayed to be admitted to his freedom by patrimony and to the clothing, and to be allowed to fine for Renter; he was granted the first two requests immediately and the third—after some debate and perhaps because he was a merchant and therefore ineligible for higher office—on July 1st. The full significance of these orders did not appear until the eighteenth century. Secondly, on April 7, 1690, a number of young booksellers asked that the financial strain on Renters might be eased by increasing the number of those fining and by allotting some of the fines to those who served. Impatience with the Assistants' failure to respond produced among ambitious Liverymen a 'combination', the details of which are missing. On December 2, 1700, the Court resolved that no one putting his name to an agreement about the Rentership would be elected to a share in the English Stock or, if he were a printer, have any Stock work; but, after a conference with the malcontents, it was agreed that fines should be limited to five at each election and that the £24 contributed by the fifth should be given to the two who served.)

The next clauses laid down the power of the Court to appoint and remove the *Clerk* and the *Beadle*, and yearly to choose, from the Society, *Whifflers* or *Ushers* 'to attend . . . in any Services to which

3 Silver presented to the Company by George Sawbridge 1677 (Master 1675), Sir Thomas Davies 1676 (Master 1668 and 1669), Humphrey Robinson (Master 1661), John Macock 1692 (Master 1680), Abel Roper 1676 (Master 1676) and Sir Thomas Davies

they shall be appointed'; reference to the duties of the officers was in similarly general terms. (The Clerk was a part-time servant of the Company and his hours of attendance—except on Court Days—were fixed in August 1662 at 9 to 11 a.m. When George Tokefield, who earned our incalculable gratitude by taking most of the Company's books to his own house when the Hall was threatened by the Fire, retired in 1673, it was ordered that in future the Clerk should be elected afresh each Lady Day. This was presumably an insurance for good behaviour, but even so both John Lilly and John Garrett were criticized in 1682 for incompetence over the Ordinances and for failure to keep the Pension Lists up to date. The early Clerks had some legal training; but only when the election of a successor to Christopher Grandorge was being discussed in 1697 was it laid down that he must have been bred an attorney. On this occasion the candidates were reduced to six by scoring and, by scoring again, to two who went to the box; Simon Beckley was successful.[1] The worries over the shortcomings of Clerks were small compared with the trouble which the Beadle gave. Randall Taylor, on his appointment to succeed John Cleaver in 1674, was threatened with the loss of his job if he worked for the Treasurer of the English Stock. Moreover, he had to be severely reprimanded in 1682 for appearing in the Court Room without his hat and without summons, and for dining with the Assistants and with the Livery; in future he was to wait upon the Master and Wardens

---

[1] On this occasion the Clerk's fees, from each source, were agreed upon and shown to all the candidates:

(a) from the Corporation	£	s	d
Yearly salary, by Wardens	20	0	0
„ „ , by Renters	10	0	0
Pens, ink and paper	3	0	0
Glove money		11	8
Admitting each Assistant		10	0
„ „ Liveryman		10	0
Loan money, for each £100	2	0	0
„ „ , „ „ £50	1	0	0
For each funeral from Hall		10	0
„ „ feast by strangers		10	0
„ „ app. indenture and t.o.		2	6
„ „ freeman			8
„ „ lease of house	2	0	0
„ „ „ „ w/house	1	0	0
„ „ leave to assign lease		5	0
Writing pensions list	4	0	0
„ pensioner's petition			6

(b) from the English Stock, etc.	£	s	d
Yearly salary	6	0	0
Writing Dividend books	1	0	0
For each admission to a share		10	0
„ attendance at Court of Law with register		3	4
„ writing mortgage of share		5	0
„ each entry of copy			6
„ „ assignment		2	6
„ „ search in register, 1st year			6
„ „ 10 years more			6
„ „ certificate of entry			6
„ „ transcript			1

L

at their houses at least three times a week. Taylor was irrepressible, and only in 1692 did his effrontery and infirmity combine to ensure Nicholas Hooper's election in his stead. It was during Taylor's tenure of office—June 20, 1681—that the practice was established of disfranchising the Beadle as a free Stationer so that he could appear as a witness in any cases in which the Company was involved. In addition to the Clerk and Beadle, there was a Porter; and there were the Cook, Carpenter, Bricklayer and Plasterer who were retained by the Company—and, at a rather higher level, the Counsel. One order affecting all of them was made in February 1662: no office was to be granted in reversion and, the Assistants added optimistically, 'this order shall for ever be inviolably observed'.)

There follow a group of clauses governing general behaviour. Stationers must pay their fair shares of an *Assessment* laid on the Company; they must not *Abuse* one another or the Assistants; they must not *Plot* against the Society nor give away any *Secrets*. The fines for offences under these heads were up to £5 for a member of the Court and up to 40s for others. (The Ordinances make no mention of apprenticeship—presumably because this was governed by the custom of the City. Throughout the period there was the old trouble of printers' binding their apprentices by foreign indentures, but there were three new features. The term of service was becoming standardized at seven years from the date of presentment. In 1681 Samson Evans, a bookseller in Worcester and a freeman of the Company, was allowed to bind a local boy with indentures sent down from London. Thirdly, on August 7, 1666, Thomas Minshall, an engraver, took as his apprentice Joanna Nye, the daughter of an Essex parson—the first girl to be formally apprenticed. This was followed two years later by the admission by patrimony of the first girl—Elizabeth, daughter of George Latham, a bookseller who had died in 1658. It was an ancient custom of the City that the widow of a freeman became a freewoman. This meant, in the Stationers' Company, the right to take apprentices and to hold a share in the English Stock; one widow, Mrs Edward Griffin, was allowed a loan of £50 in 1627 as a special favour, and others were, occasionally, granted smaller loans. During the drive against stall-holders in the 1680s four women were admitted by redemption, Sarah Andrews and Dorothy Sheldenslow paying £5 each for the privilege.)

These twenty-two by-laws, and the oaths for freeman, Assistants,

Wardens, Masters, Clerks and Beadles, might have been designed for almost any other City company; the last ten of the 1678 Ordinances and five out of the nine clauses in the 1681 Supplement (the other four dealt with elections of Liverymen and Renters) and the single by-law approved in 1683 could apply only to the Stationers' Company. In them is concentrated the history of the Company, as the keeper of copyright, from 1662 to 1710.

All internal disputes about copyright and about any matter relating to the book trade must be first brought to the Court for settlement. No freeman must set up a press, nor let premises for printing, before giving notice to the Master or Wardens. No one must erect or countenance any private press 'commonly called *A Press in a hole*', nor must anyone employ, for three months afterwards, a man who had worked at an unlicensed printing house. No master printer must knowingly allow his apprentices or journeymen to work at anything prohibited by the Act of 1662 nor must he countenance instruction in printing to any other than his own son or an apprentice bound to an authorized printer. No new printing houses must be set to work until the number be reduced to twenty, besides those of the King's Printers and those at the Universities. Any journeyman working at an illegal press without reporting its existence within two days would forfeit his claim, and his widow's, to a pension. The last clause of all was also printed separately, and a copy of it was handed to each freeman after he had taken his oath; it was a résumé of the rules about unlicensed printing. The penultimate clause, put in as a result of Streater's pressure on L'Estrange, threatened with fines of £200 all, except the King's Printer, who printed any of the law books granted to Edward Atkins and his assigns by letters patent. (This was agreed to by the Court three years before the 1678 Ordinances were finally approved.)

SUPPLEMENTARY ORDINANCES OF 1681 AND 1683

The Supplementary Ordinances of 1681 begin with a restatement of the provision in the 1662 Act (which had lapsed in 1679) that every piece of printing must bear the name either of the printer or of a bookseller with a shop in London or the suburbs.[1] Then a fine of 1s a copy

[1] This Ordinance had been approved as a separate order on August 22, 1679, by the Lord Chancellor and the Lord Chief Justices, and it was reprinted as a broadside after a summons from the King to the Court to attend him in Council on March 11, 1681 (B.M. 1887, b. 58, no. 17). Since it was embodied in the 1681 Supplement, it was not reprinted by Arber.

was set on anyone printing or importing another man's duly entered or privileged copy, or any of the items in the Company's School Book Patent, and a fine of £10 on any Stationer who resisted a search, 'at any Convenient time', ordered by the Master or a Warden. Finally, the single Ordinance of 1683 made it compulsory for every member of the Company, before printing or reprinting any book—except one protected by the Great Seal of England—personally to see that the full title was entered in the register and to put his signature to the entry, on pain of a fine of £20.

The Printing Act of 1662 received the royal assent on May 19th and came into operation on June 10th.[1] Its most immediate impact on the Company—like the impact of the 1637 Decree—was a rush at the July elections to fine for Master. In the end old Miles Flesher, who had faced worse trouble and who had retired from active business, allowed himself to be chosen. The presence of a printer in the Master's place helped the Company to defeat the printers' attempt at separate incorporation during the following year, and the disasters of 1665 and 1666, which I shall deal with in the next chapter, created an atmosphere in which men were unusually ready to co-operate. By July 1667, however, the journeymen printers were once again appealing to the Court against their masters and the following year the letter-founders and makers of presses were proving sources of trouble. But a much more serious difficulty, with its roots in the 1640s, began to require attention in 1668: the selling of books and pamphlets by those who were not members of the Stationers' Company. These might be free-men of other companies, or they might be foreigners who kept stalls, or they might be hawkers who sold from house to house and up and down the streets; whoever they were, they were sources of danger both to the Government and to the Company, and they could be controlled only with the help of the City of London.

On August 10th a letter from the King in Council was read to the Stationers assembled for Sweeting's Feast, forbidding booksellers and printers to sell to hawkers and urging frequent searches of shops and printing houses. Early the following year (1669) the City Marshal's men were voted 20s a quarter for apprehending 'Hawkers, & women crying bookes neare the Exchange'. In August 1671 the King, at L'Estrange's suggestion, proposed to the Lord Mayor that men of other companies who were working in the book trade should be

---

[1] For the renewal of the Act from time to time, see below, p. 172.

turned over to the Stationers' Company or suppressed, and that in return the latter should release to their proper companies those who plied none of the Stationers' trades. Though the Common Council had passed an Act in 1663 that all practising as innholders be translated to the Innholders' Company, the Court of Aldermen went no further on October 1, 1671, than to order all apprentices serving 'Masters of other Companies vsing printing binding or Selling of Bookes' to be made free as Stationers and to promise that all lawful means be used to translate freemen of other companies when the size of the problem was known. On the following day, Jonathan Edwin, servant to Henry Brome (L'Estrange's bookseller), and Nathaniel Hooke, servant to Cornelius Bee, both masters being Haberdashers, took the oaths of free Stationers; but numerically the result was negligible. The Stationers, after all, were of little importance in the City; Thomason, when he was Warden in 1662, grumbled that his Company was ranked below others which were junior and yet was assessed—e.g. for the coronation—at a higher rate than the newcomers. In 1665 the Lord Mayor's request that the Stationers should give up their pew in St Paul's to the Clothworkers was indignantly refused; and when the Beadle warned the vergers of what was afoot, the latter demanded 15s by way of arrears in their fees! On his election as Lord Mayor in 1676, Sir Thomas Davies was immediately translated to the Grocers. It is not surprising that, when in 1696 three Stationers who were iron-mongers asked to be translated to the Ironmongers' Company, the Court refused.

The City's actions, in the next few years, against hawkers in the markets and against freemen (of companies) who had not taken up their freedom of the City did not help the Stationers and when the failure of Parliament to renew the Act in the summer of 1679 led to an outcrop of unlicensed pamphlets they sent a deputation to the Lord Mayor to ask for the suppressing of 'Hawkers & Bawlers'. This produced a circular to constables but no diminution of the trouble. It was not until 1684, when more serious misfortune befell the Stationers' and all the City companies, that a redrafting of the Charter provided an opportunity for more rigid control of those through whom books and pamphlets reached the public.

THE NEW CHARTER OF 1684

As part of his campaign to build up support for himself in the House of Commons, Charles II demanded the surrender of borough charters and, in the new grants, inserted clauses to ensure the loyalty of those who elected Members of Parliament. He then turned his attention to the companies of London, whose Liverymen formed the City electorate. In the course of March and April 1684 *quo warranto* proceedings were instituted, and all the companies decided that the only sensible policy was to surrender their existing charters and petition for new grants.

For the Stationers events moved early and fast. Before the end of March the Assistants had tendered their resignations to the Master and Wardens, and a draft petition to the King had been approved by a full meeting of the Company. By April 7th a list of loyal Assistants had been agreed upon, and ten days later a warrant for a new Charter was issued from Windsor. Within a week a meeting of 'senior' members (for, until the Charter had been approved, there were no Assistants) had accepted the draft of the new patent. The first three weeks of May were spent on legal formalities—perusal by the law officers of the crown and by the Lord Chief Justice, Jeffreys; 'haveing the Kings hand ffower times' through the agency of the Earl of Sunderland; passing the Privy Signet and the Privy Seal. The new Charter is dated May 22nd and an English version was read to the assembled Company on the 27th. In an address of thanks to His Majesty, reference was made to 'a restless & perverse ffaction' whose 'Presumptions' the King was pleased to baffle by showing how easy it was to 'annihilate' the Charter. Two four-horsed coaches were hired for two days to carry the deputation and the address to Charles at Windsor, and it looks as if the Stationers had attracted some attention as the first company to obtain a new charter. The writer of a news-letter on May 29th thought it worth while to mention both the grant and the expedition to Windsor, and the writer of a ballad used the occasion to pull the Company's leg.

During the second half of the summer Nathaniel Thompson, a courageous Catholic printer, published *A Choice Collection of 120 Loyal Songs*, for which he provided an introduction over the initials N. T. Among the 120 was 'A new song, in praise of the loyal company of Stationers, who, for their singular loyalty, obtain the first charter of London, 1684', to be sung to the tune of 'Winchester Wedding'.

> But *Stationers-Hall* so Loyal
> the *Charter*, by which they meet,
> The gift of his Ancestors Royal
> did humbly lay at his feet:
> Whose Suit he so far befriendeth,
> their Liberties know no bound,
> Their *Charter* her Whigs extendeth,
> through *London*, & full 4 miles round.
> And now from the *Bygot* and *Whig*,
> (to distinguish the good men and true),
> The Table is purg'd, and Rabble
> with the Members excluded withdrew.
>
> With limping *Dick* the *Zealous*,
> went doting *Yea*, and *Nay*,
> And squinting *Jack* so Jealous;
> lest Loyalty got the day.
> With these *Jack Thumb* was reckon'd,
> and hungry *Will* of the wood;
> And *Frank* the first and the second
> and *George* that will never be good.
> And thus they did trip it along,
> whilst *William* led up the Brawl,
> But *John* did storm above any,
> to be turn'd out of the Hall.
>
> *Jack* gave his right hand to *Harry*,
> who almost his place had lost,
> And swore if the day they carry,
> the Loyal shou'd pay for the Roast,
> But *Bob Hog* who made a tryal,
> and found how the Jig wou'd go,
> Resolv'd to change sides and be Loyal,
> but all the *Dissenters* said no;
> Thus whilst to the *Charter* or *Law*
> they would no obedience yield,
> The glory was still, *true Tory*
> is Master of the Field.

These are the most interesting of the six stanzas. In the third verse quoted, Bob Hog is the unpleasant Robert Stephens, who had once worked for Thompson and who had just lost his job as Messenger of the Press because he took bribes. Jack and Harry, at the beginning of the same verse, are the two Wardens, John Towse and Henry Hills, the only members of the Table—with Roger Norton, the Master—who did not resign. Hills was another unpleasant and unreliable character who 'ever made it his business to be of the rising side; let what Card would turn up Trump, he would follow Suit'; he must have been anxious lest his popularity with Oliver Cromwell might be remembered against him, but he made a great show of his devotion to the Church of England in 1684 for the same reasons as he went over to Rome a year or so later, when a pamphleteer described him as 'our spick and span new *Convert*'. The names in the second verse quoted are more difficult to attach to members of the Company, and it would be foolish to expect Thompson or his ballad-monger to be completely accurate in what was meant to raise a laugh. 'George that will never be good' must be George Calvert, and Frank is probably Francis Tyton; but John was too common a name to justify the risk of a guess. The sole candidate for 'limping Dick the Zealous' is Richard Royston, the grand old man of the Court; and Edward Brewster (for reasons which will appear later) must be 'doting Yea and Nay'.[1]

It is difficult to prove that the Stationers were the first of the City companies to get a new charter, but I have found none nearly so early and the majority much later; the Merchant Tailors, for instance, received theirs in January, the Blacksmiths in March and the Goldsmiths in May—all in the following year. The reason for the speed must have lain in the unique relationship between the Crown and the Stationers. While it was inconvenient for the Drapers to be temporarily charterless, it was a source of danger to both corporate and individual copyrights for the Stationers to be without legal existence; and while the King was unlikely to lose any sleep because the Worshipful Company of Ironmongers were, for a month or two, unable to sue or be sued, he relied on the Stationers to keep printed attacks on his Government within reasonable bounds. Moreover, some previous thought had been given to the modifications which might be made to tighten control of the book trade.

The document of May 22, 1684, which is permanently exhibited at Stationers' Hall and which is headed with a vigorous portrait of Charles II, begins by recapitulating the clauses of 1557. It then makes

[1] For a more detailed discussion of the names, and of the whole *quo warranto* incident, see *The Book Collector*, Winter 1957, pp. 369–77.

provision for ensuring that the governing body shall be, now and in the future, loyal to the sovereign. These new clauses are common to all the renewed charters and insist on the Assistants' being practising members of the Church of England (which is why Hills 'most zealously took the Sacrament'), and swearing the oaths of Allegiance and Supremacy and the oath laid down in the Corporation Act. The Master and Wardens and twenty-seven Assistants, self-chosen but approved by the Court of Aldermen, are then named, along with the Clerk. Rules are added for the summoning of the Court and for the co-opting of new members, who shall be subject to royal approval. Finally, there are the clauses included at the request of the Master and Wardens and designed to give the Company complete control of the book trade. Membership is to be obligatory not only for printers, as in the old Charter, but for letter-founders and builders of presses, and all such must live in the City or its liberties; the only exceptions are the King's Printer and the Printers to the two Universities; no mention is made of printing at York. Most important of all, no one is even to bind or sell books in London and Westminster and four miles round (as in the first verse quoted) unless he is a member of the Company, and all those in the book trade are to keep open shop so as to make search easy. Finally, royal approval is given to the 'publick Register' which, for more than a hundred years, the Company had kept for the entering of books and copies 'not granted by letters Patents'; and it is laid down that any member of the Company who becomes the proprietor of a copy 'by gift or purchase from the Author' or from anyone having the right to sell or give it, shall have the enjoyment of it as heretofore, provided he enters it in the Register.

The Company lost no time in trying to enforce the terms of its new Charter. On June 10, 1684, it petitioned the Lord Mayor to order the translation of members of other companies and applied to Jeffreys to suppress hawkers. Between two and three dozen tradesmen were called before the Court to explain why they were not Stationers. Some, like Richard Sare and John Walthoe, claimed to have been apprenticed to booksellers and took up their freedoms by service; some like Charles Brome could be admitted by patrimony; some, like Robert Smith— a Merchant Tailor of Bow Lane—promised to petition their companies for translation; but some, like the French booksellers in St Martin's Lane, were warned to continue trading at their peril. Since the Stationers were trying to swim against the tide of trading development, their success was small. After an appeal to the King in December, they helped to promote a Bill in the Commons against wandering Scotch pedlars and petty chapmen, and they produced for the City a list of dealers in books who were free of other companies. Thirteen companies are represented in this list, the Haberdashers by seventeen men (including Moses Pitt and Edward Millington), the Fishmongers by fourteen and the Girdlers by eight. But the Lords threw out the Bill as a corporation racket, the Bishop of London continued to issue licences to hawkers, and the translations never took place because no agreement could be reached at Guildhall about the payment of City fees; neither the individuals nor their parent companies saw why they should pay for something which the Stationers wanted, and the Stationers somewhat short-sightedly refused to defray expenses which would be incurred—theoretically—at the King's request.

The threat of the higgler to the established shop-keeper continued to be a source of worry to the Court throughout the reign of James II. Two petitions from booksellers, signed by about a hundred on each occasion, drew urgent attention to the growing number of foreigners among bookbinders, printers and paper-stationers, and to the loss of both town and country business through the intervention of the peripatetic undercutter; and in 1687 eighteen of the biggest tradesmen promised to subscribe 10s each for a year—and the Company bound itself to put up £20 a year—for the employment of William Latham who guaranteed 'to Suppress . . . such as wander up & down Citty & Cuntry Selling or dispersing Books contrary to Act of Parliament'. In 1690 the Court resolved to ask the Bishop of London to withdraw the licences he had already issued to hawkers and not to issue any more. But the time had gone when the distribution of books could be controlled either in the capital or in the kingdom by a City company; and by 1695 the control even of printing had been abandoned.

The contrast between this state of affairs and the Stationers' peak of power is enormous. The authority achieved by the Charter of 1557 had been amplified by the Decrees of 1586 and 1637; in 1684, at the price of possible royal veto against the choice of an Assistant, the Company had increased its jurisdiction (at least on paper) beyond what even Laud had thought necessary. It is hardly surprising that the period following the Revolution, particularly after the lapse of the Printing Act in 1695, was one of considerable confusion in the book trade. Nor is it surprising that the Company was unable, even during the six years' life of Charles's Charter, to take advantage of its new authority, for there was no continuity among those who exercised it. Early in the reign of James II the Court of Aldermen ordered a new list of Liverymen—'persons of approved & unquestionable Loyalty' —to be prepared; the tests for loyalty in May 1685 were not quite those of twelve months before, but agreement was eventually reached on the names of a Livery of eighty, including thirty Assistants. In the autumn of 1687 the King, using the powers in the new charters, commanded the Lord Mayor to remove large numbers from the governing bodies of the City companies. Seventeen of the Assistants of the Stationers' Company were thus unseated and those who had been turned out in 1684 were restored; nearly three-quarters of the Livery were displaced and those previously excluded were given back their original precedence. Six months later almost the same thing happened again; seven Assistants were turned out (Calvert—George that will *never* be good—for the second time) and forty-six Liverymen. The one result of permanent effect was the resolution of the Court to co-opt in future only such members of the Company as were working printers, booksellers or bookbinders at the time of their election.[1]

The confusion of the year 1688 was completed by an order of the Court of Aldermen on October 7th that all Liverymen thrown out at the time of the *quo warranto* be restored yet again to their places. On November 27th the 1684 Master, Roger Norton, and the reigning Master, Henry Hills (who had been Under Warden in 1684), summoned such of the pre-*quo warranto* Assistants as were still alive. Twelve turned up and were informed by the Clerk that Jeffreys now regarded the surrendering of the old charters as void and their provisions as still valid. This verdict did not suit the Stationers, who had gained more than they had lost by the change; the meeting therefore formally declared that the Company had made no surrender of its new Charter and proceeded to elect a new Master and new Wardens. But after legal opinion had been taken, the co-option of new Assistants in February 1689 was according to the by-laws and not according to the 1684 Charter.

There remained the ticklish question of seniority at the Table. Even in normal times there were squabbles about this; the present con-

---

[1] March 1, 1688; see above, p. 158, for the reaction of certain Liverymen to this.

fusion was settled with remarkable speed by the decision that those who had not served as Master or Warden should sit according to their service or fining as Renter. The only grumbles came from men like John Starkey, Daniel Blague and Giles Sussex, who argued about their right to places on the Court. The final tidying up did not come until 1690. On May 20th the *quo warranto* was reversed by Act of Parliament and on June 2nd a Master and Wardens had to be elected for the last four weeks of the Stationers' year. There were thus eleven elections in seven years, only four of which were conducted in the customary way. The following Table shows the confusion caused by the action of Charles II in March 1684.

ELECTIONS OF MASTERS AND WARDENS, 1683–90

Date	Method	Master	Upper Warden	Under Warden
June 30, 1683	Hands	Roger Norton	John Towse	Henry Hills
July 5, 1684	Box	Roger Norton	Henry Hills	James Cotterell
July 4, 1685	Hands	Henry Herringman	John Bellinger	Ambrose Isted
July 3, 1686	Hands	John Bellinger	John Baker	Robert Clavell*
July 2, 1687	Box	Roger Norton	John Baker†	Thomas Bassett
Oct. 12, 1687	Box	Henry Hills	Edward Brewster	Christopher Wilkinson
June 30, 1688	Hands	Henry Hills	John Sims	Benjamin Tooke
Nov. 27, 1688	Hands	John Towse	John Baker‡	Robert Clavell
July 6, 1689	Hands	Edward Brewster	Ambrose Isted	Thomas Parkhurst
June 2, 1690	Hands	Edward Brewster	Ambrose Isted	Henry Clarke
July 5, 1690	Box	Ambrose Isted	Henry Clarke	Henry Mortlock

* John Sims was elected *in absentia* but at the next meeting asked to fine because he was living out of Town.

† Baker and Isted received seven votes each in the ballot-box; an open vote—by a show of hands—chose Baker.   ‡ On Baker's death, his place was taken by Isted.

THE PROTECTION OF COPYRIGHT

Whatever other problems may have exercised the minds of whatever combination of Master, Wardens and Assistants, the fundamental and perennial worry was the protection of copyright. Even before the expiry of the two years for which the Act of 1662 was due to run, the Court was taking advice about measures to make a new Act still more rigorous. But the Cavalier Parliament had little time for the necessary consideration of a new Bill and took the easier course of renewing the old Act from session to session until its dissolution in 1679. The Company and Sir Roger L'Estrange were therefore forced, in uneasy partnership, to control the press with such powers as they could derive from the 1662 Act. The Assistants hated the association with the Surveyor of the Press; an example of their attitude was their immediate rejection of his suggested Law Patent by-law, not because they disagreed with it but because acceptance might suggest that they were not fit to manage their own affairs. Even if they had worked amicably together, the control of the press was bound to be incomplete; one reason was that the Court, as it pointed out to L'Estrange in 1671, regarded its powers as inadequate, and another that the problem of printing-house supervision had grown in size and complexity since the time of Laud; a third reason was the difficulty—and delay—in getting a verdict in the courts; but the most important reason of all was that the main interest of the Court was the guarding of English Stock rights. No printer who had set up in contravention of the Act was prosecuted by the Company unless he printed almanacks, as did Mrs Maxwell and the printers at York, or psalters, as did Nathaniel Thompson. When, on July 4, 1676, Robert Everingham was summoned to a Private Court to explain by what authority he had set up a printing house, he merely answered 'because hee served his time at the trade & for no other reason'; and no further action was taken then. Urged on by L'Estrange, the Wardens seized Quaker pamphlets and Catholic books and had them burned in the garden at Stationers' Hall or damasked;[1] and in the Michaelmas Term 1681 no fewer than twelve cases were pending, seven instituted by the Crown and only five by the Wardens who were known to send warning of impending searches to such members of the Company as were foolish enough to be caught dealing in unlicensed books yet not knavish enough to handle counterfeit primers. Mearne told the Catholic bookseller Anthony Lawrence that he would never have been troubled if he had not behaved saucily to the Company's officers;[2] and although the Assistants frequently resolved, after a note or even a visit from L'Estrange, or on the strength of a note from the Council, that Ichabod Dawks or some other 'irregular' printer should be indicted at the next sessions of the King's Bench, the proceedings were seldom pressed and, as a general rule, the Company did not interfere with those who did not offend the Company.

[1] When books or pamphlets had been folded and stitched they could be made unreadable only by destruction; but the reading matter on printed sheets could be obliterated, and the sheets, thus 'damasked', could be used by bookbinders or for wrapping.

[2] S.P. Dom. Car. II, vol. 366, no. 263. The State Papers are full of reports by L'Estrange of the unsatisfactory behaviour of the Company, of the distribution of unlicensed books by Grocers, Mercers, etc., of search-warrants and indictments. For an account of the failure to suppress irregular printing, see 'The Censorship of the Press during the reign of Charles II' by J. Walker in *History*, vol. xxxv n.s., 1950, pp. 219–38.

One of the obvious sources of copyright trouble came, as before, from the Continent, and it was aggravated by the destruction of books in the Fire; in March 1669 it was suggested (without success) that imports of books should be cleared only after viewing by the ecclesiastical authorities and the Company.[1] Another source of such trouble was disputed claims to copies, and in August 1674 it was ordered that no assignments were to be entered in the register without the authority of the Court and without a saving clause that no established right was being infringed; by two further orders, assignments which had not been drawn up by the Clerk were not to be accepted.

By 1679 even L'Estrange recognized that the Printing Act was unworkable, and it lapsed; in its place were the new by-laws of 1678 and there was the chance, for a few weeks during the following summer, that the printers might be separately incorporated.[2] Though the bookselling section of the Company, aided by the continued disgruntlement of the journeymen printers, was able to prevent this amputation, the loss of statutory support for copyright was serious enough, even without the impending threat to the Charter. Time and money were devoted to the promotion of a new Bill and, when the worst happened, to the introduction of new powers in the 1684 Charter; but it was not until the accession of James II that Parliament renewed the Printing Act. Meantime, something had to be done to supplement the Company's ability to protect copyright. On Wednesday, August 17, 1681, a Common Hall was held at which the nine additional by-laws, with their emphasis on respect for copies, were formally adopted; and just before Christmas in the following year another Common Hall adopted the 1683 Ordinance. Judged solely by the increased use of the register, the Company had re-established some confidence in the minds of its members that it could protect their rights. But the confidence was short-lived, and the booksellers as the chief copyright-holders were already devising their own machinery for mutual protection.

The title-pages of law books printed, from 1669, by John Streater, James Flesher (the son of Miles) and Henry Twyford, as the assigns of the Atkins family, contain the names of a dozen or more distributors who between them controlled the market in books of this kind and who could put a copyright infringer out of business by refusing supplies to him (in his capacity as wholesaler or retailer) and by refusing

---

[1] This echoes clause vi of the 1637 Decree; see above, p. 121.　　　[2] See above, p. 151.

to distribute the books which he promoted. When Richard Royston made his will in the autumn of 1682 he advised, with the Law Patent arrangement as an example, that new impressions of the copies he was bequeathing should immediately be divided between six or eight of the leading London wholesalers. Out of these ideas evolved the joint-copyright-owning and joint-distributing groups of booksellers called Congers,[1] the main purpose of which was the protection of copyright through control of wholesaling. A few weeks before Royston made his will, the Court gave the first of a series of permissions to book-sellers to sue, in the name of the Company, anyone who pirated a copy which had been properly entered—provided the Company was not financially involved; the first two to obtain this concession were Henry Herringman and Robert Scott, the biggest wholesalers in the trade, the one of London-produced books and the other of impor-tations. In such ways the booksellers were learning to rely on their efforts rather as tradesmen than as freemen of a City company for the preservation of their rights in copies, and these early experiments had a considerable effect on the booksellers' attitude to the Stationers' Company in the next hundred years.

The accession of James II brought a renewal of the 1662 Act, for a period of seven years; but its warmest advocates made no greater claim for it than that it was better than nothing. Confidence in the efficacy of entering copies at Stationers' Hall declined and London printers—masters and men—protested more than once against unfair competition from the presses at Oxford and York and from an illegal press at Chester. When in 1687 the Court ordered David Mallet to cease printing until he was licensed to do so, he bluntly refused and resorted, along with other unrecognized masters, to binding his apprentices at scriveners'; and when William Bonny, a Blacksmith, married a printer's widow and demanded work on English Stock books, the Court acquiesced and withdrew its permission only in 1690 when he openly criticized the Company.

THE FIRST COPYRIGHT ACT, 1710

The Printing Act, after further extensions, lapsed for ever in April 1695, and for the next fifteen years there was a stream of Bills, petitions

---

[1] For a full description of this kind of development see *The Notebook of Thomas Bennet and Henry Clements*, Oxford, 1956, pp. 76 ff.

for Bills, pamphlets for and against control of the press, and committees to watch over the Company's interests.[1] I have come across no indication of the Court's official attitude; it is not improbable that it was still thinking in terms of another Printing Act which would give more power to the Company. But the setting up of printing houses in provincial cities (Bonny opened one at Bristol in 1695) made nonsense of the old control from London, and the joint pressure on the House of Commons of 'learned men' and of enterprising booksellers like Jacob Tonson and Awnsham Churchill put the emphasis directly on the protection of copyright instead of indirectly—through the control of printing. Though the Court voted £30 towards the expenses of the Bill which became 'An Act for the Encouragement of Learning by Vesting the Copies of Printed Books in the Authors or Purchasers of such Copies, during the Times therein mentioned' on April 4, 1710; though the register at Stationers' Hall was a part of the machinery of the Act; and though Stationers were the immediate beneficiaries, the Company—apart from keeping the register and forwarding 'deposited' books to the nine copyright libraries—was not mentioned and was given no part in the operation of the Act. I need therefore say no more here than that, from April 10, 1710, the author of any book then in print (or anyone to whom he had transferred his rights) was to enjoy the printing and reprinting of it for twenty-one years; that the author (or the purchaser) of any book printed after April 10th was to enjoy fourteen years from the date of publication, provided he entered it in the register before publication, with a further fourteen years for the author if he were still living at the end of the first period; and that the Act applied equally 'in that part of Great Britain called Scotland'. The Company was, of course, guaranteed the same protection for the books in the English Stock as any other copyright owner—and the same chance of vindicating its claims in the law courts of England or Scotland.

It is strange that within a dozen years towards the end of the Stuart period the Stationers' Company should both achieve the maximum of theoretical authority and experience the minimum of practical power. In May 1684 it received its augmented Charter and by the summer of 1695 it had lost not only this augmentation but the support of the revived Printing Act; it was back where it had been in 1557

---

[1] Harry Ransom, in *The First Copyright Statute*, Austin, 1956, gives on pp. 89 ff. a detailed account of the steps which led to the Act of 1710.

and the additional strength which might be derived from the new Ordinances was more than offset by the changes which had taken place in England during the century and a half between the reign of Queen Mary and the reign of Queen Anne. The first reason for this strange closeness in time of zenith and nadir is that the contrast between the two was more apparent than real; the additional powers in the 1684 Charter existed only on paper and bore little relation to the context in which they had to be operated. For the age of rule by decree had passed; the Revolution of 1688 proved that the Tudor methods of government, under the shadow of which the Company had begun to play a real part in the world, were no longer workable. In the next place, 150 years of printing had given the products of the press quite a different weight in the life of society; even news-papers, in the provinces as well as in London, had become by 1710 part of the pattern. The Stationers' Company, on the other hand, took no official cognizance of this change; its corporate ideas about the exploitation of the printed word were as out of date as its political philosophy. But this was not true of individual members of the Company; and the last reason is the tendency of men to support, as members of a committee, policies which they would not think of following in their own businesses. I shall show in the next chapter how a two-standard approach operated in the management of the English Stock; I have given examples in this chapter of book-sellers acting more realistically in their capacities as private tradesmen than as Stationers. The Company lost a great opportunity, in the second half of the seventeenth century, of becoming, through a rethinking of the copyright problem, a central and essential rallying point for all members of the book trade throughout the country; that it retained some importance in the eighteenth century was due, paradoxically, to the pull of its most parochial interest—the English Stock—and to the enterprise of that section in the Company which was to give it progressively less support—the booksellers.

CHAPTER X

CORPORATION AND ENGLISH
STOCK FINANCES

MINUTES OF COURT MEETINGS

THE last chapter emphasized the formal aspects of the Company's life in the second half of the seventeenth century—the royal grant which made it a corporation, the rules by which it governed its members, the statutes for the control of printing. In this chapter I want to show something of its day-to-day work during the same period and to indicate how it dealt with its economic problems: how it financed its normal corporate activities and how it managed its unique trading organization, the English Stock. Since the earliest Treasurer's Stock Book opens in March, and the Wardens' Accounts begin again from July 1663, the gild year 1663–4—the last twelve months before the disasters of the Plague and the Fire—is an obvious starting point.

Saturday, July 4, 1663, was Election Day, and when the three candidates for each office had gone 'to the box' the key was given to William Lee, the most senior Assistant not standing for election. The only subject debated that day was the propriety of presenting apprentices and admitting freemen when it was not known who the officers were; and on Festival Day, Thursday, July 9th, the fees for those presented at the beginning of the meeting were paid to the late Wardens and, after the return from church and the opening of the box, the fees then taken were handed to the new Wardens. These were Andrew Crooke, who was still involved in the Law Patent negotiations with Miles Flesher (re-elected Master), and Luke Fawne, who had played a part in Sparke's movement of 1645.

The August meeting of the Court was on Monday the 3rd, when Rapha Harford chose to fine for first time Under Warden. Matters discussed were the printing house owned by the English Stock in Scotland, a squabble between Samuel Speed and Mrs Alsop (about which the Master and Wardens met the next day) and the tenancy of a Company house. It was decided to lend Robert Stephens, the 'Bob Hog' of 1684, £50 from the Norton bequest, to prosecute William Leybourn for the refund of his £50, to fine Henry Hall, one of the Oxford printers, 40s for not binding an apprentice in London, to hold the Clerk responsible for money stolen from his study, to call Roger Norton and Thomas Davies (Lord Mayor in 1676) to the Livery, to buy a piece of plate worth £10 out of John Sweeting's bequest and to appoint four bachelor booksellers as stewards for the first Sweeting dinner to be held on September 21st. It is clear from the 'waste' book minutes of the next meeting (Monday September 7th) that the business could be interrupted by the arrival of a master with an apprentice to enrol or turn over or make free. Among the items discussed were debts for rent or on loans, and permission to Robert White to mortgage his Livery share to George Sawbridge, the Treasurer; and the Court made a special order that the assignment of Drexelius's *Upon Eternity* by Margaret Alsop[1] to Thomas Rookes be entered in the register of copies. Normally one of the Wardens took sole responsibility, so far as the Company was concerned, by signing the manuscript copy of a book, 'that it might be entered on the company's register';[2] assignments were liable to be disputed and to require consideration by the Court, but normal entries could be made whenever the Clerk could be persuaded to make them.

On September 29th a special Court was summoned, on a precept from the Lord Mayor, to choose ten men, substantially horsed and wearing velvet coats and chains of gold, to wait on the King and Queen when they visited the City. Warden Crooke with four other booksellers among the Assistants and five printers from the Livery were selected. At the Quarter Day Court on Monday, October 5th, there were two copyright disputes, four problems brought up by tenants, and permissions to mortgage a share and to take a loan. An injunction from the Court of Chancery concerning the Law Patent was presented to the Table 'but no further dispute theruppon'. An old man called John Robins petitioned to be made free as the apprentice (in Oxford) of Leonard Lichfield who had been the apprentice of Joseph Barnes; since Lichfield was never free, as Robins very well

---

[1] Probably the Mrs Alsop whose dispute was heard in August. The Clerk made the entry in the register on the 10th.

[2] Andrew Crooke, then Under Warden, in evidence given to Mr Secretary Nicholas, March 23, 1661 (*C.S.P. Dom. Car. II, 1660–1*, p. 546).

knew, the petition was refused. The Assistants then moved into the hall for the reading of the Ordinances and, on returning to the parlour, appointed auditors of the Wardens' accounts for the two previous years.

The Court met on twenty-four occasions in the course of the year and had an average attendance of twelve out of a possible nineteen members.[1] John Chapple, who died in 1664, did not attend at all and Ralph Smith (for what reason I do not know) only once; but the Under Warden and George Thomason were there every time, while Crooke, Samuel Man and Humphrey Robinson each missed only once. The subjects discussed, in addition to those already mentioned, were the supply of books to libraries under the 1662 Act; tips to Custom House officers; the shoddy (and in one case the piratical) printing of almanacks and the irresponsible habit among the elected Stock-keepers of acting without the knowledge of the Master and Wardens; the election to two half-Yeomanry shares; a bookbinder's complaint against a powerful partnership of booksellers; the allowance to a journeyman printer of an apprentice 'lame of one of his hands'; two special elections of Liverymen, with the refusal of some who were ironmongers or distillers; the stopping of John Martyn's Dividend for selling a school book printed on the Continent; the complaint of John Dever that L'Estrange had 'indirectly disposed' of a copy which he had recently bought and which someone else might even then be printing; the invalidity of share mortgages which were not registered. The Treasurer and Stock-keepers were as usual elected on March 1st and the Renter Wardens on March 26th; but Richard Tomlins, having been elected Renter *in absentia*, did not formally accept the office until June 6th. The poor were paid only twice instead of quarterly, but a few minor charitable donations were made. At the Quarter Day Court on April 4th it was not possible to read the Ordinances in the hall 'in respect of some Inconveniences' (a leaking roof, I suspect) and the freemen had to adjourn to the Council Chamber.

A reading of the full minutes of all the meetings in 1663–4 leaves a number of impressions. The first is that the Ancients were dealing fairly and thoughtfully with the problems put before them but that, immersed in the present and guided by the past, they were no more inclined to look to the future than their predecessors had been a

---

[1] For the Court 'by special summons' on September 29th there is no list of those present.

hundred years before. The second is that items relating to the English Stock did not take up as much of the time as in some years they were apt to do; it was quite exceptional for only one share to come up for disposal in twelve months. The third is the small sign of discord in the trade; the only breeze to ruffle the smoothness of the minutes was the refusal of a few members of the Company—particularly those not engaged in the book trade—to be saddled with the expense of becoming Liverymen. The fourth is the 'relaxed' attitude of the majority; at its best this was a determination not to be rattled by the first threat to the Charter, but at its worst it was an over-readiness to defer a decision to the next Court or to put off paying the poor until next quarter.

WARDENS' ACCOUNTS

I have already mentioned this frame of mind where it affected the auditing of the Wardens' Accounts; those for 1663–4 were not finally squared until more than five years later and they themselves contain items which refer back four years. Most entries were presumably covered at this time—as they certainly were later in the century—by vouchers, but there must have been a certain amount of fiddling; in March 1665 Samuel Gellibrand was elected second Renter and on July 2nd of the following year he paid to the Under Warden £6 13s 4d, the balance of his account; at some later date he paid a further 15s 'for some Quarteridges besides some of whose names he put downe, he forgott'. It is not surprising that, for this reason among others, there is considerable fluctuation in the amount of cash which passed through the Wardens' hands; in the fifty years from 1663 total annual receipts were as low as £90 (1667–8) and as high as £1,416 (1692–3) and the balances ranged from a debit of £71 (1710–11) to a credit of £513 (1690–1). No year can be called typical, but an analysis of income and expenditure for 1663–4 (set out on p. 182) will throw some light on the problems facing an Under Warden during the latter part of the seventeenth century.

The first point to notice about this year's accounts is that the sale of old books—(11) and (o)—was made on behalf of the English Stock and that the loans repayed by Richard Hodgkinson, John Burroughs (£100 each), William Leybourn after threat of prosecution, Underhill, Keynton (£50 each), and five others, amounting to

	£	s	d	
By balance from Wardens' Accounts, 1661–2*	51	9	4	(1)
cash from Renter Wardens (in two sums)	51	2	0	(2)
licensing of copies, 138 at 6d each	3	9	0	(3)
presenting of apprentices, 63 at 2s 6d each	7	17	6	(4)
admission of freemen, 61 at 3s 4d each	10	3	4	(5)
Livery fines; 14 at £20, 2 at £10, 1 at £5†	305	0	0	(6)
fines for breaking ordinances		8	6	(7)
letting of the Hall for funerals	2	0	0	(8)
repayment of loans made to Stationers	399	0	0	(9)
assessment for coronation	36	1	0	(10)
sale of old books from Wardens' room	113	6	0	(11)
miscellaneous, including £5 for Livery attendance at funeral	6	0	0	(12)
fines for not serving as Warden	21	0	0	(13)
bequest money	96	13	4	(14)
rents from Company houses, £92 and £24 19s 6d	116	19	6	(15)
repayment of subsidy	31	15	0	(16)
dividend on Londonderry Estate	54	4	5	(17)
money borrowed	100	0	0	(18)
Total	£1,406	8	11	

	£	s	d	
To wages	38	10	2	(a)
retaining fees for Cook, etc.	14	5	6	(b)
repairs to property	49	8	8	(c)
contributions towards feasts	22	17	4	(d)
loans made to Stationers	374	0	0	(e)
subsidy for coronation, paid to the City	50	0	0	(f)
rates and taxes	29	6	8	(g)
legal expenses	12	19	8	(h)
repayment of money lent to the Company	365	5	0	(i)
entertainment	31	10	8	(j)
sermons	81	13	0	(k)
bequests	51	11	0	(l)
parish dues	5	11	6	(m)
quit rents, etc.	13	2	5	(n)
English Stock for sale of books	113	6	0	(o)
repayment due on Wardens' Account for 1658–9	12	0	0	(p)
„ „ „ „ „ „ 1660–1	42	18	2	(q)
interest on money borrowed	61	10	0	(r)
miscellaneous	3	0	3	(s)
balance paid to Mr White, Under Warden 1669–70	33	12	11	(t)
Total	£1,406	8	11	

* Not from the previous year but from the year before that.
† Liverymen were allowed to pay their fines by instalments.

£399 (9) were paid out (*e*), less £25, to Robert White (£100),[1] Robert Stephens, John Playford, Christopher Eccleston, Thomas Lambert, Nathaniel Calvert (£50 each), widow Alsop and Thomas Sheeres (£12 each). The second point is that the indebtedness of the Company was not as bad as an interest figure of £61 10s (*r*) suggests; this is, rather, an indication of the unbusinesslike method of account-keeping and is made up of 2½ years' interest on £250 repaid this year, of 3¾ years' interest on £100 also repaid, and six months' interest on the £100 borrowed (18) to repay the last £100. The third point is that if the sum of £305 (6) collected on Livery fines is brought in to balance the repayment of money borrowed (*i*), self-cancelling items amount to about £900 and reduce each side of the account to £500; the average for the last twenty years of the Stuart period, when the books were kept with rather more care and regularity, was about £570.

Even if these allowances are made the account for 1663–4 looks very different from that of the previous year analysed, 1577–8.[2] The first ten headings on the credit side and the first eight (and the last) on the debit side are represented in both years, and three or four items on either side in the later example could be found in other years in the sixteenth century. But only half a dozen of them are comparable in magnitude and only the fees for entering of copies (roughly), for the presenting of apprentices and for the admission of freemen are the same in both years. There are three reasons for the great increases: the drop in the value of money, the growth in the number of Stationers and the expansion in the activities of the Company. The first will largely explain the increases in the wages (*a*), the retaining fees (*b*), the repairs (*c*) and the donation of Ralph Triplet, a distiller, for the attendance at his father's funeral (12). The second will explain the greater contribution towards the Company's dinners (*d*) and for more spending on entertainment (*j*), the rises in the yield of fixed fees, (3) to (5), and in the cash received from the Renters (2);[3] but this last figure was never as high again, partly owing to the tendency of members to avoid paying quarterage if, as journeymen, they never went near the Hall, and partly owing to the increased expenses to be met by the Renters.

---

[1] Loans were not intended for Stationers of such standing; White was Under Warden five years later. But he was one of the master printers who did not sign the petition for separate incorporation in 1663. [2] See above, p. 56.

[3] Owing to the loss of the Renters' Books it is impossible to say when the quarterages payable by Liverymen and Assistants were put up to 6d and 8d respectively.

The biggest changes came from the development of the Company along normal gild lines. Whereas the fining to avoid offices (13) was an exceptional occurrence at the beginning of the century, by 1663 it had become common; the remarkable feature this year was that no one fined for the Renter Wardenship. This was a jolt to the Company's finances, and I feel that the institution of a 'special call' to the Livery towards the end of April, a month after the loss on Renters' fines was known, may have been an attempt to milk one group of cows when another had failed, and to create, in the process, a larger number for a second milking. On the other hand, the policy of enlarging the Livery may have been not an example of foresight but an attempt to vie with other companies. In either case, the results were, at once, an annual income of £200 to £250 and, by the eighteenth century, a complete change in the pattern of the Company. The problem as always was to collect the money; those elected in 1664 paid quickly, but in July 1711 £412 was still due from Liverymen. The remaining items on both sides of the account require no further comment than that the dividend on the Londonderry Estate (17) ought to have been paid to the Treasurer of the English Stock (and was not until after the Fire), that the bequest money (14) was largely made up of £80 from Mr Sweeting, that almost the whole of the fantastic sum spent on sermons (k) was an accumulated debt to the City for preachers at St Paul's—an obligation under George Bishop's will—and that I shall deal in Chapter XI with the Company's property and the property managed for the partners in the English Stock.

ENGLISH STOCK ACCOUNTS

Since the Treasurer's year ran from March 1st, the following accounts do not exactly synchronize with those of the Company.[1]

The English Stock, as crystallized by the grant of 1603, was now sixty years old; it had survived the difficult 1640's and, with the Restoration, was recovering some of its initial prosperity based on the sales of a few quick-moving books and almanacks. On p. 187 is a reproduction of a broadside listing the books available in about 1695 and giving their wholesale prices; all but a dozen of these formed the

---

[1] For a description of the books of account and of the Treasurer's method of keeping them, and for a detailed analysis of the figures for the period 1650–1715, see 'The English Stock of the Stationers' Company in the Time of the Stuarts', *The Library*, 5th ser., xii, 1957.

ENGLISH STOCK ACCOUNTS

THE TREASURER'S ACCOUNTS
MARCH 1, 1663, TO MARCH 1, 1664

Receipts

	£	s	d
By sales of books	3,074	11	4
„ „ almanacks	2,417	0	7
„ „ waste paper	7	18	8
permissions to print	30	0	0
dividend from Londonderry Estate	–	–	–
money borrowed	–	–	–
rents	412	19	8
allowance for almanacks given away	10	7	11
Total	£5,952	18	2

Disbursements

	£	s	d	£	s	d
(a) Costs of production						
To authors of books	11	5	0			
„ „ almanacks	143	0	0			
paper	1,211	10	4			
printing	1,920	2	5			
engraving and printing cuts	44	3	0			
binding	2	13	6	3,332	14	3
(b) Overheads						
To wages	51	0	0			
carriage and postage	3	15	2			
entertainment	25	0	1			
legal expenses	44	5	11			
other patentees	165	4	3			
repairs to property	–	–	–			
rent and allowance for tenants' taxes	150	0	0			
interest and loan repayment	53	16	0			
miscellaneous	2	2	6	495	3	11
(c) Variation in 'Sundry Debtors'				230	0	0
(d) Profit						
To the poor	100	0	0			
dividend	1,795	0	0	1,895	0	0
Total				£5,952	18	2

main stock-in-trade thirty years earlier and, apart from the law books (which were again being handled by the Stock for a few years from 1661) there were not more than a dozen publications which were in print in 1663 but no longer available in 1695. In order to show which books were regarded as the most profitable, I give below a list of those which were reprinted in the autumn of 1666, immediately after the devastation; the printing numbers represent about twelve months' sale at the pre-Fire rate, and the wholesale prices already reflect the shortages at the end of 1666.

BOOKS REPRINTED IMMEDIATELY AFTER THE FIRE

Number	Title	Wholesale rate
5,000	Psalter*	16s for 25
5,000	Psalms, 12mo for Bibles	12s „ „
12,000	Old Primer	20s per gross of 150
5,000	Scotch Primer	15s „ „ „ „
20 reams	ABC	16s 8d per ream
3 „	Print for Horn Books	10s „ „
1,500	English Schoolmaster	10s for 26
3,000	Aesopi Fabulae	12s „ „
3,000	Pueriles Sententiae	3s „ „
3,000	Pueriles Confabulationes	4s „ „
1,500	Sturmii Epistolae	7s „ „
1,500	Ovidii Epistolae	20s „ „
1,500	„ Metamorphoses	20s „ „
1,500	„ de Tristibus	7s „ „
1,500	Corderii Colloquia	10s „ „
1,500	Textoris Epistolae	9s „ „
2,000	Catonis Disticha	5s 6d for 26

together with 20 almanacks printed in London and 5 at Cambridge

* Every item except the Scotch Primer is to be found in a large English Stock entry in the register for March 5, 1620; the last ten items were part of the School Book Patent. It will be noticed that the wholesale rates allowed one or two extra books per two dozen, and six per gross. Opposite is a printed advertisement of *c.* 1695.

I have mentioned the Court's conservative policy in handling the gild affairs of the Company; since, of the nine Stock-keepers who managed the Company's trading business, five were Assistants, an equally conservative outlook dominated the management of the English Stock. The creation of a back-log is the essence of survival in publishing; but a list which is all back-log is dead, or at the best moribund. It is therefore to be expected that the sales of English Stock books were never again as high, even at the enhanced post-Fire prices, as

BOOKS Printed for the Company of STATIONERS, and ſold at their Ware-Houſe in *Stationers-Hall, London.*

	l.	s.	d.
Æſopi Fabulæ 8o ——	0	07	00
Aphthonii Progymn. 8o	0	14	00
Barton's Pſalms 12 ——	0	16	00
Caſtalionis Dial. 8o ——	0	07	00
Catechiſmus Parvus, 8o	0	00	10
Cato, 8o —— ——	0	03	00
Corderii Colloq. 8o ——	0	06	00
Engliſh Schoolmaſter, 4o	0	05	00
Flores Poetarum, 12o	0	14	00
Hawkin's Spelling book 8o	0	04	00
Hool's Æſop, 8o ——	0	16	00
——*Cato,* 8o ——	0	04	00
—— *Century of Epiſt.* 8o	0	06	00
——*Corderius,* 8o ——	0	16	00
—— *Pueril. Confab.* 8o	0	04	00
——*Sententiæ Puer.* 8o	0	04	00
Iſocratis Orat. 3. 8o *Gr.*	0	04	00
—*ad Demon.* 12o *G. Lat.*	0	07	00
Juſtini hiſtoria. 8o ——	0	07	00
Ludovicus Vives, 8o ——	0	04	00
Mantuan. 8o —— ——	0	07	00
Nomenclatura brevis, 8o	0	04	00
Nowel's Catech. 8o *Lat.*	0	04	00
—— 12o *Gr.* and *Lat.*	0	14	00

13 per Doſen (all of the above)

	l.	s.	d.
Ovid. Metam. 8o ——	0	12	0
—*Id. Notis Minellii* ——	1	02	0
—*Epiſt.* 8o —— ——	0	12	0
— *de Pont. Faſt. &c.* 8o	0	10	0
— *de Triſt.* 8o ——	0	03	0
— *Id. Notis Minell.* 12o	0	12	0
— *Epiſtles Engliſh* 8o	0	12	0
Pſalter, 8o Black Print	0	06	0
— 8o White —— ——	0	06	0
Poſſelius Col. 8o —— ——	0	07	0
Pueriles Confab. 8o. ——	0	02	0
Sententiæ Pueriles ——	0	01	6
Smetii Proſodia, 8o ——	1	07	0
Terentius Chriſtianus, 8o	0	07	0
Terentius Com. 8o ——	0	07	0
Terentius Minellii, 12o	1	00	0
Textor's Epiſt. 8o ——	0	05	0
Textor's Epith. 12o ——	0	12	0
Tullies Offices, 8o ——	0	12	0
— *Select Epiſt. Lat.* 8o	0	04	0
Teſtam. 12 *Patriarchs* 8o	0	07	0
Tuſſer's Husbandry, 4o	0	09	0
Virgilii Opera, 12o ——	0	14	0

13 per Doſen (all of the above)

The *Pſalms* in *Folio* 2s. *Nett.*

	l.	s.	d.
Pſalms, 4o for Par. Cler.	0	10	00
——8o *Pica* —— ——	0	12	00
——8o *Brevere* ——	0	08	00
——8o *Nompareil* ——	0	12	00
——*Large* 12o ——	0	07	00
——12o *Nompareil* ——	0	06	00
——24o *Pareil* ——	0	06	00

13 per Doſen (first three); Per Quartern (last four)

	l.	s.	d.
A B C. —— ——	0	00	8
Catech. with Proofs ——	0	02	0
Horn-Book Prints ——	0	00	6
Engl. Primer Bl. Print	0	15	0
——*Prim.* White Print	0	15	0
Cambridge Primer ——	0	12	0
Child's Guide ——	0	15	0

per Quartern (first three); per Groſs (last four)

FIG. V.—Broadside, *c.* 1695 (*reduced*).

they were in 1663–4—except for a brief period from 1703 when the Treasurer was handling the Oxford editions of Clarendon's *History*; and in 1683–4 the figure was only just over £1,000. Almanacks, on the other hand, came out as new books every year, even though the 'Gadbury' for 1664 contained little that could not be found in the 'Gadbury' for the previous year. Moreover, the Company's monopoly covered *all* almanacks; whereas Charles Hoole could offer his *Accidence* to a bookseller of his choice, John Partridge had little alternative but to bring his *Merlin* to the Company. Of the twenty-seven 1692 almanacks offered for sale in November 1691 (see p. 189), ten were first published for 1672 or later; and a dozen of those put out for 1664 were dead before 1692. For these reasons the sales of almanacks show a steady increase from £2,250 for 1670 to an average of well over £3,000 during the reign of Queen Anne, and go some way to offset the decline in the sales of books. What these figures do not immediately show is the vast quantity of almanacks handled between the end of November and the end of December each year; this was seldom less than 350,000 and was often more than 400,000; the sales of Wing's alone for 1669 were well over 50,000.[1] In addition, copies found their way into the market from the presses at York and, in spite of every precaution, direct from printing houses in London.

The remaining items on the Receipts side of the Treasurer's account did not normally contribute more than 10 per cent to the Stock's income. There was a good market for waste paper in the seventeenth century; though the £113 in the Wardens' Accounts provides some evidence of this, there is no corresponding entry in the Treasurer's books until the following year, when it appears as less than £70! But sums of £30 or more occur fairly regularly, and in 1715–16 the figure was nearly £50. The dividend from Londonderry (shown as received by the Wardens) did not reach the Treasurer on this occasion, but he could normally rely on an income of £40 to £50. From permissions to print, the return was variable; in some years there was nothing, but in 1684 the lessees of the Oxford privilege paid £147 in satisfaction for having printed 66,000 copies of the psalms. A new and sensible source of income was created in 1689. There was a tradition that a successful candidate for a share should treat his fellow partners; the

---

[1] For a detailed study of this business, see 'The Distribution of Almanacks in the second half of the Seventeenth Century', *Studies in Bibliography*, Charlottesville, xii, 1958.

ON Day of this present *November*, 1691. Will be published at STATIONERS-HALL, thefe feveral ALMANACKS following, for the Year 1692.

𝕭𝖑𝖆𝖓𝖐𝖘.	𝕾𝖔𝖗𝖙𝖘.
Andrews.	*Trigg.*
Coley .	*Fly.*
Chapman:	*Woodhoufe.*
Dove.	*Swallow.*
Gadbury.	*Fowle.*
Partridge.	*White.*
Poor Robin.	*Rofe.*
Proteftant Almanack.	*Perkins.*
Pond.	*Dade.*
Salmon.	*Turner.*
Saunders.	*Culpeper.*
Tanner.	*Davis.*
Woodward.	
Wing.	

Parker ; with Obfervations, a Table of Houfes, and the Planets Places; newly Calculated from the *Caroline* Tables; with an exact Tide-Table, *&c.*

Publifhed inftead of Lilly, *and of the fame Price and Number of Sheets with that.*

Thofe that will have Parcels, are defired to give in t ɥr Notes before the Day of Publication.

FIG. VI.—Broadside, 1691 (*reduced*).

new order brought into the Stock funds the rough cash equivalent, which produced £35 each time an Assistant's share changed hands.

The full annual rent-roll in 1663 was over £500 for the thirty houses and warehouses huddled round Stationers' Hall, and there ought to have been another £50 which the Court had agreed, in October 1659, to pay for the gild's use of the Hall itself;[1] but the £412 collected in 1663–4 exceeded both the total amount received in the remaining thirty months before the Fire and also, as a result of the rebuilding arrangements after the Fire,[2] the income from this source in any year during the next half-century. The returns from the sale of books and almanacks outweighed the interest from the capital—i.e. from the property—as heavily as the Company's perennial absorption in the means to preserve copyright—on which profit from the sale of publications depended—outweighed any attempt to increase an investment which was not subject to the whim of a monarch or to an unfavourable decision in the courts. The attitude even to the collection of rent, the income from the capital, was extremely casual, partly because it was largely due from Stationers but chiefly because there was no place in the accounting system for rents outstanding.

Equally unrealistic, in our eyes, was the attitude to borrowing. Early loans were fairly quickly repaid and in 1653 the Stock was unencumbered. Of £150 borrowed in 1654, £50 was repaid within three years; the balance was not disposed of until 1667 and the £6 due on it did not appear in the 1663–4 accounts because two years' interest had been accounted for in the previous period. Towards the end of 1669, £800 was borrowed, £500 at 6 per cent and the rest at 5 per cent. New loans were raised to repay bills as they fell due but additional borrowing was not necessary until the summer of 1684, at the time of the new Charter. By 1688 the debt amounted to over £2,000 and by 1698 to over £4,500. In 1712 Thomas Guy provided—in return for annuities, first to himself and then to his hospital—£1,600 for the cancelling of bonds and £800 for paying printers' bills; in the same year the Dividend was reduced to half the normal rate. Only five times in the previous forty years had the Dividend been cut, on each occasion to three-quarters of what was expected; and once, as a result of the Oxford trouble, it was not paid at all. Even in the difficult

---

[1] On March 11, 1644, this was fixed at 40s, and on April 1, 1650, it was raised to £22 in order to offset certain testamentary obligations under George Bishop's will; see below, p. 209.
[2] See Chapter XI.

winter of 1688–9, when distribution of almanacks to country chapmen was impossible, £500 was borrowed so that the full Dividend might be maintained. A steady adherence to a 10 per cent Dividend over the period would have disposed of all loans without Guy's assistance and added £5,000 to the capital of the Stock.

The Treasurer's attitude to the keeping of accounts, even though he was a paid servant of the partners, was not unlike that of the Wardens. He produced his books for quarterly auditing as infrequently as possible—in some years only twice; his budgeting was limited to providing, just before Christmas, £1,800 for paying the Dividend, and since the almanacks were nearly all sold in December this was normally not difficult. Otherwise he settled his bills as and when the cash came in. Many, therefore, of his Disbursements do not relate to goods supplied or services performed in the current year; paper merchants and printers often had to wait three years for their money. Since, in addition, we do not have the detailed production costs for a single English Stock publication at this period, the calculation of the profit margin is difficult. But for the ten years from 1673, when the effect of the Fire had worn off, 40 per cent of the net sales was paid out for the production of books, 40 per cent was spent on Dividends and the remaining 20 per cent went towards overheads. (The rest of the overheads were covered by income from other sources.) The Dividend, in fact, at the usual rate of $12\frac{1}{2}$ per cent on the capital of £14,400, took all the profits and precedence over all obligations. In 1663–4 the poor received only half the sum mentioned in the 1616 grant and, ten years before, the Stock-keepers had protested against paying a Dividend while their liabilities were so heavy; but a Dividend of 5 per cent was nevertheless paid. Only at Christmas 1694 did the Court have the courage to deny the partners what they had come to regard as their right.

The break-down of the production figures for the decade from 1673 shows that printing accounted for slightly more than half the total and paper for 38 per cent; since books and almanacks were sold by the Treasurer in sheets, the expenditure on binding was confined to preparing sets of almanacks which were given as New Year presents[1]—to the Archbishop of Canterbury, for instance—and special gifts like that of Foxe's *Book of Martyrs* which the Company presented to Charles II on his return to London; the total under this

---

[1] Hence the allowance on the Receipts side for almanacks given away.

heading was never more than £40. The standard fee for compiling the simpler kind of almanack was £2; but for the more informative sort Lilly received as much as £48 and Gadbury £40; in 1697 nearly £300 went to almanack authors. Because it was not the policy to bring new *books* into the English Stock, the amount spent on this branch of authorship was minute; the £11 5s in 1663–4 was Hoole's fee for editing Terence.

Most of the entries under the heading of Overheads require little or no elaboration. The Treasurer's salary was back to £40 a year and the balance comprised payments to the Clerk and Beadle for occasional help. The legal expenses were due almost entirely to the trouble over the Law Patent. The rent was paid to the Bishop of London for a piece of ground in Ave Maria Lane which was given up after the Fire; but in most years there were small allowances to English Stock tenants for taxes. Under entertainment fell the expenses at meetings of the Stock-keepers and at meetings of sub-committees of the Court when Stock matters were discussed; this item increased considerably after 1690 when the Assistants decided that the Stock should pay for their dinners on Court days, and in 1697–8 it was over £130. The figure under interest was made up of the meeting of a £50 bill (probably on the Company's account) and the interest on it.

There remain two entries on the Disbursements side of the 1663–4 account, Other Patentees and Variation in 'Sundry Debtors'. The latter might have appeared on the credit side if at this time the attitude to the paying for books bought from the Treasurer had been any different from that to the paying of rent. But the tendency was the other way; in the following year the outstandings increased by over £100 and on August 31, 1666, the figure was £7,354 2s 2d. The disastrous events of the next few days produced a complete change of policy; about £650 worth of debts were written off as never to be recovered and in twelve months £2,000 of good debts were collected. Slowly but surely during the next eleven years the Sundry Debtors figure was nibbled away and by September 1678 it stood at less than £1,300. Between then and July 14, 1679, when John Leigh (having been elected on March 1st) took over the Treasurership from George Sawbridge, the figure dropped to £42. It is difficult to measure what loss the Stock suffered by the Fire; there was no destruction of almanacks and the value of the books in the Treasurer's warehouse was, at wholesale rates, about £1,000; the books kept by the Stock-keepers may have been twice as many. The cost of replacement, since much of the stock was of law books which were not reprinted, may have been no more than £1,000; but money had to be found not only for this but for the satisfaction of the Stock's creditors in August (no record of which was ever shown in the accounts but which may have amounted to £2,000) and for rebuilding the Hall and the other property which had been burned down. All this was achieved with a resort to borrowing of a mere £800; it was a remarkable achievement on the part of Sawbridge. Moreover, an important lesson had been learnt; never again were Sundry Debtors allowed to get out of hand.

RIVAL PATENTEES: SEYMOUR AND THE UNIVERSITIES

Among the other patentees, the Atkins family and Streater were in 1663 the most vocal, but they involved the Stock in worry and intermittent legal expenses rather than in the regular levies to which the University of Oxford and the printers at Cambridge were entitled and which a fresh competitor exacted. This new story begins in 1631 when George Rudolph Weckherlin persuaded Charles I to grant him the reversion of the School Book Patent for thirty-one years from the end of the Company's[1] current privilege in 1634. Weckherlin came from Stuttgart and settled in England after a diplomatic visit to this country. He was taken into Government service and, because of his proficiency in languages, became an Under-Secretary of State. His patent was dated April 5th and by May 16th the Company had come to such satisfactory terms with him that the Court voted him a piece of plate 'for his extraordinary paynes'. Whatever the arrangement was (almost certainly an outright payment) Weckherlin did not disturb the Company in the enjoyment of his privilege; the Court even accepted his intervention in 1635 on behalf of an unlicensed printer. On November 30, 1664, when the patent had only a few months to run, the Assistants decided to petition the Lord Chancellor for its renewal. But an unrewarded Royalist, John Seymour, had already established some claim to a new patent and just after Christmas the Court had a private meeting to debate an order from Secretary Bennet

---

[1] The privilege was, of course, granted to the Master, Wardens and Commonalty, but it was worked by the English Stock and it benefited only the partners. In what follows, the Company, and the Court, will often appear as acting not for the whole corporation of Stationers but for the shareholders in the Stock.

that no more school books be printed for the Stock.[1] Fortunately Sir William Morice, one of the other Secretaries, was approachable; he had written a book on the administration of the sacrament, the first edition of which had been brought out by Richard Thrale and the second by Richard Royston; Thrale was Master of the Company from July 1664 and Royston had been co-opted to the Court, at the King's wish, the previous year. It was therefore possible to prevent for the moment the passing of the grant to Seymour. Morice received £10 in gold and his secretary 40s. A year later, however, it was admitted in the minutes that the Company and Seymour were still 'in competition' for the patent and a committee was appointed to treat with the latter's envoys, one of whom was Streater! By mid-April a grant in favour of the Company had been drafted and certain alterations made at the suggestion of Andrew Crooke, Thrale's successor as Master. While this was finding its way slowly through the administrative machine, Streater agreed that, in return for £100 when the Company's patent had passed the Great Seal, neither Seymour nor any of his friends would do anything to hinder this process. On October 11th the patent was sealed and the Company once again had a monopoly, for thirty-one years, in the production and distribution of a score of school books, half of which were already being reprinted after the Fire and all of which were in the original grant from James I.

But John Seymour did not give up the struggle and in the autumn of 1669, as a reward for his long service to the King and the King's father, he obtained two grants.[2] The first gave him, for forty-one years, the right to thirty-seven classical books—such as the Justinus and Isocrates, which were not then part of the Company's monopoly but which appear in the 1695 advertisement—and to any almanacks which were offered for publication to him and not to the English Stock or Cambridge. The second, also for forty-one years, was a reversion of the School Book Patent when the recent grant to the Company expired and this, though irritating, was not an immediate threat. The first, however, was very dangerous, not because of the classics in it but because of the breach in the almanack monopoly; and negotiations were at once opened with a meeting at the Swan Tavern in Old Fish Street. Since no agreement was reached Seymour financed a printing

---

[1] *C.S.P. Dom. Car. II, 1664–5*, pp. 5, 13, 34 and 119.
[2] S.P. Dom. Car. II, vol. 450, f. 141, and Entry Book 25, f. 127; October 17 and 19, 1669.

house in Westminster (there is a strong smell of Streater in this) and put in charge George Larkin, a journeyman free of the Company since 1664. The Wardens had no difficulty in finding an excuse, under the 1662 Act, for raiding the press, seizing the almanacks found there and defacing the type used. In the summer of 1671 there was a possibility that Seymour might sell his rights to the University of Oxford[1] and in January 1672 the validity of the Company's claim to monopoly in almanacks was argued before the Privy Council by the Attorney-General, Sir Heneage Finch, the Solicitor-General, Sir Francis North, and two other counsel. No judgment is recorded, but in July the Company offered Seymour £200 for the grant of almanacks and a further £200 (towards which Roger Norton, the holder of the Grammar Patent, promised £150) for the reversion of the other. But in spite of more raids on his printing house, which he had moved to Putney, and of further action at law, Seymour held out, and in 1677 the tide began to run his way. In June the Court ordered the Beadle, on behalf of the members of the Company indicted for smashing Larkin's type, to plead guilty and submit to a fine; and in March 1678 a committee was empowered finally to come to terms.

By an agreement of June 28th, John Seymour assigned the patent which touched almanacks for annual payments of £200 for his life and thereafter of £100 for the life of the grant. In October Seymour agreed that, at his own expense, he would secure for the Company a reversion of the School Book Patent for a fee of 500 guineas, half to be paid on delivery of the patent and half at midsummer 1679. This bargain was faithfully carried out. After John Seymour's death in 1681 his executor, Sir Joseph Seymour, set his hand to an agreement for the residual annuity of £100, and the Court composed an ordinance —on the lines of that for the Law Patent—which was included in the Supplementary By-laws. All was now neatly, and expensively, settled; it was a pity that the sales of the books were falling.

The second holder of a privilege which the English Stock paid to keep out of the market was the University of Oxford. The 1637 covenant of forbearance[2] was renewed in 1639 but was allowed by the Company to lapse in the uncertain conditions of 1642. It was not until the autumn of 1655 that the basis for a new agreement was hammered out at the Christ Church lodgings of the Vice-Chancellor, Dr John Fell. The Company took no exception to the printing of

[1] *C.S.P. Dom. Car. II, Add. 1660-85*, p. 445.   [2] See above, p. 104.

Bibles at Oxford because Hills and Field[1] appeared certain to secure this monopoly, but, with Roger Norton, it was ready to pay the University £60 a year for three years to prevent the printing there of almanacks and *Grammars*. It also agreed, in return for the reduced consideration, to employ the University printers if they were short of work. The arrears, which the Vice-Chancellor claimed, were to be the subject of arbitration, the Stationers arguing that, since there was no protection for copyrights after the dissolution of the Court of Star Chamber, it was unfair to expect them to pay for a safeguard which anyone could ignore. No formal articles of agreement have survived, though they were despatched from London in August 1656; but the payments were made with fair regularity and Henry Hall did some work for the English Stock. A new agreement, signed at Oxford on January 6, 1659, operated from the previous September; its terms were those of 1655, except that the University printers were to have enough work every year for 200 reams of paper. In February, after a dinner at the Feathers,[2] the Oxford representatives settled at £50 for the outstanding dues from the Company, and this was paid ten years later.

The Restoration brought the King's Printers back into partnership with the Company and on October 1, 1661, the conditions of 1637 were re-established on the basis of an annual payment of £200, the share of the English Stock being fixed at £85. This agreement was renewed in 1664 and 1669; but about a year before the second renewal ran out the University leased their printing rights to Dr Fell and three partners, who first of all doubled the price of their forbearance (on the strength of a possible agreement with Seymour) and, when the Stationers refused to treat, set about exercising their newly acquired rights by printing privileged books at their newly acquired printing house. The reaction of the King's Printers and the Company was exaggeratedly, but perhaps deliberately, plaintive, for they must have realized that, though it was easy enough to have almanacks and Bibles and school books printed in Oxford, it was exceedingly difficult to distribute them through the only possible trade channels; for these channels were in London and most of the controllers of them were shareholders in the English Stock. In October 1672 Fell was forced

---

[1] The University made a separate agreement with them in 1656, *Print and Privilege at Oxford to the year 1700* by John Johnson and Strickland Gibson, 1946, p. 34. This study contains a fully documented account of printing at Oxford and of the University's relationship not only with the Company but also with individual Stationers and booksellers.
[2] The tavern in St Paul's Churchyard; from 1554 to 1606 it was the Company's Hall.

to come to terms and he signed an agreement with the Company alone, back-dated to March; the tribute was to be £120 and the Stock would buy up at cost the school books printed at Oxford in the summer. On March 9, 1675, the terms were modified to £100 in return for the University's right to print the famous Oxford sheet almanack.

When, three years later, the agreement came up for renewal, Fell, now Bishop of Oxford, and his partners found that they had built up a stock—of Bibles and slow-moving learned works—which was valued at £3,800 and which the £100 a year from the Company did not *sell*. They therefore made the purchase of this stock a condition of renewal. When the Company sensibly refused to bargain, the farmers of the University privilege turned to four London booksellers who, for private reasons, were willing to challenge the Company by operating the privilege as sub-lessees of the farmers. The four capitalists were Moses Pitt, William Leake, Thomas Guy and Peter Parker. Pitt was a Haberdasher whose large ideas, in real estate as well as in the production of books, soon led him to bankruptcy. The other three were Stationers; but Leake was dead within three years, and it was left to Guy and Parker to bear the brunt of the fight. This was largely with the King's Printers since the Company had quickly made a covenant of forbearance with Pitt and his partners, for an initial fine of £200 and an annual payment of £100.

Aided by an increased subsidy from 1681 this treaty worked reasonably smoothly until Guy and Parker printed the psalms to bind up with their Bibles; they were probably forced to do this because the Company, under pressure from the King's Printers, were dilatory in the supply of psalms from the English Stock. Even Fell, in admitting that the Company had 'for many years continued in agreement with us', described the action of his tenants as 'a little foul'; and he contrived a revision of the arrangements at Oxford so that the University withdrew from him and his partners all but the right to print Bibles. It was therefore possible for the Company, on September 30, 1685, once again to make an agreement direct with the University. The payment by the Stock was now to be £160; moreover, the University could print newly annotated editions of the classics in formats not intended for schools and the psalms were to be supplied to the sub-lessees on the same terms as to the King's Printers. After the death of Fell in 1686 the whole complicated arrangement broke down: the Stock found an excuse to withhold the quarterly payments; Guy and Parker printed primers in retaliation; Henry Hills, one of the King's Printers, used his position as Master of the Company from October 1687 to draw the King's attention to the danger from the excessive number of presses at Oxford and their 'deluge of Workmen'. Only a sudden change of mind on the part of James II saved the University from answering a charge of *quo warranto*. In March 1689 a compromise was reached by which the Company was to buy up the Stock's books printed at Oxford and to pay the arrears of rent in return for £180 from Guy and Parker for their offence of comprinting.

But some more permanent solution was still to be found and the finding grew into a matter of University politics, in which one of the Proctors challenged the action of the Vice-Chancellor, and senior members went from college to college canvassing votes for the Stationers and 'blemishing' Parker and Guy as criminals. The big guns of Christ Church again carried the day and on January 27, 1692, the University made an agreement with Ambrose Isted, Henry Mortlock and John Bellinger—the Master, one of the Wardens and a past-Master—acting secretly as trustees since the Company was almost as unpopular academically as the late sub-lessees. In return for £200 a year the three agents were empowered for five years to take charge of the trade printing at Oxford and to enjoy the benefits from all the popular books to which the University had any right and which were listed; they were also to buy, for about £1,850, the learned books then in stock and to purchase not more than 500 copies of such as the University might print in future. Other clauses, and a supplementary agreement of March 23rd, gave to the Vice-Chancellor the right to fix prices and to criticize quality, and to the three agents the responsibility of saving all previous parties harmless from lawsuits, of seeing that copies of books due to the Bodleian were punctually despatched, of maintaining in full employment four good presses in Oxford (having bought them from Guy) and all the journeymen at work in January, and of printing certain quantities of Bibles in four different sizes. This was the old covenant of forbearance with the additional burdens to the Company of running a printing house set up to make forbearance unnecessary and of buying slow-selling or unsaleable works of scholarship over the production of which it had no control. Isted and his colleagues had bound themselves to conditions which were obviously unworkable; but they had plunged thus deeply under the joint pressure of competition from Guy and fear of the chaos which the lapsing of the Printing Act would create, and with the knowledge of an agreement made two years earlier for printing at Cambridge.

In order to understand this last arrangement it is necessary to go back to the death, in August 1668, of John Field, printer to the University of Cambridge, who had enjoyed for the previous twelve years a favourable contract of service from the Stationers' Company.[1] Field died in possession of the printing materials and of the leasehold of the printing house with thirty-four years to run. The executors of his will were his son and George Sawbridge; the latter so arranged it that he bought up these two valuable assets without his action being generally known. Sawbridge was the son of a husbandman at Hilmorton near Rugby and, after a seven-year apprenticeship to Edward Brewster, was free of the Company on April 14, 1645; when his master died two years later he succeeded him as Treasurer of the English Stock. He could not take Field's place and still retain the Treasurership but he might get most of the benefit if he appointed the official Cambridge printer as his manager; and this he did. John Hayes, a master printer put out of business by the Fire, was, with the backing of old Thomas Buck, chosen by the University in October 1669 on condition that the negotiations with the Company, which had been going on for the last twelve months, were broken off. Sawbridge arranged for Hayes to pay the £100 a year which the University demanded, and to give out that he was the lessee of the printing house and the owner of its contents, when all the time he was no more than the Treasurer's servant at £60 a year with free quarters. Sawbridge had undertaken, secretly and as a private individual, what the Court had decided, during the 1669 negotiations, to avoid at all costs— saddling itself once again with the printing house at Cambridge—and he completed the arrangement by persuading the University to allow its printer to conclude an agreement with the Company. On April 21, 1670, Hayes accepted the Livery and put his name to articles of agreement very much like those with Field: he was to print almanacks and school books up to a maximum of 500 reams a year at 20s a ream[2]

---

[1] See above, p. 145.

[2] For the 2½-sheet almanack this works out at £5 per 1,000, the post-Fire wholesale price being £6 per 1,000. This indirect reward, being payment to a printer for a service, works out at more than the cash paid to the University of Oxford or its lessees. The King's Printers were not parties to the Cambridge agreement.

and be paid for additional English Stock work at the cost of paper and printing only; he was to pay carriage to and from Cambridge and £20 a year for warehousing his books at Stationers' Hall; he was to be responsible for all waste and he was not to sell privileged books in Cambridge except at London rates. Since this guarantee of work enabled its printer to remain in business and be available for the printing of learned books when required, the University of Cambridge—the third of the patentees who had to be rewarded, directly or indirectly, for keeping out of the market—was reasonably content.

The great merit of the arrangement was that, for all its complexity, it worked without serious interruption for thirty-five years and even without discovery for nearly ten. It was not until January 31, 1679, that Sawbridge, sitting at the Table as a past-Master,[1] was asked if he were in partnership with Hayes. Though he denied having any share in the printing house he admitted to dealing direct with Hayes over almanacks and school books, which he did not bring in to the English Stock account. The loss to the Stock was not great since the profit on most of the Cambridge business was 16 per cent instead of the usual 40 per cent; but the discovery showed up the incompetence of the auditing and decided Sawbridge against standing for re-election as Treasurer on March 1st. He died intestate two years later and in May 1683 his widow paid the £158 which the investigating committee (Sawbridge himself being an original member!) decided was owing. Meantime the Sawbridge family continued to control the Cambridge business, and only after the deaths of Mrs Sawbridge and her son Thomas (both intestate) in 1686 did the Court attempt to alter the pattern. Edward Brewster—perhaps the 'doting Yea and Nay' of Nathaniel Thompson's ballad and certainly the son of George Sawbridge's master—was given the administration of Thomas's estate, but for more than three years, during which he was Upper Warden and Master, he put off coming to terms with his Company. At last on April 1, 1690, he assigned the remainder of the printing house lease to three trustees acting on behalf of the Company, and sold the interest in the appointment for 100 guineas and the printing materials for £300. This enabled the trustees and the Company to make a joint agreement with Hayes whereby he became the servant of the English

[1] He had the unusual distinction of being chosen Master two years after election to the Court.

Stock and not of a member of the Sawbridge family. The relationship between the Stock and the University Printer continued as laid down in 1670 and as reaffirmed after Sawbridge's retirement. Both arrangements were to end with Hayes's death.

THE NEW STOCK

The three trustees in 1690 were Ambrose Isted, Henry Mortlock and Henry Clarke, and it is understandable that, though John Bellinger came in on Clarke's death in 1691, the Cambridge experience influenced the Oxford bargaining less than two years later. By 1692, therefore, the Company—through the English Stock—found itself the owner of the trade presses at the two Universities. But whereas at Cambridge there was more than twenty years' evidence that the plan worked and as yet no learned press (though the idea for one was in the air), at Oxford the Company inherited twenty years of expensive and unhappy experiment and saddled itself with the responsibility for a large proportion of the output of the co-existing learned printing house. It was however decided to run the acquisitions as a joint venture and, because the Oxford side of the business needed capital, to create a new Stock. On October 6, 1693, were signed an indenture between the Company, the trustees and the new partners, and articles of agreement among the partners themselves; the first created the new Stock—a trading venture open only to those who already had shares in the English Stock—and the second laid down rules for its management. In return for £2,097 3s 5d[1] paid to the Treasurer and a promise to pay the rent on the printing house at Cambridge and the annual £100 due to the University, the trustees and the Company gave the partners in the new Stock all the printing privileges which they then

---

[1] The final instalment was paid in February 1695. The expenditure by the Treasurer had been as follows:

	£	s	d
Cost of type and other printing materials already bought in London and sent to Oxford	324	7	10
Ditto bought from Guy and Parker	471	12	5
Cost of paper sent to Oxford	267	17	4
Printing work at Oxford	518	17	6
Alterations to and rent (at £16 p.a.) on new printing house	53	7	0
Cost of type, etc., bought at Cambridge	300	0	0
Cost of paper sent to Cambridge and of almanack copies	161	1	4
Total	£2,097	3	5

had or might in the future receive from the Universities, for as long as these might last, provided there was no printing of English Stock books and *Grammars* at Oxford and the printing of no more than 500 reams of such books at Cambridge. The Company would be responsible, through the Treasurer, for the £200 a year due to Oxford. There were to be ninety shares of £50 each which could be divided; no Stationer might have more than two shares, one of which he was free to assign to another partner in the English Stock; no other shares could be assigned without the consent of the rest of the partners, twenty-one forming a quorum; widows were to have the usual rights. A warehouse was to be rented in London and five Stock-keepers elected every Lady Day, the senior being chairman. A balance, show-ing state of the Stock and the value of the shares (an interesting departure from English Stock practice), was to be drawn twice a year and there were to be full annual accounts. Sixty-seven Stationers and widows subscribed the necessary capital; the Stock-keepers, with Mortlock at their head, were elected on October 24th and, having been re-elected on March 26, 1694, are heard of no more. Though the articles lay down what books of account are to be kept, none has survived and the evidence for the running of this new Stock does not exist.

Long before the first term of the new Oxford agreement expired the Court realized that it was economically unsound. Five times committees were appointed to visit Oxford and bargain for adjust-ments. Finally new articles,[1] signed in June 1698, gave some relief; the University refused to accept less than £200 a year but the drawing off of learned works was limited to £1,000 in the five years of the agreement and to 200 copies of a single book. In October 1699 the English Stock bought back the Cambridge equipment at the regular price of £300 and resumed control of Hayes and his establishment; I assume that, since the presses at Cambridge were kept busy on the printing of almanacks and school books which, by agreement, could not be printed at Oxford, the managers of the English Stock found it inconvenient to be at the mercy of another group of Stock-keepers. In addition, it was likely that the English Stock partners who had no shares in the new Stock objected to the absorption of the small profits from Cambridge by the—probably large—losses on the Oxford venture. This last was extended by further agreements in 1703 and

---

[1] The trustees were now Henry Mortlock, William Phillips and Samuel Lowndes.

1708[1] on exactly the same lines as that of 1698. In the autumn of 1711 William Phillips, the Master of the Company and one of the trustees, reported to the Court that the University was on the verge of leasing its privilege once again to individual Stationers when the Company's agreement ran out. Since these were known to be John Williams and John Baskett (who, though not an original partner in the new Stock, had shown great interest in the running of the Oxford business), a committee was appointed to meet them. But twelve months passed before the parties reached agreement whereby the annual payment to Baskett for not printing school books and almanacks was to be £230 (including £30 for the Norton share), and Baskett, who was chiefly interested in Bible printing, was to pay royalties of 6d and 1s a copy to the English Stock on quarto and folio psalms printed by him at Oxford. Neither the interference of Eyre nor Baskett's bankruptcy[2] upset this arrangement, which was renewed in 1734 with a contribution of £250 from the Company towards the expenses of a new concession from the University. The Stock-keepers resisted two suggestions, the second arising from Baskett's death in 1744, that they buy that part of the Oxford privilege which cost them £200 a year to nullify, and in 1766 they agreed to the enhanced rent of £550 asked by Wright and his partners who were then the farmers.

At Cambridge the story was similar except that individual London Stationers did not appear as third parties. John Hayes's death in 1705 brought to an end the old arrangement, and on March 11, 1706, the University undertook for twenty-one years, at an annual cost to the English Stock of £210, not to print any of the books in a schedule based on the Oxford list of 1692. Extensions of this, which raised the payment to £250 in 1747 and to £500 in 1767, carried the Company and the University of Cambridge in reasonable amity through most

---

[1] Robert Andrews had taken Lowndes's place as a trustee in 1703 and he retained it in 1708. The agreement of 1703 is printed in *The First Minute Book of the Delegates of the Oxford University Press 1668–1756*, edited by Strickland Gibson and John Johnson, Oxford, 1943, pp. 90 ff.

[2] The Company may not have been unduly disturbed at Baskett's intervention, since the terms exacted by the University—even as modified in 1698—were liable to prove dangerous. In 1701 Samuel Buckley went to the Continent as bagman for the English Stock in an attempt to dispose of some of the learned works from Oxford. Only the surprise appearance from 1702 of Clarendon's best-selling *History of the Great Rebellion*, which more than absorbed the £1,000 worth of books written into the agreement, can have kept the new Stock going. It must be assumed that, in 1712, Baskett bought up the physical assets in Oxford and that the shareholders were gradually repaid some of their investment; but no evidence survives, except the receipt by the Treasurer in September 1712 of £51 17s 10d from the Oxford Stock and his borrowing from the partners of £463 for stamps in 1718.

of the eighteenth century. The unprotesting acceptance of the doubled forbearance money demanded by the Universities (or their lessees) points to the value of the almanack monopoly in the middle of the eighteenth century.

THE TREASURER OF THE ENGLISH STOCK

It is easy to criticize the Court of Assistants and the Stock-keepers for concentrating their resources rather on preserving existing monopolies than on keeping the English Stock 'list' up to date; but all the evidence in the second half of the seventeenth century pointed to their ability (even if it meant borrowing) to spend at least £500 a year in order to keep rivals out of the field, to find—usually—£200 a year for the poor of the Company, to stand the charges of expensive lawsuits and still to pay, in most years, a Dividend of £1,800. But the ease with which George Sawbridge had deceived them gave their complacency a jolt and, before they chose his successor from the five who applied for his (obviously) lucrative post, they compiled a set of rules which the new Treasurer would have to agree to keep. He must give up his own business as a bookseller within six months and furnish security of £1,000 through guarantors outside the Company. He must keep regular hours at the warehouse—8 a.m. to noon and 2 to 6 p.m. in the summer, 9 a.m. to noon and 2 to 4 p.m. in the winter, six days a week—and be absent only with permission. He must sell Stock publications at the warehouse only, and no others, and keep a Day Book showing names of purchasers and rates of sale. He must provide monthly accounts of receipts and stocks, and hand over cash when instructed. Without written authority he must not buy paper nor deliver it to printers, nor must he pay any bills. He must keep careful account of all books received direct from printers and check 'overs', and he must not sell almanacks before the date of publication fixed by the Stock-keepers. He must collect the rents each quarter and render a written account of them, and he must immediately pass on to the Master or Wardens any information affecting the welfare of the Stock. His salary is to be fixed by the Court, and that of John Leigh, the successful candidate, was wisely put up from £40 to £100. It is clear from these rules where Sawbridge had erred, but I believe that his thirty-two years of service as Treasurer were, on balance, of great value to the English Stock; he organized the recoveries after the Civil War slump and after the Fire, he abolished the customer credit abuse, he left a reputation in the trade which led John Dunton to describe him as 'the greatest Bookseller that has been in England for many years',[1] and he made the endearing suggestion, six months after his retirement, that the problem of his account should be referred to Mr Collins, the mathematician.

John Leigh died in the summer of 1686 and Obadiah Blagrave, who was unsuccessful in 1679, was appointed as a stop-gap. But on March 1, 1687, Benjamin Tooke, yet another who had stood before, was elected and agreed to certain modifications in the rules. He was to be called the Warehouse-keeper, with a salary of £80 and free quarters, but he was to be allowed to deal in those books of which he owned the copyright. If he were elected an Assistant, he could enjoy the privileges but not sit at the Table. He must, if required, produce, any Saturday night, an account of the week's business and he must not allow quick-selling lines to be out of print. The warehouse must be opened at 8 a.m. throughout the year but the Warehouse-keeper was to be trusted with petty cash payments without authority. The books of account, which he must keep, are listed.[2] It was, however, one thing to lay down rails for the Warehouse-keeper to run on and quite another for the part-time and annually changing Stock-keepers to see that he did not leave them. In March 1702 Benjamin Tooke assigned to the Company for £50 a half-share in *Gradus ad Parnassum*, the only school book obtainable to this day at Stationers' Hall. He did this not out of generosity but from want of money, for on June 1st the Court appointed a committee of investigation to report on his accounts. On July 16th the report was read to the partners; Tooke had been paying printers for a great deal more stock than he showed as received and had been selling the balance to his own profit.[3] He was, of course, suspended but he was otherwise treated leniently; though his Dividends were stopped he was allowed to retain his Livery share. The gentle treatment of erring Stock servants is one of the pleasant aspects of the casualness with which Stock and corporation affairs were conducted during the reigns of the later Stuarts.

[1] *The Life and Errors* (1818 edition), p. 211. Dunton was free of the Company half a dozen years before the death of Sawbridge.

[2] A Day Book, for receipts of paper and books, and for cash sales with prices; a Posting Book, for cash received and paid, to be kept 'by way of Debtor & Creditor'; a Bought Book, for paper; an Acquittance Book, for all payments; a Book for the Universities' business; a Book for share transfers and fines; and a Rent Book, showing receipts and (at last) dues. None of these, as kept by Tooke, has survived except that for share transfers.

[3] As early as 1695 a complaint had been made against him for trading on his own account in books which did not bear his imprint.

CHAPTER XI

THE PROPERTY

THE HALL IN ST PAUL'S CHURCHYARD

THE surveys made after the Fire give an exact record of the lands which were in the possession of the Company and of the English Stock partners in the middle of the seventeenth century; but it is possible to give some account both of the acquisition of properties during the previous hundred years and of the buildings standing thereon up to September 1666. Of the first Hall in Milk Street, however, nothing is known either of its exact location or of the terms on which the gild occupied it.[1] The second Hall, bought probably in 1554, was Peter's College, which had been a foundation for Chantry Priests and had belonged to St Paul's.[2] It stood immediately to the east of the Deanery at the point where Ludgate Hill opened into the Churchyard on the south side. In 1557, after alterations costing about £60, the building contained the main hall[3] where the freemen assembled, a great parlour measuring 32 feet 8 inches by 21 feet, a council parlour 20 feet by 20 feet 6 inches where the Court normally met, a chapel used as an armoury, a kitchen, a buttery and cellars; there were also good rooms over the two parlours, the smaller of which looked south and west into the Dean's garden. I hazard the guess that the chapel (which was so small that it fetched only £1 a year for rent in 1601), the kitchen and the buttery were in a semi-basement facing north into the Churchyard, with the hall over them at slightly above ground level. The parlours would then have been

[1] See Appendix II for 'The Milk Street Myth'.
[2] On November 24, 1548, John and Richard Keyme, gentlemen of Lewes, paid £1,154 15s into the Court of Augmentations and obtained possession, along with other property, of 'the site, house and mansion commonly called Peter College' (*Cal. Patent Rolls Ed. VI*, i, 362–3). Four years later, William Sparke, a Merchant Tailor, conveyed the property to the executors of Matthew Wotton, clerk, but retained the right to reclaim it on payment of £340; this figure may approximate to that paid by the Stationers two years later still (Hustings Roll 246, 63). For a short period before 1553 William Seres used the building for a printing house.
[3] The Hall, with a capital H, denotes Stationers' Hall; the hall is the room within the Hall where the Company met.

behind the hall and, since the ground slopes down towards the river, at a slightly lower level; the cellars would have been below, and the rooms above (with their garrets) would have reached the level of the hall roof.

In 1557 the great parlour was carpeted and wainscotted, and it was furnished with two long tables, two benches, a dozen stools, and cupboards for silver; the new glass in the windows was paid for by individual Stationers. The council parlour had, besides similar furnishings, chests with locks for the cash and account books, iron casements to the six glazed windows, the hearse cloth (the gift of John Cawood) in a special box, an honours board with the names of Assistants and two whips 'for reformacyon'. The hall was panelled, with crests above and benches below; the main table was 16 feet 6 inches long and there were two side tables painted red and black; there were scutcheons, a banner, a screen, a 'Deske' for plate, and glazed windows; the amenities were improved in 1593 by the purchase, for 20s, of a copper pan on wheels 'to make fyer'. The armoury was, in 1557, poorly stocked—one bow with arrows, ten pikes, a few swords and daggers with several pieces of armour, and three guns. In the buttery were, amongst other things, four stone jars lined with pewter, a horn with a silver-gilt lid and copper-gilt feet, twelve dozen trenchers, and a new table-cloth and napkins given by Robert Toy's widow. The kitchen had a pair of iron roasting racks, three spits, a few other crude cooking utensils and a 12-foot table; there were also four cressets on staves, for processions.

The building and its equipment were of necessity modest, and such spare space as there was had to bring in a little income. The Dean rented a room in the cellar for 4s a year; John Walley and his partners had a warehouse for 13s 4d and John Pont a 31-year lease of the flat over the parlours at a rent of £3. Within the next few years two other small rooms were let at £1 apiece and when Pont renewed his lease in 1577 his rent was doubled. Between April 1570 and July 1572 nearly £150 was spent on a new kitchen and buttery and on new stairs into the Hall. These alterations created more accommodation in which Timothy Rider, the Beadle, lived and in which John Wolf, in his early years as Beadle, kept a printing-press. After this had been removed by order of the Court in 1591, £15 was spent on making 'the Lower Rowme' habitable for him by putting in a chimney and panelling; a few years later the Clerk was living on the premises.

During the 1590s the Hall became the headquarters of the partners in two of the most important monopolies in books, and from 1603 room had to be found for the English Stock. It must quickly have become obvious that the building was too small; but there is no reference in the Court minutes to a search for, or the removal to, new premises until, on October 20, 1606, the Assistants discussed the allocation of rooms for the Clerk and the Stock-keepers. These must have been in Abergavenny House[1] because, on November 10th, it was agreed that Edward Kynnaston, a Vintner, should have a lease of the old Hall in St Paul's Churchyard for twenty-one years at £40 a year and be responsible for all repairs; he was also to buy the fixtures, for which he paid £20 two years later. From now on this property in the Churchyard was known as the Feathers Tavern, and for sixty years it provided both a steady revenue and a surety against which money could be borrowed. Three times it was mortgaged in order to raise loans for the King, and on each occasion redeemed; the first time was in 1628 for £280; the second time was for £500 in 1640, when Miles Flesher was the mortgagee; and the third time was in 1664. In March 1639 Mr Dell, Archbishop Laud's secretary, had been accepted as tenant on assignment from the lessee, and because of his good service to the Company was freely allowed another ten years on his lease; but normally the tenant was a Vintner. Nothing came of Henry Walley's proposal in 1653 to sell the Feathers, although Alderman Andrews and Mr Browne, the surgeon, were interested in buying; and it was not until over five years after the Fire that the land was sold to Alderman Sir William Turner for £420.

THE DARK HOUSE

The second piece of Company property came by bequest. In June 1573 died Jane, the widow of Stephen Kevall, and released for her husband's Company a house in Salutation Alley off Thames Street, Billingsgate, on condition that £5 a year was paid to the poor of the parish of St Mary-at-Hill. There was, however, some dispute over the property and it was not until 1580 that the Company made any contribution to the parish. The house was divided and in 1588–9 21-year leases were granted for fines of £30 and £20. Little more is known of this building before the Fire than that it was called,

[1] See below, p. 212.

4   *The Hall in 1781*

The Hall in 1802, with Stock Room wing (right)
and houses on Ludgate Hill

appropriately, the Dark House and that the rent of one tenement was £10.

NEWTON FARM

Since Abergavenny House was paid for out of English Stock funds and since nothing came of the negotiations to buy a house from the Dean and Chapter of St Paul's in 1578 and a house from Adam Bland[1] in 1590, the third piece of corporation property was a small estate called Newton Farm, at Milbournstoke in Shropshire. George Bishop, whose will was proved in January 1611, left it to the Company, after a life interest for his widow, at a peppercorn rent for 500 years on the conditions that, every year, Christ's Hospital received £6, the fund for preachers at Paul's Cross £10 and a young Stationer a loan of £6. In the following year the Company granted John Norton, a Shropshire man, a lease of Newton Farm for 499 years at a rent of £22, the exact obligation under Bishop's will. No doubt Norton made the most of his position as Master, his generosity in lending £900 at 10 per cent and the difficulty the Company would have in managing a distant property. Mrs Bishop died early in 1613 and John Norton a few months before. His cousin, Bonham Norton, promptly conveyed the estate back to the Company in return for all the expenditure incurred by the Nortons—including the rent paid. By the middle of 1618 Bonham had acquired a new lease, the rent on which he ingeniously linked with a pension to Mrs Joyce Norton, John's widow, and the fine for which was paid in £400 worth of books belonging to the Grammar Patent. Out of the sale of the books the Stock was supposed to buy property to bring in £22 a year; but for the twenty years of Joyce Norton's life there was no need to do anything and at her death there were no books. It is not possible to tell how much more than the annual obligation of £22 the Company might have received from Newton Farm, but the Norton cousins were not men to lose on a deal; the complicated story is worth mentioning only as an illustration of the way in which an individual—operating, so to speak, along interior lines—could outmanœuvre a body of men whose experience lay in the distribution of books rather than in the handling of real estate.

[1] A Skinner who acted as the Company's Butler.

WOOD STREET

The Nortons were also involved in the fourth piece of Company property. John left £1,000 for the purchase of land, the income from which was to provide £50 a year to be lent to Stationers, and £4 a year for the trouble taken by the officers of the Company over the bequest. Bonham Norton, as executor, was in no hurry to part with the money and six years passed before, in 1619, the purchase for £1,200 of property in Wood Street was completed. The extra £200 came from John's bequests to the parishes of St Faith's and St Martin's Vintry, the first involving the payment every Wednesday of 2d and a penny loaf to twelve poor people and the provision of cakes and ale for Liverymen on Ash Wednesday, and the second the payment of 52s for distribution by the churchwardens. There were six or eight tenements lying either side of Friar's Alley and abutting southward on Wood Street Counter; the annual yield was over £90, which gave the Company a further net income of about £30, with the bonuses of fines at the renewal of leases. Owing to the complexity of the arrangement, the collection of rents and the doles to the poor were taken out of the hands of the Renter Wardens and given to the Clerk for a yearly payment of 26s 8d and the odd loaf each week from the baker's dozen.

By 1620 the unencumbered rents from the Feathers Tavern, the Dark House and Wood Street amounted to between £80 and £90, and there was the hidden advantage of having the Hall and its upkeep paid for by the English Stock. Before I deal with this important branch of the property I want to mention two deals into which the Company entered as tenants rather than as landlords. On September 2, 1616, a committee was appointed to agree with the workmen for the building of a new shop and warehouse for the Latin Stock on Amen Corner. For three years, at a rent of £40, the accommodation was adequate, but late in 1619 a house in St Paul's Churchyard was leased for twenty-one years at double the rent with a fine of £110. Within eighteen months the Company realized its mistake and was trying to dispose of the lease. The property was divided and one of the sub-tenants was William Bladon, later the agent in Ireland, who took part of the house for fifteen years at £15. More modest accommodation was found for the Latin Stock in Old Change with a rent of £5 and

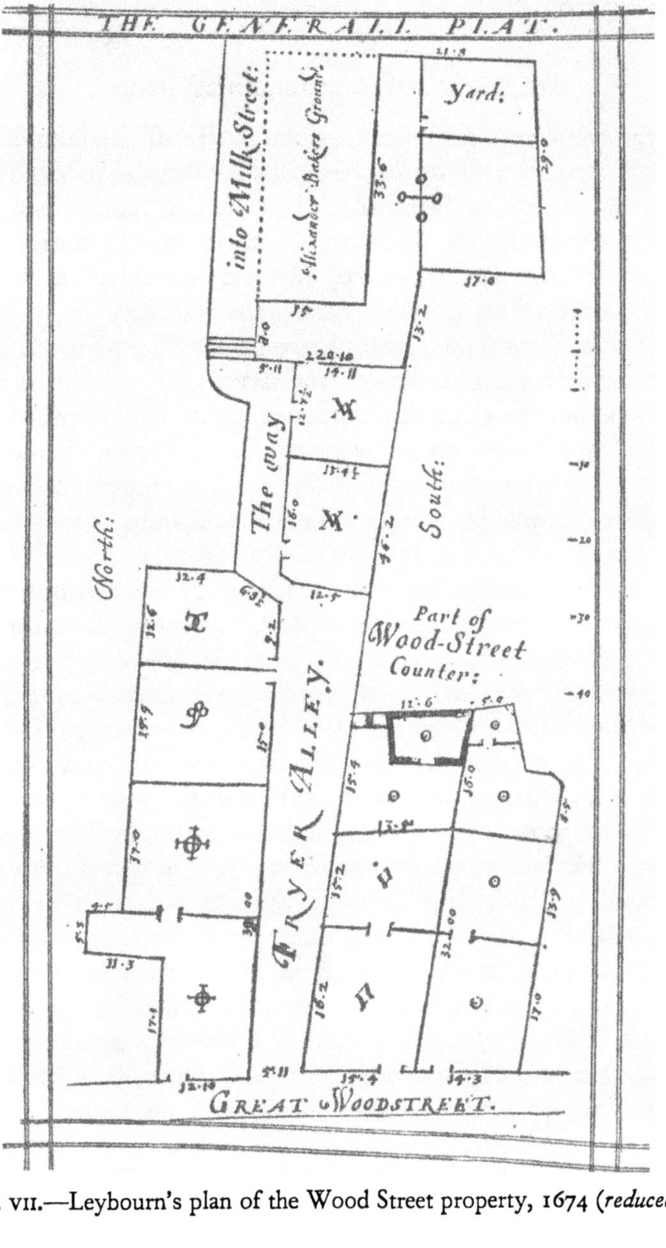

FIG. VII.—Leybourn's plan of the Wood Street property, 1674 (*reduced*).

a fine of £66 13s 4d.[1] By 1626 Bonham Norton had his hands even on this property.

THE HALL AT ABERGAVENNY HOUSE

Abergavenny House belonged to the Earls of Richmond in the fourteenth century and to the Earls of Pembroke in the fifteenth, when it was known as Pembroke's Inn. It then passed to a branch of the Neville family, the Barons of Bergavenny, the third of whom was beheaded in 1538; the estate, however, remained in the family and passed to the Company by a conveyance of March 26, 1611, from Edward, Lord Bergavenny, and his two sons.[2] The price was £3,500. The house, according to Stow, was large and built of stone and timber; it stood in about three-quarters of an acre bounded on the north by Amen Court, on the west by the old City wall, and on the south by a line from the vestry of St Martin's Ludgate to Ave Maria Lane, which formed the eastern boundary and along which tenements had been built.

It is, however, quite clear that the Company had taken possession of the new premises by Christmas 1606, for seven 'Chambers' were allotted as warehouses at rents of £2 or 26s 8d payable from Lady Day 1607; but it is not clear why more than four years passed before the conclusion of the agreement with Lord Abergavenny. On April 8, 1611, the Court decided that the partners in the English Stock should pay for the purchase out of profits and have the value of their shares written up by 50 per cent. But the cash was not immediately available and three weeks later the Company borrowed £900 from John Norton and £200 from Humphrey Lownes, which may have been either for the payment of the last instalment on the house or for its refurbishing. The £4,500 by which the values of the shares was increased allowed for £1,000 to be spent on improvements. Since the Company achieved a rent-free Hall and the English Stock obtained adequate warehouse and office accommodation and since, in addition to fines, the rent roll was over £450 by 1663,[3] the investment was a good one.

Anthony Munday, in bringing Stow's *Survey* up to date in 1618, described how the Stationers had converted 'the Stoneworke into a new faire Frame of Timber'; but the minutes of the Court suggest

[1] Bridge House Rentals.   [2] Hustings Roll 288, 9.
[3] This figure does not include the rents from the houses built on land acquired later; the figure may well have been as high in 1640.

that, though the Assistants—after their initial enthusiasm—might order
the Beadle to remove his chickens from the garden and might threaten
to withdraw permission to hang out washing from any tenant who
allowed a stranger's linen to be dried in the grounds, they preferred
to spend the Stock's money, not on the Hall but on building which
yielded a profit; six warehouses, for instance, were put up in 1630 on
the bowling alley (probably in the front, or eastern, part of the
garden) and were let—one of them to the partners in the Irish Stock
—at £4 apiece. In 1633 £90 had to be spent on rebuilding the chim-
neys and staircase on the garden side of the great house, but twenty
years later the hall was in such disrepair that the dinner on Lord
Mayor's Day could not be held in it. Early in 1656 there was a drive
to sell Foxe's *Book of Martyrs* in order to raise funds for the most
urgent repairs; but very little was spent and in 1664 the hall was unfit
for the reading of the ordinances.

Similar neglect was not tolerated in the tenements which were let
off; tenants entered into bonds to keep their houses in good repair.
When Mr Locke took over the 'Corner House', which the Latin Stock
had rented, he paid a fine of £250 for a 31-year lease at £10 a year,
and he was, at his own cost, to rebuild the overhanging upper storeys
should the City demand it; and, if this did happen, he was to have
twenty years added to his lease for £50. Some tenants made handsome profits from their tenancies. When Mrs Dallison applied in
September 1664 for an 18-year extension of her lease and offered
a fine of £430 in lieu of her £15 rent, she admitted to earning £70
a year from her sub-tenants; and it was rumoured that she was getting
£120. The Court, however, procrastinated and lost what the Fire
would have turned into a bargain.

Four alterations were made to the shape of the property which
had been Abergavenny House. In 1616 the Stock bought a small piece
of ground on the southern boundary for £20 and in 1647 the Court
put out feelers to the contractors who were negotiating the sale of
the Bishop of London's house and garden on the opposite side of
Ave Maria Lane. The following year a strip of ground facing the
street was bought; but there was no money with which to exploit
the purchase. It was therefore decided, after a half-hearted attempt
to dispose of the acquisition,[1] to sell part of the old property and on

---

[1] Henry Walley's suggestion in 1653 (already mentioned) to sell the Feathers Tavern must
have been prompted by the same need.

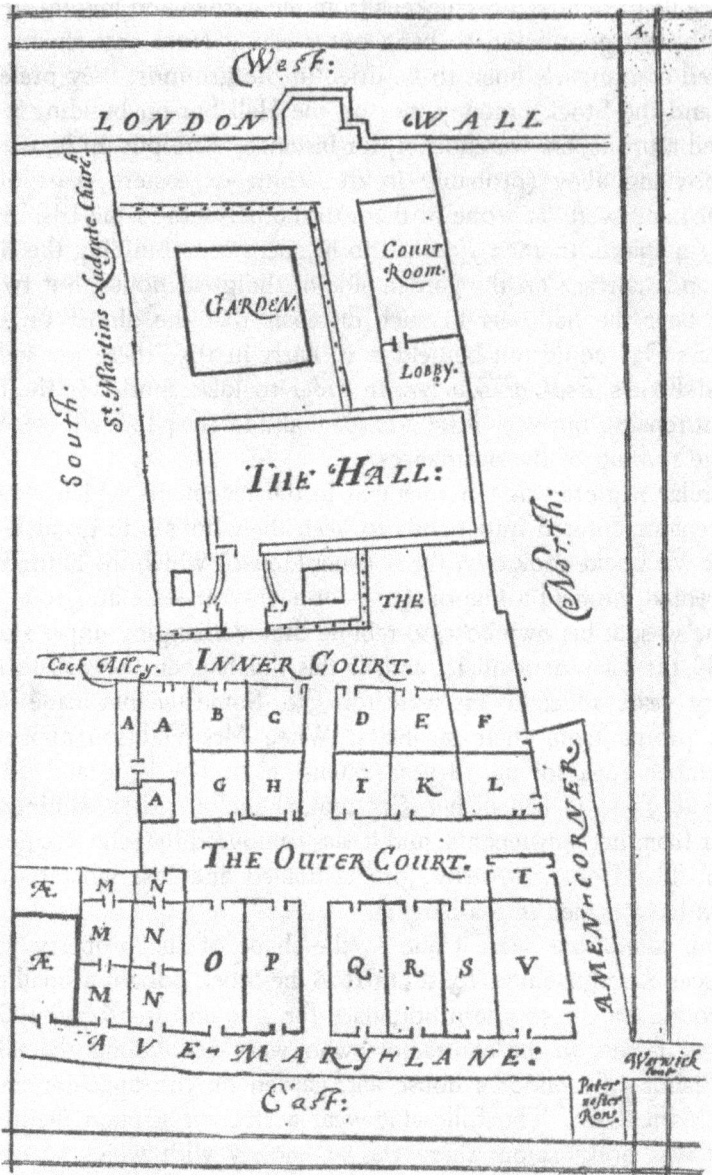

FIG. VIII.—Leybourn's plan, 1674 (*reduced*).

August 7, 1654, Jeremiah Halfhide, a Clothworker, bought for £1,200 the two houses he was occupying immediately east of the Hall gate; the expenditure on four new houses was limited to this amount. By May 28, 1655, Andrew Crooke was able to report that the new shops, with living quarters above, had each been leased for twenty-one years at a rent of £10 with a fine of £100; the tenants were two Cloth-workers, a Haberdasher and a Grocer. Crooke must have been personally involved in the transaction for, after the Restoration, he was made responsible for securing the Stock's title to the new property, for which a rent of £120 was then being paid. He was unsuccessful, and in vain the Stationers waited upon and petitioned the Archbishop during the following summer, pleading that, while others had obtained leases for valuable buildings, they stood to lose £1,500 for making use of a bit of waste ground. When the Fire demolished the houses, the land on which they had stood reverted automatically to the Church. The fourth and last modification was the addition in 1665 of a small piece of ground on the west side of the garden,[1] on the site of a bastion in the old wall. The Mount, as it was called, was leased from the City on payment of a fine of £8.

THE GREAT FIRE AND THE REBUILDING

By the evening of Monday, September 3, 1666, the Company's property in Billingsgate had been burned and its houses in Wood Street threatened. Tuesday, 'the worst day of all',[2] engulfed St Paul's Cathedral and, with it, the Feathers Tavern in the Churchyard and Abergavenny House to the north-west. Within thirty-six hours the Stationers—as a corporation and as partners in the English Stock—had apparently lost everything, and many of them, as individuals, had suffered total destruction of shops, houses and stock-in-trade.

George Tokefield, the Clerk, had managed to remove most of the Company's records to his house in the suburbs, and he made the entries immediately after the Fire just as if no disaster had occurred.

[1] In a list of such documents as were in the Company's possession in 1772, there is mention of the plans and elevations of a chapel 'formerly at the West side of the garden'. This document no longer exists, and I have found no other reference to this chapel, which certainly did not survive the Fire.
[2] T. F. Reddaway, *The Rebuilding of London after the Great Fire* (1951 ed.), p. 25. In what follows, the parts played by the City and Charles II's Government are based on this exciting book.

Only in the Treasurer's Stock Book is there a break, and a new page is headed:

'After the sadd and neuer to bee forgotten Judgment by the ffire which vpon the 2d. 3d. 4th. and 5th days of September 1666 destroyed the greatest part of this City, and in the comõn calamity our Hall, Warehouses and stock of Bookes & other goods therein.'

The first record of a meeting is for Tuesday, September 18th, when the Clerk, Humphrey Robinson, Richard Thrale, George Sawbridge (the Treasurer of the English Stock), and the two Wardens conferred about a fine of £40 which the Court, at its previous meeting, had imposed on Richard Lambert of York for printing almanacks; this subject was not as irrelevant as it may appear for there was the urgent need of cash and there was the danger, intensified by the recent disaster, that Lambert would repeat his piracy during the next few weeks. On October 2nd a full Court of Master, Wardens and seven Assistants, an attendance only one smaller than in August, met at Cooks' Hall just outside Aldersgate; after debating four items affecting the Stock, the Court ordered that labourers be hired for digging over and searching the ruins of Stationers' Hall and that a watch be set while the work was being done. A week later Mrs Elizabeth Ward, a widow and the tenant of the Dark House in Billingsgate, asked for a shed to be built on the ruins of her tenement so that she could continue in business; the Court agreed and ordered Robinson and Thrale, who had lost their shops in St Paul's Churchyard and their warehouses in the Cathedral crypt, to take a carpenter to the site and arrange for the construction at the Company's expense. By November 6th, when the Court met in the hall of St Bartholomew's Hospital—its headquarters for the next twenty-eight months—a lease for Mrs Ward was being discussed.

The steps which the Company took to rehouse itself and to re-create the income derived from its properties could be taken only as part of the general rehabilitation of the City, which was controlled by Statutes and by Acts of Common Council passed early in 1667. The first was an Act for setting up the Fire Court by which summary justice could be done between landlord and tenant; this was followed by a series of Acts which aimed to make the circulation of traffic easier by widening and realigning certain thoroughfares; to minimize the likelihood of devastating fires in the future by banning jerry-building and insisting on brick or stone for exterior structure; to encourage rebuilding by making the provision of materials and labour as easy as possible; and to facilitate the supervision of rebuilding by standardizing private houses in one of three sizes. Three further points are relevant; Ave Maria Lane was one of the streets to be widened, but only to 18 feet; the cost of rebuilding, as laid down in the usual kind of lease, was the responsibility of the tenant; and the value of land was roughly half the value of the building on it.

The Stationers made little progress during the eighteen months succeeding the Fire. The Abergavenny ground was not cleared and measured in spite of a Court resolution, but a warehouse was hired in St Bartholomew's Court, close to the Assistants' place of meeting, and the English Stock publications were removed from the Treasurer's house on Clerkenwell Green; the enterprising Mrs Ward began rebuilding. It was not, however, till the spring of 1668 that the first warehouse was put up in Stationers' Hall garden and tenants were approached about rebuilding the Feathers Tavern and the houses in Ave Maria Lane. In August Mrs Ward at last obtained a lease for sixty-one years at £14 a year on condition that she completed, within a year from Michaelmas, a brick house on the lines laid down by Act of Parliament; her rent was to be a peppercorn one for the first seven years provided the parish of St Mary-at-Hill agreed to forgo its £5 for the same period. In the autumn a permanent committee for building and debts was appointed and three significant names appeared in the Court minutes: Peter Mills,[1] the City Surveyor, reported on a drain and a party wall which had been in dispute; William Leybourn began his survey of Company and Stock property; Robert Wapshott, the contractor, gave an estimate for the building of a house in the garden.

It is understandable that the first buildings should go up on sites which were completely or relatively free of rubble, some of which might be cleared by being used in such building. The first warehouses were therefore put along the northern wall of the main garden and over them was built a room where, from March 26, 1669, the Assistants met and thankfully re-established the first Monday in the month for Court-keeping. It was in this way that the position of the present Court Room was fixed. The next area to be used was the old bowling

---

[1] He was one of the six Commissioners appointed in 1666 to watch over the rebuilding and he, with three assistants, was responsible for surveying and marking out every site before rebuilding could begin. See *The Survey of Building Sites in the City of London after the Great Fire of 1666*, vols. 1 and 2, ed. by W. H. Godfrey, London Top. Soc., 1946, 1956.

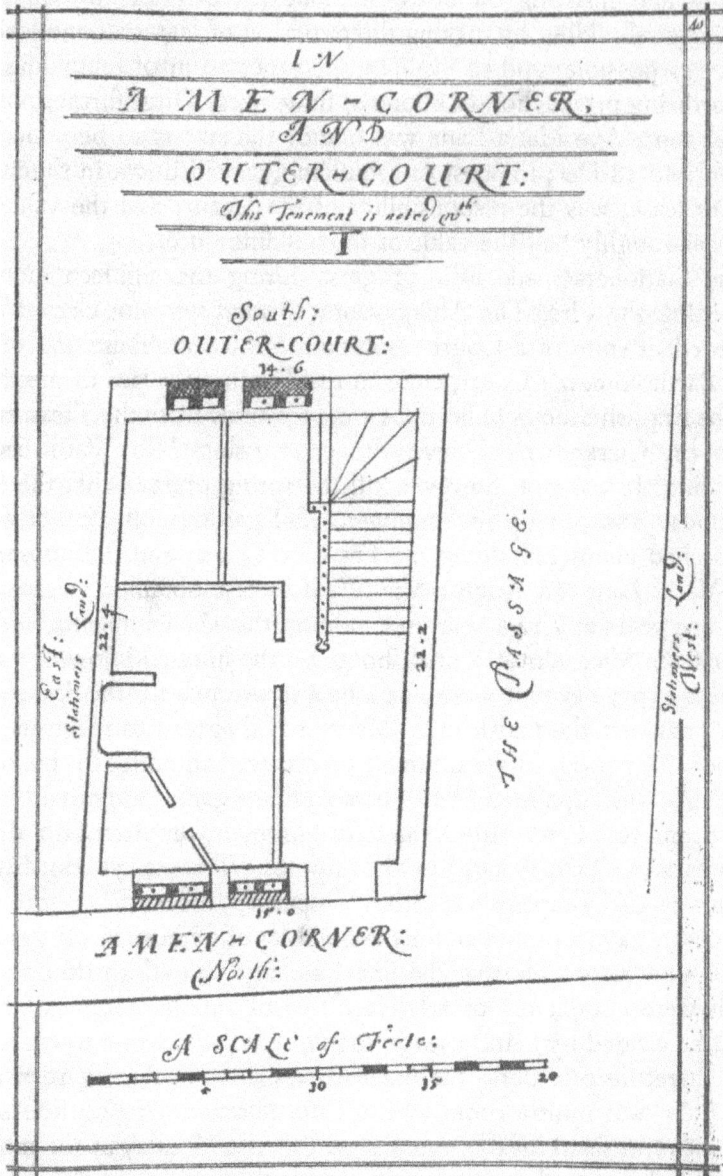

I N

A M E N - C O R N E R,

A N D

O U T E R - C O U R T:

This Tenement is noted wᵗʰ

I

South:
OUTER-COURT:
14.6

East:
Stationers Court:

THE PASSAGE.

Stationers Court West:

A M E N - C O R N E R:
North:

A SCALE of Feete:

FIG. IX.—Leybourn's ground plan (*reduced*) of the house next to, and partially over, the entrance to the Outer Court, as rebuilt in 1670. There were cellars, two good rooms each on the first and second floors, and two garrets.

alley on which single-storey warehouses had been erected in 1630; hence the approach to Wapshott. It was only in the summer of 1669 that the Court turned its attention to the hall, the foundations of which Mills was asked to survey, and to the houses in Ave Maria Lane, whose tenants were ordered to surrender their leases or pay their full rents; by September 6th there was sufficient agreement for work to begin on six tenements facing the street. One of these was the Corner House, the site of which the Stock bought back from Jeremiah Halfhide in August for £525, on the understanding that he should have the first offer of a lease and that, if he refused it, the new tenant should use a sign quite distinct from Halfhide's.[1] The cost of this purchase was largely offset by the sale in 1671 of the land on which the Feathers Tavern had stood, the site of the Company's second Hall.

By the autumn of 1670, four years after the Fire, the houses in Ave Maria Lane were ready for occupation. The lay-out of the Corner House, as described by Leybourn, was as follows. In the cellar was a house of office under the stairs; the kitchen, on the first floor over the back shop, had a large sink and a pipe bringing water from the street. Over the front shop was a well-windowed dining-room looking into Ave Maria Lane and Amen Corner, and, at the stairhead, a withdrawing-room. On the second floor were three bedrooms and on the top floor were three garrets, with fire-places and lantern windows, and a second house of office with a pipe to the vault in the cellar. A double skylight lit the staircase. This was the best house[2] of the six and one of those erected at the expense of the Stock; the total cost of the six houses was £3,000.

During the same year, 1670, work on the hall began. The foundations were laid, the walls of the ground-floor warehouses built and the joists of the hall floor set. Then the money ran out. During the winter a proposal to build the Prerogative Court in the garden came to nothing, and in April 1671 an area of 1,500 square feet was let to Wapshott on a 60-year building lease at £40 a year for the erection of the second class of house as laid down under the Act; it was agreed that Wapshott should have any usable materials and £20 towards

---

[1] I do not know what he used; among those set up in Ave Maria Lane in the earlier part of the century were Hand and Dagger, Three Mermaids, Pineapple, and Holy Lamb.

[2] Leybourn's ground plan of the house to the west of it (part of which was built over the entrance to the Outer Court) is reproduced on opposite page. The plan of the Corner House is unfortunately not fit for reproduction.

the cost of removing the rest, that he should build at the rate of £38 per 100 square feet, and that he should let none of them to tallow-chandlers, braziers, blacksmiths or flax-sellers. In August 1672 the sight of the unfinished hall and its deteriorating timber-work goaded the Assistants into fresh activity. A new committee for building and debts was instructed to meet at two o'clock every Friday; slowly the money came in—largely through the efforts of Sawbridge—and the walls rose. By the autumn of the following year the roof was on and the hall was used for the dinner on Lord Mayor's Day; but a further twelve months passed before Stephen Colledge contracted to panel the hall, in the style of the panelling at Grocers' Hall, for £300, a third of which was to be held back for a year after completion.

The work of Colledge's joiners and carvers can still be seen in the hall; the work of Colledge himself can be seen in *The Raree Show* and other anti-Popish broadsides for which (with other activities) he was executed at Oxford in 1681. He completed the work in December 1675[1] and gave the interior, apart from the windows, very much the appearance it has today. The exterior is more difficult to be certain about; the earliest elevation to survive is the engraving for the 1781 *London Almanack*, which is reproduced opposite page 208 along with an easily recognizable engraving by John Lee, of 1802, after the refacing in Portland stone. The accounts for the work on the hall and kitchen after August 1672, that is for everything above the first floor, have survived. Henry Foord, for all the woodwork (except the panelling), charged £732, and Mr Pollard, the painter, £33. Wapshott, for draining and brickwork, plastering and slating, put in a bill for £905. The cost of panelling and glazing would bring the total to over £2,000 and the cost of the foundations and the rest of the early work to perhaps £3,000. In the ten years following the Fire the Company and the English Stock (the accounts, as usual, inextricably mixed) spent about £5,000 on building—in addition to the hall and kitchen—warehouses, Court Room, Stock Room and tenements. £800 of this came from borrowing, but by far the greatest contribution was made by those who owed money to the Stock at the time of the Fire.[2]

In 1674 William Leybourn made a survey[3] of all the property—the houses belonging to the corporation and the central block rebuilt

---

[1] And received his last £25 on May 18, 1678.
[2] See above, p. 192   [3] Reproduced in part on pp. 211, 214, 218.

by the partners in the English Stock; this neatly completed the post-Fire reconstruction, but more than fifty years passed before the Company bought its own fire engine. In the end, the houses between the Inner and the Outer Court were taken over from Wapshott, who had overtaxed his financial resources; by April 1674 he was in debt to Henry Foord and to Samuel Gellibrand, a well-to-do Stationer; and by December Henry Herringman, another Stationer, was lending him money. For the next hundred years there is little to record but the renewing of leases, the attempts to get money out of dilatory tenants, the trouble with boys in the garden and pigeons in back-yards, and the hiring out of the premises. Until the church of St Martin's Ludgate was finished the parishioners used the hall for services, in return for contributions to the poor box and 'rubbing' the new panelling; but in 1688 the proposal to let the hall to a Non-conformist minister was defeated. Dances were safer and more profitable; the drawing of lotteries,[1] particularly when books were the prizes, more appropriate. Before the close of the seventeenth century, began the long succession of musical dinners on the Feast of St Cecilia, which were organized at first by Mr Glover, a Vintner, and for which the hiring of the Hall cost £5. In 1712 the Company of Clockmakers had the use of the premises when the Stationers did not want them, at twelve guineas a quarter; in 1745 the Company of Surgeons, having recently separated from the Barbers, were per-mitted to hold meetings of Assistants but not anatomical lectures. The hall was not usually let for political gatherings.

Just over a century after the Fire there occurred three events of rather greater importance. The first clarified the legal possession of the Abergavenny property. Although, in 1611, the corporation had made the purchase (out of the funds of the English Stock), it had no right, in the terms of its Charter, to hold land of such value; it there-fore appointed five or more senior Stationers as feoffees, who held the property in trust for the Company; from time to time the old feoffees conveyed it to new feoffees while some of the former were still alive to do so. A further complication arose because the payment to Lord Abergavenny had been made not out of the general funds of the corporation but out of profits earned by those members of the Com-pany who were partners in the English Stock; out of Stock funds

---

[1] The best 'let' was in 1734 to the Manager of the Charitable Corporation Lottery who had to pay £200 and £25 to the Company's servants.

additional pieces of land were bought (in the name of and under the common seal of the Company), and buildings were erected or re-erected. By letters patent on March 1, 1745, George II graciously forgave the Master, Wardens and Commonalty of the Stationers' Company for accepting estates, either themselves or through trustees, without licence, and he gave them permission to hold their existing property in mortmain. But the use of feoffees was still continued; on May 6, 1746, Daniel Midwinter,[1] the sole surviving feoffee, made the usual conveyance to John Knapton and others. In his turn, Knapton became the sole survivor but died in 1770 without the appointment of successors. Finally, on June 21, 1771, Knapton's residuary devisees conveyed the property back to the Company. From now on Stationers' Hall belonged indisputably to the Company of Stationers, whatever arrangements might be made for the upkeep of the fabric or for the disposal of the rents from the adjacent houses.

THE PROPERTY SINCE THE SURVEY OF 1773

The second event was the purchase in May 1772 of no. 1 Cock Passage (or Stationers' Alley). The price was £288 and it was, as usual, paid out of English Stock funds. This was a sensible addition to the property, and the third occurrence was a sensible addendum to the legal settlement of 1771. In the course of 1773 a complete survey was made of all the property, with the terms on which each warehouse and tenement was held. Since this matches Leybourn's visual survey of almost exactly 100 years earlier, I give it in full on pages 223 and 224 except for odd notes about the tenants' liability for repairs and the length of their leases.

The houses still, almost certainly, had shops on the ground floor and living quarters above, and those on the Abergavenny land show an interesting concentration of members of the book trade; all four branches are represented. The total rent-roll amounted to £686 7s, not counting the house just purchased; of this £519 3s was collected by the English Stock.

The later history of the two outlying pieces of property is soon told. The Dark House abutted on to houses belonging to the City, with whom there was a dispute about a party wall in 1817 and to

---

[1] For his part in English Stock affairs, see below, p. 238. The houses in Wood Street were held by the feoffees under a second deed. (Liber A, ff. 191–2.)

1773 RENTAL

Location of property	Tenant		Rent
	name	trade	£
At the Hall (Company's)			
Warehouse no. 7, in garden under little room behind Court Room	} Mount & Page	[b-sellers]	29*
Ditto nos. 8 & 9, w. side of garden			
Ditto no. 10, ditto	Robert Horsfield	[b-seller]	5*
Ditto no. 11, ditto	Thomas Caslon	,,	2 10s*
House no. 6, w. end of Court	[George Hawkins]	Treasurer	nil*
Wood Street			
No. 11, east side	Cuthbert Wilkinson	haberdasher	21
No. 12, ,, ,,	Thomas Meyrick	—	21
No. 13, ,, ,,	Robert Hall	—	24
Fryer Alley			
No. 1, e. side & one adjoining to east	Francis & Elizabeth Knight	—	18
No. 2, north side	John Apethorpe	—	4 4s
No. 3, ,, ,,	Major Williams	carpenter	7 10s
Dark House Lane			
House called Dark House	Letitia Smith	widow	35
At the Hall (English Stock's)			
Warehouse no. 1, under hall in passage to garden	Lockyer Davis	[b-seller]	4*
Ditto no. 2, ditto	Tonson & Millar	[b-sellers]	6*
Ditto no. 3, at foot of stairs from lobby to garden	Thomas Longman	[b-seller]	5*
Ditto no. 4, under Court Room	,, ,,	[,,]	5*
Ditto no. 5, ditto	Samuel Bladon	[,,]	3 3s*
Ditto no. 6, ditto	Bedwell Law	[,,]	3*
For window of house in Ludgate St.	Powell Garway	Esq.	2
Cock Passage or Stationers' Alley			
No. 1, east side (purchased 1772)	—	—	—
No. 2, east side	Elizabeth Stevens	b-seller, widow	28*
No. 3, east side	Nicholas Pennington	dealer in coals	16*
No. 4, east side	Thomas Caslon	b-seller	35*
No. 5, east side, 2 houses as one	Mary Harrison	printer, widow	32*

* Land Tax paid by the Company. The properties listed were houses unless otherwise described.

Location of property	Tenant name	trade	Rent £
Stationers' Court			
No. 1, n.w. corner of Gateway into Amen Corner	[Edward Littleton]	Beadle	nil*
No. 2, west side	John Boys	b-binder	20*
No. 3, west side	Edward Johnson†	b-seller	15*
No. 4, west side	John Courtier	peruke-maker	20*
No. 5, warehouses n.e. of Gateway	Various tenants	—	33*
For back-door & lights, Sun Tavern	James Lee	[vintner]	10
Amen Corner			
No. 5, east side	William Cooper	—	21*
Ave Maria Lane			
No. 9, n.w. corner	Charles Wright	silver-smith	35*
Nos. 10 & 11, west side	Charles Green Say	printer	40
No. 12, west side	Edward Johnson†	b-binder	30*
Nos. 13 & 14, west side	Bedwell Law	b-seller	55*
No. 15, west side	Joan Bryant	butter-woman	30*
No. 16, west side	Robert March	stationer	38
No. 17, west side	Edward Barnard	,,	33*

* Land Tax paid by the Company. The properties listed were houses unless otherwise described.

† It is not possible to say whether there were two Edward Johnsons or one man with two places of business.

whom the tenement was unsuccessfully offered for sale. For the next half-century the tenants were—not surprisingly—fishmongers, and when the Billingsgate Market Act of 1871 made its sale compulsory the Company asked for £5,000. This was refused and the Company, reviving an ambition first mooted in 1806, proposed to exchange the Dark House for property of similar value in the Old Bailey (to the west of the warehouses built on the Mount) so as to create a more imposing entrance to Stationers' Hall. The Corporation refused this also (as it did again in 1877) and in January 1874 paid £3,400 for the Billingsgate house. Out of this sum 3 per cent Consols to the value of £166 13s 4d were purchased in order to provide the £5 a year, under Stephen Kevall's bequest, for the parish of St Mary-at-Hill. The houses in Wood Street were repaired, refaced and rebuilt; they changed hands and the rents steadily increased;[1] but the ground plan

[1] The employment of the rents for the provision of a school is dealt with below, p. 256

5 *The hall in 1830*

did not alter until, in July 1888, C. R. Rivington, the Clerk, bought at auction for £4,200 a narrow piece of property which lay along the eastern boundary of City land (the site of the old Counter) and opened into Feathers Court. His offer of it to the Company was gratefully accepted at the next meeting of the Court. The management of all these awkwardly shaped and not easily accessible buildings was difficult and was, perhaps, not always as prudent as it might have been. They were sold in 1946 to Messrs I. & R. Morley, who had long been the tenant of the largest portion of them, for £25,000.

The story of the Abergavenny property from 1773 falls into three parts. The first was dominated by the Mylne family, architectural advisers to the Company for over a century, and the centre of attention was Stationers' Hall itself. The second began in 1858 and included a complete redevelopment of that portion of the land from which the income was derived. The third aimed at extending the property southwards to Ludgate Hill, and the main part of the purchases was made after the Second World War.

Robert Mylne, the architect of Blackfriars Bridge and Chief Engineer to the New River Company, became Surveyor to the Company of Stationers in 1776. His journals[1] show how much time he spent on ordinary surveyor's jobs; reporting on a tenement lately vacated; advising on the terms of a new lease and the repairs to be done by the incoming tenant; explaining to the Assistants the necessity of reslating part of the roof; discussing with Alderman Cadell the stained-glass window which the latter was putting in at the northern end of the hall. But he did have one small chance to show his architectural ideas, which can be seen in the present frontage. So long as the Company was of little significance in the life of the City, the simple brick exterior, designed and erected by Wapshott, was good enough; the buildings stood well back from Ave Maria Lane and were invisible from Ludgate Hill. When, however, the promotion of Stationers to the Court of Aldermen began to bring Sheriffs and Lord Mayors to the Hall, Robert Mylne was asked to give it a more dignified appearance. He put in new windows along each side of the hall and put a stone facing on the east wall. The work was finished in the autumn of 1800 and cost a little over £1,300. Robert Mylne died in 1811 and his son William was immediately elected to succeed him. His opportunity came in 1825 when it was decided to improve the amenities

---

[1] Printed by A. E. Richardson in *Robert Mylne, Architect and Engineer, 1733 to 1811*, 1955.

of the Court Room. After consulting Robert Smirke, he put his proposals before the Assistants who agreed to spend the necessary £1,600. The main alterations were the conversion of the little chamber at the western end into a card room, the improvement of the entrance lobby and elaborate redecoration of the Court Room itself. This wing of the building was severely damaged by enemy action in October 1940; the restoration has in the main followed the Mylne designs, but the panelling, which had been added in 1757, was lost.

The major work of the third Mylne, Robert William who succeeded his father in 1863, was the reshaping and the partial rebuilding of the eastern wing of the Hall. On July 4, 1871, it was decided to pull down the houses of the Treasurer and the Beadle in order to make more room for the Company's offices and the copyright registry; but it was not until October 6, 1885, that the Court adopted a report from the Stock Board and ordered the work to be put in hand. At a cost of something over £7,000 the Stock Room was given its present shape —the original panelling being carefully put back—and a new entrance from Amen Corner, made possible by an exchange of strips of land with the Dean and Chapter of St Paul's, was created. This access to the Hall was the only one possible after the continued failure to obtain a right of way from the Old Bailey and the blocking (except for pedestrians) of the way through from Ludgate Hill to the true main door. The offices were tucked in under the Stock Room and a flat for the Beadle was fitted in above the new entrance. Three ambitious projects—put forward in 1903, 1918 and 1935—for alterations which would increase the earning capacity of the Hall, came to nothing; and the considerable improvements, completed in 1957 along with the reconstruction of the war-damaged buildings, did not affect the exterior of the Hall. The purchase from the Corporation in 1954 of the strip of land under the warehouses in the garden and under the card room was £4,500 very well spent.[1]

I must refer briefly to the redevelopment of the area lying between the Hall and Ave Maria Lane which became the centre for the distribution of English books all over the world. In 1858 it was agreed that Messrs Simpkin and Marshall, who had been tenants of the English Stock for nearly half a century, should have a building lease of the

[1] By the last lease, which ran from Christmas 1872 to Michaelmas 1951, the rent had been fixed at £50 p.a. The only other piece of leasehold property is a small area of ground at the southern end of the hall, on which stand the old pantry and cloakroom; the landlords are the Merchant Tailors' Company.

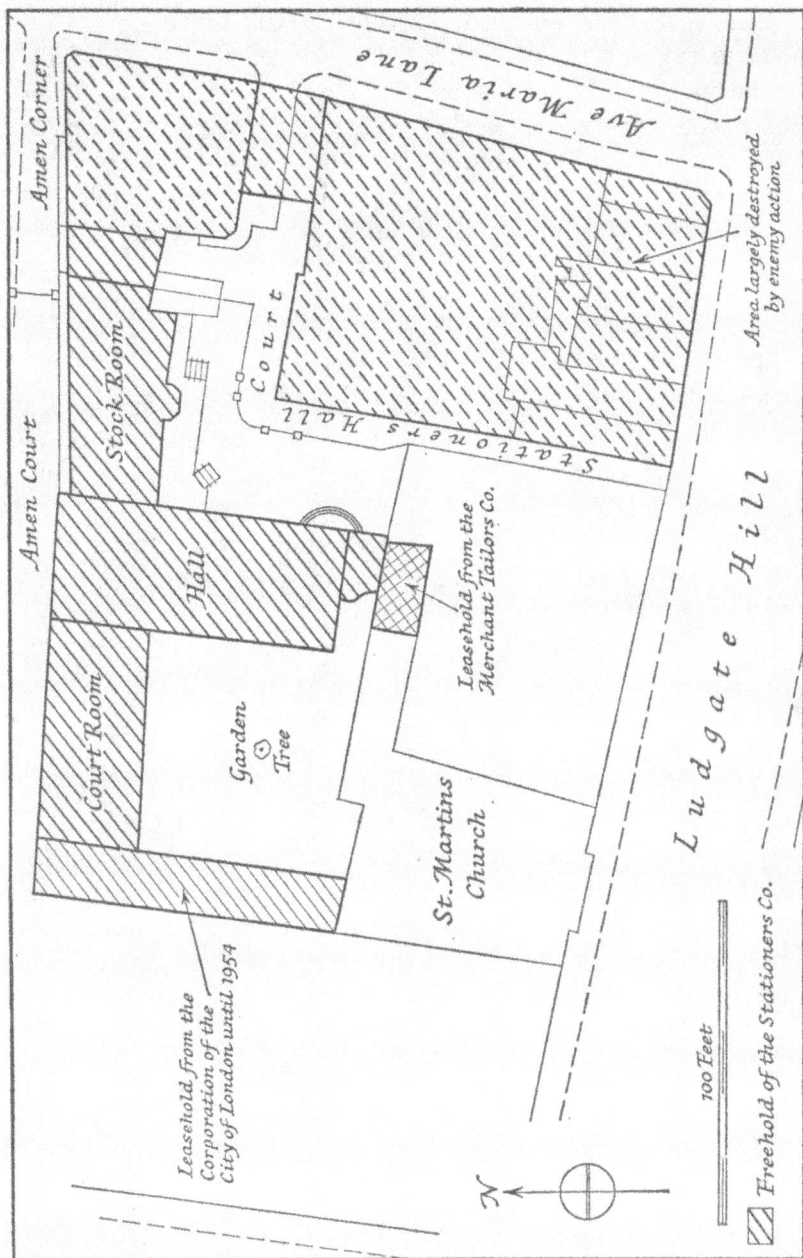

Amen Corner

Amen Court

Ave Maria Lane

Stock Room

Hall

Court Room

Garden
⊙ Tree

St. Martins
Church

Court

Stationers Hall

Leasehold from the
Merchant Tailors Co.

Area largely destroyed
by enemy action.

Leasehold from the
Corporation of the
City of London until 1954.

Ludgate Hill

N

100 Feet

▨ Freehold of the Stationers Co.

FIG. X.—Sketch plan of Stationers' Hall and surrounding property in 1953.

houses in Stationers' Hall Court for eighty-one years (i.e. until 1939), the Stock advancing £5,500 towards the cost of the new block. In 1860 a similar bargain was made for four houses in Ave Maria Lane (nos. 10 to 13), and the old Outer Court, created after the Fire, began to be built over. Twenty years later the Oxford University Press offered to take a 37-year lease of a new building on Amen Corner at a rent of £1,000 and in October 1883 took possession of the Bible Warehouse, erected out of Stock funds. In May 1884 Cambridge University Press made an almost identical arrangement for a warehouse further south in Ave Maria Lane (nos. 14 to 16). In 1890 the Company had agreed to erect a new building still further south (no. 17) and to let it to Simpkin Marshall until March 25, 1939, at a rent of £65 plus 6 per cent of the cost of construction. When Simpkins in 1905 took over the property used by Cambridge, which it had previously surrounded on three sides, the solid block of wholesaling warehouses achieved the shape which it retained until its destruction in December 1940.

The expansion of the Company property southwards began in 1811 with the purchases of the freehold of no. 32 and of the leasehold of no. 38 Ludgate Hill in the hope of improving the approach to the Hall. In 1824 the Merchant Tailors' Company, the landlord of no. 38, granted a 26-year lease at a rent of £140, on condition that the Stationers spent £500 on repairs. An attempt to buy the property in 1850 was unsuccessful, and even before the building of the new entrance in 1886 the interest in this approach had died; no. 32 was resold in 1881. But interest in the houses to the east of Cock Alley steadily increased. No. 22 Ludgate Hill was bought, rebuilt and let to Simpkins in 1900; no. 20 was purchased in 1930, nos. 24 to 28 (mostly destroyed by enemy action) in 1951 and no. 18, at the corner of Ave Maria Lane, in 1953. The total cost of rounding off this block was a little over £40,000. I shall tell of the outcome of these purchases in Chapter XIV.

CHAPTER XII

THE COMPANY IN THE EIGHTEENTH CENTURY

———

THE CHALLENGE OF THE LIVERY: MESSRS OSBORNE AND NUTT

IN the course of about 100 years the Stationers' Company had to face four crises which, in different degrees of severity, affected many aspects of its gild and trade life and many aspects of the gild and trade lives of its members. The first was the lapsing of the Printing Act in 1695; I have dealt in Chapter IX with the way in which the booksellers and the Company repaired this gap in their defences. The second and third were minor disturbances within the Corporation, in 1741 and 1762, which showed where the growth of the Company created grievances. The fourth was a severe threat, in 1774, to the almanack monopoly and therefore to the prosperity of the English Stock. Out of these troubles the Company emerged a more powerful and prosperous—though a somewhat different—organization.

In the early winter of 1741 two booksellers, Thomas Osborne father and son, and a printer, Richard Nutt, advertised their intention of calling a meeting of the whole body of Stationers and of taking legal action against the Assistants.[1] The Court immediately co-opted fifteen Liverymen—ten booksellers, four printers and a stationer; this was the first election for nearly six years and it almost doubled the size of the governing body. Early in 1742 the Osbornes published a pamphlet[2] (printed by Nutt); in this they condemned 'The *Pomp* and *Grandeur* of the *Master*, *Wardens* and *Assistants*, and their Relations and *Dependents* [who] have long stood upon the *Miseries* of the FREEMEN', particularly poor printers and bookbinders. The authors printed the Charter and the English Stock grants, and asked why, on the strength of these, the rank and file of the Company should not

---

[1] Many of the points in this chapter are discussed more fully in 'The Stationers' Company in the Eighteenth Century', *Guildhall Miscellany*, 10, 1959.
[2] *The Charter and Grants of the Company of Stationers . . . now in force.* MDCCXLI. This was reprinted in 1825, when there was a good deal of outside interest in the affairs of City companies.

elect their own governing body and officers, reduce the fees (for enrolling an apprentice and presenting one for his freedom) to the ancient level, make an equitable division of English Stock profits and call to account those who were misappropriating corporation funds. These were much the same criticisms as Sparke and Underhill had made a century before,[1] but the real grievances were somewhat different; for when the Osbornes and the other complainants in a Chancery suit against the Company agreed to withdraw their case and submit to arbitration, they were content with £100 towards their legal expenses and two promises: that seniority should be given more weight in the choosing of Assistants and that Stationers who did not work in the book trade should stand equal chances with other Liverymen of election to shares in the English Stock.

The Osbornes were senior to nearly all the ten Assistants 'called' on December 1, 1741. The father had not been clothed until eighteen years after he had taken up his freedom in 1703 (seven years after he was entitled to it); the son, on the other hand, was made free by patrimony, clothed and allowed to fine for Renter Warden within a single week in 1728. In the seventeenth century the experience of the elder Osborne would have been normal and that of the younger exceptional. But as a result partly of the growth of the Company and partly of the exploitation of the fine as a regular source of income,[2] clothing gradually ceased to be a minor honour conferred on senior members of the Yeomanry and became a step taken by nearly all those with prospects of independent mastership, the day they became free Stationers. From quite early in the eighteenth century the Yeomanry was regarded as a status proper only for wage-earners, but it was not until February 2, 1762, that this was, by implication, acknowledged in a formal resolution debarring journeymen from the Livery; seven years later it was resolved that all pensions not reserved for printers were to be kept for Liverymen. As part of the same process, the turnstile through which men had to pass—fining for or serving as Renter Warden—dropped further and further down the list of Liverymen. In 1721 the Renters were numbers 88 and 89; in 1800 they were numbers 266 and 267. When, on August 1, 1775, it was resolved that no one be elected to a share in the English Stock until

---

[1] See above, pp. 131-7
[2] The best example occurred a little later—in 1766—when thirty Liverymen were called upon to fine for the Rentership in order to provide money for rebuilding the barge.

he had passed the barrier, the revolution was complete. Liverymen above the Renter Wardens corresponded, at an additional cost of £24, to the ordinary Liverymen of 100 years earlier, and the rest were £20 worse off than the Yeomanry of the seventeenth century. Moreover, each section of the new Livery was, like the old Livery and the old Yeomanry, divided into those with ambitions to climb higher and those without. The satisfying of these ambitions rested, as the century passed, less and less on the preferences of the Assistants and more and more on patiently waiting. In 1741 the fifteen elected to the Court ranged from 21st to 81st in the Livery list; in 1763 the eighteen elected ranged from 19th to 46th and in 1792 only one in six was passed over from number 24.

Within the Court itself the same process was at work. Traditionally, the Mastership was open to those who had served or fined twice as Under and twice as Upper Warden; a man might be chosen Master three or, as James Roberts was, four times.[1] This meant that, even when the Court was small, some Assistants never attained the highest honour. But on September 1, 1752, Thomas Ridge, a stationer who had just been elected Master, suggested that quicker rotation might be healthier for the Company. His proposal was debated at two succeeding meetings and then dropped. At the Court before the 1754 election Thomas Page, the sitting Master, announced that he would decline to stand for a second term and proposed that no one should hold an office for more than a single year. Reference to the by-laws revealed no impediment, but a final decision was postponed until July 2nd, when the resolution was carried and Page was thanked, *nem. con.*, 'for his candid behaviour'. To Ridge and Page, therefore, we owe the present pattern of office holding by which survival and willingness to serve are the sole criteria. Though the formalities of election, by 'scoring' and 'going to the box', were long preserved, the only exceptions made in the operation of seniority were the immediate promotion of those who were elected Sheriff.

It is impossible to say how much of this hardening of the gild pattern was due to the Osbornes' protest and how much to the general tendency among City companies; but the modest results of the other concession must be credited to them. At least three of the plaintiffs with them in the 1742 suit against the Company were haberdashers who were understandably annoyed that, because they were not

[1] 1729–32.

employed in any branch of the book trade, they were traditionally passed over in elections both to shares in the English Stock and to the Court. In a Company so closely interested in the occupations of the majority of its members (six out of seven of the masters binding apprentices at Stationers' Hall were booksellers, printers, bookbinders or stationers throughout the century), the second deprivation was probably inevitable; but the right to invest in a business paying 12½ per cent was worth fighting for, and by the end of the century a couple of dozen had been elected to shares. The policy of keeping the Stationers' Company, and all it had to offer, for members of the book trade may have been good when applied to the admission of freemen by redemption; and it shows a confidence in numerical strength which many other companies must have envied. But it was of greater importance to avoid losing Stationers to more glamorous or more easy-going companies. The loss by translation was very small and was confined to those engaged in other trades; part of the potential loss through apprenticeship channels was ingeniously prevented by binding a boy to a Stationer and, a month or two later, turning him over to the master for whom he was really intended—a Merchant Tailor who was a bookbinder or a Fishmonger who was a stationer—on condition that he be presented for his freedom as a Stationer. Since so few companies were still trade-conscious there was apparently little difficulty in persuading the new master to put his name to these conditions.

THE CHALLENGE OF THE YEOMANRY: JACOB ILIVE

The third piece of trouble occurred in 1762. The ringleader was Jacob Ilive, a letter-founder turned printer, an eccentric in his theological views and remarkable for his habit of working in his night-gown. Shortly after the Court order which excluded journeymen from the Livery, he asked for and was refused permission to examine the records of the Company; he thereupon summoned a general meeting of Stationers 'and, standing on the upper table in the hall, he thanked the freemen for the honour they had done him' in making him chairman of the assemblage. He proposed that, 'to rescue their liberties' and return to the intention of the Charter, they should elect their own master and wardens, and appoint a committee of twenty-one to meet on the first Tuesday in each month at the Horn Tavern for an enquiry into the state of the Company. Christopher Norris was chosen master; Thomas Norwood Ashfield and Ilive were chosen wardens; the first two were bookbinders who were still members of the Yeomanry.[1] The story goes that they met for the second time at the Hall on July 6th and summoned the Clerk to swear in the new 'master'; when John Partridge refused to do this, Ilive deputized for him. At their next meeting they bound apprentices, admitted men to their freedoms and called freemen to the Livery. When, in September, the Chamberlain of the City questioned the right of Norris to bind apprentices, Ilive challenged the by-law under which the officers of the Company were normally elected; the Chamberlain, however, expressed himself satisfied with an ordinance which had operated uniformly for eighty years and refused to enrol the indentures.

How much longer the game was played, I do not know; but in the following year Ilive stirred up members of the Yeomanry to refuse to pay quarterage on the grounds that the by-law under which it was collected had gone the way of the new Charter of Charles II. When the Company sued defaulters in the Court of Requests, Ilive acted as defence counsel and argued that, since the Commonalty was no longer summoned to Quarterly Courts for the reading of the by-laws, there was no obligation to pay the quarterly dues. The Company won its case without difficulty and quarterage was not abolished until 1884, though its collection became more and more difficult. One of the results of the case was that the Court strengthened its own position by making, in December 1763, one of the biggest—and broadest based—calls of Assistants. The number first proposed was twelve; this was increased to fifteen and finally to eighteen. Only half of these were booksellers. Another result was that from this date the Yeomanry, as one of the 'estates' in the Company, is heard of no more.

Ilive died in 1765, supported in his last months by Company charity. Though he was unbalanced and unsuccessful, he spoke up for the wage-earning Stationers—compositors, pressmen and journeymen bookbinders—for whom their Company no longer had any meaning. It was too late for a resurgence of the Yeomanry whose corporate

[1] William Bowyer, the printer, told the story to Richard Gough who printed it in *British Topography*, i, 1780, p. 597 n. According to him the meeting was held on Saturday, July 3rd, when John Lenthall, Esq., a stationer, and John Wilcox, gent., a bookseller, were elected 'wardens'. The first was the senior Liveryman outside the Court, having been clothed in 1721; the second took up his freedom in 1708 and remained in the Yeomanry. The 'wardens' who appeared before the Chamberlain were, however, Ashfield and Ilive.

feelings were engaged either within the expanding printing houses where they spent their days or with their fellow-workers in the same trade. Loyalty might still exist vertically in a well-run business like that of Samuel Richardson, but in the second half of the eighteenth century a stronger loyalty was crystallizing horizontally over the whole printing trade—a fellow feeling between *all* compositors, whether or not they had ever been near Stationers' Hall. A working printers' trade union existed, in all but name, by 1785 when it was able to negotiate with the masters a new scale of payments for piece-work in London.[1] The Company refused to play any responsible part in this development and thereby lost the second of its opportunities to become a meeting ground for different interests in an expanding trade. The Court merely showed that it was on the side of the masters by refusing to pay attention to the petition of the journeymen and by debarring from pensions those who took part in the combination. Jacob Ilive —the compositor with the reputation for setting type by the feel of the letters—may have had an inkling of what was happening, but he was incapable of making his point in an effective way.

THE CHALLENGE TO THE ALMANACK MONOPOLY: THOMAS CARNAN

Ilive's successor in the line of challengers to Company authority—the prime mover in the fourth of the eighteenth-century crises—was quite a different man. Thomas Carnan[2] came to London from Reading in 1744 when his step-father, John Newbery, opened a shop in St Paul's Churchyard. Here he learned how to distribute cheap publications (many of them books for children) and patent medicines, not only in the capital but throughout the provinces; and here he was close to Paternoster Row, the centre of the wholesale trade, and to the warehouse of the English Stock from which about half a million almanacks were sold during the last two months of each year. This business was tempting enough to encourage interlopers up and down the country; after 1695 it was not difficult for printers in Exeter or

---

[1] For the documents in this movement see Ellic Howe, *The London Compositor*, 1947. The scales of binding prices agreed on during the seventeenth century were quite different from the printers' rates for work; the former were the results of negotiations between separate trades, the latter between employers and employed within the same trade.

[2] What follows is based on 'Thomas Carnan and the Almanack Monopoly', *Studies in Bibliography*, Charlottesville, xiv, 1960.

Chester or Newcastle to reprint the more popular almanacks and sell a small impression before effective action could be taken against them. But Robert Dodsley, Thomas Carnan and Richard Baldwin were the first to invade the Stationers' territory, not by direct piracy but obliquely. Whereas the standard almanack had to be turned into our idea of a diary by being interleaved at the binding stage, these three booksellers published in 1748 and 1749 *The New Memorandum Book*, *The Ladies Complete Pocket Book* and *The Gentleman's and Tradesman's Daily Journal* which were already diaries but which also contained useful information.

The threat was not at first direct enough or serious enough to worry the Company; but when in 1755 Carnan, armed with a formal resolution of the Court of Aldermen, applied for his freedom by redemption, the Court voted against admitting him. The decision was probably unwise, because it drove Carnan to challenge, as a matter of principle, the Company's almanack monopoly; but it was nearly twenty years before the unwisdom was apparent. In 1772 a general warning was issued against publications which were almanacks in all but name. On November 13, 1773, Carnan published Reuben Burrow's *A Diary for the Year of Our Lord 1774*, and two days later he received a call from William Strahan, the son of the Upper Warden. Carnan always maintained that Strahan brought him an offer from the Company which he contemptuously refused; Strahan, when questioned two years later, could not remember exactly how the conversation went but he denied having authority, from his father or any senior Stationer, to negotiate. On November 18th the Company asked for and obtained an injunction in Chancery to prevent Carnan from selling further copies of the *Diary* until his answer to the bill was received and the court had made its order. He continued, of course, to sell his other diaries.

February 1774 is a very important month in the history of copyright for in the course of it the Lords gave their reasons for upholding Alexander Donaldson's appeal against an injunction granted by the Lord Chancellor to restrain the sale of a 'pirated' edition of Thomson's *Seasons*. This judgment destroyed the contention of the London booksellers that copyright was a perpetual property which could be bought and sold, as a whole or in lots, like a piece of freehold land. Under the shadow of this verdict the same Lord Chancellor had to make an order in the case of the Stationers' Company *v.* Carnan who admitted, in his answer of February 4th, that he had sold 1,900 copies of the *Diary* (out of 2,500 printed), but who boldly asserted that James I had no power to grant a perpetual monopoly in almanacks. The Lord Chancellor, therefore, allowed Carnan to sell all his almanacks (under certain conditions) and referred the question of the monopoly for argument in the Court of Common Pleas.

Nearly fifteen nonths later, on May 29, 1775, the judges decided that the monopoly could not be exclusive, that the King had no power to confine the publishing of all almanacks to one organization. Carnan was on the verge of a great victory and he is said to have driven his lofty phaeton and pair, again and again, through St Paul's Church-yard, down Paternoster Row and past the entrance to Stationers' Hall. On that very Monday William Waller, his counsel, and George Robinson, his partner in recent almanack publishing, called upon him. According to Carnan, Waller offered him £10,000 from the Company if he would allow the Chancery injunction to stand, and Robinson, whose interest in the struggle—like Dodsley's and Baldwin's—was economic rather than emotional, advised him to accept; he repeated his advice before witnesses in the Globe Tavern later in the week. Carnan swore to the truth of this story before the Lord Mayor; Waller, through the Clerk of the Company, dismissed the whole thing as a leg-pull (carefully explained to Carnan later); and Robinson, in the columns of an evening newspaper, declared that no offer was made which a sane man could entertain seriously.

Pretending that a rejected proposal was never meant to be taken in earnest is a manœuvre which has often been employed; but though it relies on that usually telling gambit, the suggestion that one's opponent has no sense of humour, it is seldom convincing. Carnan may have exaggerated the sum named, but he was right, I am sure, in asserting that the Company wished to settle; it had been making such financial arrangements with rivals for nearly 150 years and it was still paying the Universities, or their assigns, over £1,000 a year to refrain from printing certain classes of books, almanacks amongst them. The wisdom of trying to buy out a rival in the shadow of the Common Pleas decision may seem doubtful, but the history of the next sixty years proved that, on this occasion, the Assistants had been right. Whether wise or not, the attempt in 1775 was unsuccessful; the Chancery injunction against Carnan was, on his application, dissolved, and the almanack market was wide open for general exploitation.

It has usually been assumed that the English Stock never recovered from this blow; but after an initial period of panic, expense and severe competition, it enjoyed nearly half a century of great prosperity. That it weathered the storm at all was due to a previous half-century of good fortune and, more surprisingly, good management. The sums advanced, conditionally, by Thomas Guy in 1716[1] and a short period of more realistic Dividend policy, coupled with the benefits from an expanding market, meant that English Stock affairs, having been put in order, were kept in order. Part of the new policy was to invest

ENGLISH STOCK ACCOUNTS, 1766–7

Dr.	£	s	d	Cr.	£	s	d
To disbursements Lady Day to				By books in warehouse	316	19	1
Midsummer (1)*	3,257	15	11	„ good debts	2,607	4	6
„ Midsummer Dividend (1)	1,440	0	0	„ books and cash recd from			
„ disbursements Midsr to				Stock-keepers (1)	3,340	16	1
Michaelmas (2)	4,043	8	9	„ dividends recd (1)	655	0	0½
„ ditto Mich. to Lady Day (3)	1,996	12	10	„ rents recd (1)	433	0	0
„ Christmas Dividend (3)	1,440	0	0	„ Irish dividend (1)	50	2	1
„ allowance on psalms	5	11	6	„ books & cash recd (2)	3,404	7	9
„ good debts	571	5	5	„ dividends recd (2)	300	0	0
„ books in warehouse	504	18	4	„ rents recd (2)	197	10	0
„ balance due to E.S.	1,965	4	6	„ books & cash recd (3)	2,847	10	3¼
				„ dividends recd (3)	745	0	0
				„ rents recd (3)	207	0	0
				„ Irish dividend (3)	120	7	5¼
	£15,224	17	3		£15,224	17	3

* The Treasurer's accounts were, at this period, made up three times a year; the figures in brackets denote the accounting period of the entries.

profits in Government stock. The summary of accounts for 1766–7 shows a profit of nearly £2,000 over and above the half-yearly Dividends of 6¼ per cent; but what really demonstrates the strength of the financial position is the receipt from investments of £1,700 which, with the rents from the property and the dividend from the Londonderry Estate, was within £200 of providing the Dividend for the partners. The turn-over in books and almanacks this year was not outstanding at about £9,500; but the English Stock would have survived even if the whole of the almanack business had been lost.

One of the bases of the good management was the appearance of professional Stock-keepers. In the seventeenth century the partners took these jobs in turn, and a man might serve two or three times

[1] See above, p. 190. For a piece of bad management at a later date, see below, p. 244.

during his life as a partner. But in the following century only death or election as Warden interrupted[1] the service of a successful Stock-keeper, and in the sixty-five years from 1736 only forty-one men held the six elected offices between them; all but six of these became Assistants and two of the six became Treasurer; over half lived to be Master. Since the full Stock Board included the Master and Wardens, service as a Stock-keeper was a useful step—so long as such a step could be useful—towards the highest places in the Company; in 1773 Robert Horsfield (Treasurer from 1785), having missed election to the Court by one vote, was chosen a fortnight later by special resolution, on the grounds that he had been a faithful Stock-keeper.

These men were successful in their own businesses, usually as wholesale and copyright-owning booksellers, and were able to work out the policy of the Stock in terms rather of years than of months. One group remained unbroken for eight years from 1742 under the chairmanship of Daniel Midwinter,[2] one of the most prosperous booksellers in the first half of the eighteenth century. His father was a member of the Leathersellers' Company and he was apprenticed, for eight years on September 9, 1689, to Richard Chiswell (translated from the Haberdashers under the policy to concentrate members of the book trade in the Stationers' Company). Midwinter took up his freedom and was clothed on February 7, 1698, and he fined for Renter Warden six years later. In September 1706, when he was about thirty, he achieved a half-Yeomanry share and on March 1, 1709, he was elected a Stock-keeper in the Yeomanry interest. From that time until 1753 he was on the Stock Board, either as an elected member or as a Warden, for all but six years. When the Court called for a report on the state of the Stock in 1737, Midwinter wrote it; so confident were the partners in their committee of management that, though they turned up in strength for the election of a new Treasurer, only five attended the ordinary annual election on March 1, 1752, the last time Midwinter stood.

Good management and money in the bank could not of themselves protect the Company's almanack monopoly, though they ensured a certain freedom of manœuvre; some action had to be taken. The first

---

[1] The interruption was only nominal, for Wardens were *ex officio* members of the Stock Board.

[2] The other representative of the Assistants was James Roberts who finished his fourth consecutive year as Master in 1733 and returned to the Stock Board in 1737 to sit, according to rule, as the Assistant who had served as Master. Midwinter died in 1758 without ever being Master.

objective was to substitute statutory protection for that hitherto given by royal prerogative. Before the end of February 1774 a Bill, sponsored by two of the members for the City of London, was introduced in the House of Commons; since its purpose—the establishment of perpetual copyright—would reverse a legal decision of the Lords, the Lords threw it out. Then the retail prices of a dozen of the Company's almanacks were reduced by 1d (for three years) and the discounts to trade customers were increased. A mathematical expert was retained to check inaccuracies complained of in the almanacks. But Carnan, even after his partner Robinson had left him, forged ahead and by the autumn of 1777 he was publishing twelve different almanacks, one of which had separate versions for twenty different areas in England. In addition, London booksellers published over a dozen others—eight specially for the ladies—which Carnan's enterprise had encouraged. The turnover in the Company's almanacks fell by a third and, for the three years of lowered prices, the English Stock made a loss on that part of its business. To offset this there was a gain of over £1,000 a year in the general account when the payments for the Universities' rights in the monopoly were cut off because the monopoly no longer existed.

Since, however, the Company would much rather have made these payments if by making them the monopoly could be restored, it persuaded the Universities to join in promoting a Government Bill. In May 1779 the Prime Minister, Lord North, who was also Chancellor of the University of Oxford, introduced a measure to invest the sole right to print almanacks in the three original claimants. This time the Bill was defeated in the Commons. There remained one more device: an increase in the Stamp Duty on almanacks. This had been imposed in 1711 and after the increase in 1742 a book almanack had to carry a 4d stamp and a sheet almanack a 2d stamp. Unless a man were ready to risk cheating the revenue (as provincial printers no doubt did) he must have access to capital to be a dangerous competitor to the Company. Carnan, with Robinson's assistance, had been able to raise the capital; but even he might flinch, and some others would certainly give up the race, if the initial outlay (on which there was no profit to be earned) were raised still further. In April 1781 Lord North, once again thinking of Oxford and Cambridge, proposed to double the duty on sheet almanacks in order to discourage the recent practice—employed both by the Company and by Carnan

Stationers'-Hall, Oct. 1, 1793.

THE FOLLOWING

A L M A N A C K S,

Fo2 the Year 1794,

Printed for the COMPANY of STATIONERS,

Will be publifhed at *Stationers'-Hall*, on *Tuefday* the 19th of *November* next, *viz.*

The Gentleman's Diary
The Ladies' Diary
Francis Moore's Almanack
John Partridge's Almanack } 10d. each.
Poor Robin's Almanack
Seafon on the Seafons
Tycho Wing's Almanack
White's Cœleftial Atlas; or, } 1s.
New Ephemeris
Rider's Britifh Merlin - 10d.

Wing's Sheet Almanack
Cambridge Sheet Almanack
Price Eight Pence each.

London Sheet Almanack, on a }
Copper-Plate }
Goldimith's Almanack }
Price Nine Pence each.

The Free-Mafons' Calendar, }
publifhed under the Sanction }
of the Grand Lodge of Eng- }
land - - - }
Price One Shilling.

A New London Sheet Almanack }
printed on a Royal Paper, with }
Court and City Regifter - -}
Price Ten Pence.

COUNTY ALMANACKS, Price *Eight Pence* each,

With various ufeful TABLES, particularly adapted to each County, *viz.*

1. Middlefex, Hertfordfhire, }
Effex, Kent, Surrey, and }
Suffex - - - }
2. Cornwall, Devonfhire, So- }
merfetfhire, and Dorfet- }
fhire - - - }
3. Gloucefterfhire, Worcefter- }
fhire, Herefordfhire, Mon- }
mouthfhire, and South Wales }
4. Norfolk, Suffolk, Cam- }
bridgefhire, Ely, Hunting- }
donfhire, and Bedfordfhire }

5. Warwickfhire, Northampton- }
fhire, Leicefterfhire, Rutland- }
fhire, Lincolnfhire, Notting- }
hamfhire, and Derbyfhire - }
6. Chefhire, Lancafhire, Shrop- }
fhire, Staffordfhire, and North }
Wales - - - }
7. Wiltfhire, Hampfhire, Ox- }
fordfhire, Berkfhire, and }
Buckinghamfhire - - }
8. Yorkfhire, Durham, Nor- }
thumberland, Weftmoreland, }
and Cumberland - - }

All the above Almanacks are diftinguifhed by the following Words:
" *Printed for the* COMPANY *of* STATIONERS,
" *And fold by* ROBERT HORSFIELD, *at their Hall, in* LUDGATE-STREET,"
Whofe Name is printed on the TITLE PAGE *of the* Book Almanacks, *or at the* TOP *of the* Sheet.

☞ No bound Almanacks or Pocket-Books will be fent, nor any Orders in Quires exécuted under Five Pounds, for ready Money or Bills at a Month.

In order to prevent the many Complaints of not receiving the Parcels in Time, you are requefted to fend your Orders by the 12th of November.

Almanacks unfold muft be returned by the 28th of February; after which Time they will not be allowed.

FIG. XI.—Broadside, 1793 (*reduced*).

—to print the sheets in such a way that the binder could fold them into books. He proposed further that out of the additional revenue, estimated at £2,500, the Universities should receive £500 each as compensation for their recent losses. In spite of a vigorous protest by Carnan, the Commons approved both proposals.

This additional discouragement to almanack publishing put most of the small men out of the running and left the field almost entirely to Carnan and the Stationers. During the next seven years Carnan steadily improved his position, and he was defeated only by his own mortality—a weakness to which his opponent was not susceptible. He died on July 29, 1788, and three weeks later the Company acquired all his almanack interests for £1,500. The result was immediate; the English Stock handled fewer than 350,000 of the 1788 almanacks, but over half a million of those for 1789, which brought a profit of £1,000. Two years later a general price increase caused no drop in sales and doubled the profit. The doubling of the Stamp Duty in 1797 led to a slight recession but by 1802, after a further increase in prices to offset a rise of 5s a ream in the cost of paper, the profit was over £3,000. Nearly all of this was earned by one famous publication, Francis Moore's *Vox Stellarum*, better known as *Old Moore*. Within a dozen years of Carnan's death the Company was selling a greater number of Moore than of all its almanacks together at the end of Carnan's life. There can be no clearer proof both of the weight of his challenge and of the wisdom in trying to buy him out at the beginning. But beneath this evidence of prosperity there are signs of an ancient weakness; all the old favourites, except Moore, were declining in popularity, and the only almanacks of which the sales increased during the last ten years of the century were the new ones—the County Almanacks taken over from Carnan and listed in the broadsheet reproduced opposite, if Carnan had been bought out in 1774 or 1775, these might not have existed. However, so long as the Stamp Duties were imposed, the English Stock enjoyed once more the enervating advantages of a monopolist, which Lord North had made possible in 1781 and for which his successors provided additional safeguards. Only when the Company petitioned the Chancellor of the Exchequer to take more vigorous action against publishers of unstamped almanacks (the Duty having risen to 1s 3d), did the Government, by now widely criticized for taxation of this kind, decide that the best way to prevent the breaking of the law was not to return to seventeenth-century methods but to do away with the need to break it. In 1834 the Stamp Duties on almanacks were suddenly abolished and the English Stock had to face the cold winds of competition once more. Carnan's bold stand was at last justified.

THE ENGLISH STOCK

The almanack side of the business prospered because and so long as it rested on a monopoly—real or contrived—in a whole *class* of publications. The other side of the business, since it relied on monopolies in individual books—grammars, editions of the classics, metrical versions of the psalms—began to run down earlier; tastes changed and booksellers put more up-to-date publications on the market. By 1830 only five books were being sold from Stationers' Hall; the average sales of these for the years around this date are set against corresponding averages during the previous 100 years:

	1730	1775	1830
Gradus ad Parnassum	675	825	756
ABC	23,500	18,750	500
Greek Testament	350	850	216
Tate and Brady's Psalms*	8,000	10,000	196
Tully's Offices	125	140	78

* In 1766 Mrs Magdalen Barugh claimed, through her father James Holland, a quarter of the copyright in these Singing Psalms and sold it to the English Stock for £300 and an annuity of £100; she lived until 1793!

The surprise is that any demand still remained in the nineteenth century. The list had been kept alive in Stuart times only by the taking over either of other groups of patent books, like the second of Seymour's, or of single titles, like the *Gradus* from Tooke. But it was most unlikely that Midwinter could bring himself, in his capacity as a Stock-keeper, to buy a good 'copy' at a sale or from an author when it meant bidding against himself as a private bookseller. The English Stock list was therefore certain, in due course, to die.

But, as I have already mentioned, there was time during the eighteenth century to build up resources of a different kind. Though most of the new capital came from ploughed-back profits, some was derived from small increases in the number of shares. The following

BOOKS

PRINTED for the

COMPANY of STATIONERS,

And SOLD

At their HALL near *Ludgate-Street*.

	13 *per* Dozen.	l.	s.	d.		13 *per* Dozen.	l.	s.	d.
50	Æsopi Fabulæ, 8°	0	07	0	44	Minellius in Virgil. 12°	1	02	0
45	Bailey's Ovid. Epist. 8°	1	10	0	58	— in Ovidii Metam. 12°	1	02	0
15	Castalionis Dial. 8°	0	07	0	54	— in Ovidii Epistolas, 12°	0	12	0
75	Catechismus Ecclef. Angl. 8°	0	01	3	44	— in Ovidii Tristia, 12°	0	12	0
34	Cato, 8°	0	03	0	36	Ovidii Metamorph. 12°	0	12	0
53	Corderii Colloq. 12°	0	06	0	43	— Epistolæ, 12°	0	12	0
5	English School-master, 4°	0	05	0	56	Ovidius de Tristibus, 12°	0	03	0
52	Florus, 12°	0	07	0	56	— Ditto, Notis Delphini, 8°	0	18	0
106	Gradus ad Parnassum, 8°	1	10	0	68	Possfelii Colloquia, 8°	0	07	0
102	Greek Testament, 12°	1	01	0	33	Sallustius, 12°	0	07	0
64	Hawkins's Spelling-Book, 8°	0	04	0	108	Sententiæ Pueriles, 8°	0	01	6
31	Hoole's Æsop, 8°	0	16	0	60	Sturmii Epistolæ, 8°	0	04	0
106	— Cato, 8°	0	04	0	20	Terentii Comediæ, 8°	0	12	0
19	— Corderius, 8°	0	16	0	83	Textoris Epist. 8°	0	05	0
107-400	— Sententiæ Puer. 8°	0	04	0	39	Tully de Officiis, 8°	0	12	0
24	Justini Historia, 12°	0	07	0	14	— Epist. Select, 8°	0	06	0
36	Nomenclatura brevis, 8°	0	04	0	72	Testament. Nov. Lat. 24°	0	08	0
25	Minellius in Horatium, 12°	1	04	0	42	Testament of Patr. 12°	0	04	0
48	— in Sallustium, 12°	0	16	0	21	Virgilii Opera, 12°	0	12	0
67	— in Terentium, 12°	1	01	0					

	13 *per* Dozen.	l.	s.	d.		13 *per* Dozen.	l.	s.	d.
45	Psalms in Folio, for Service	1	04	0	23	Tate's Psalms Demy Fol.	1	04	0
57	— Ditto, Large Quarto	0	12	0	70	— for 4to Bible	0	12	0
23	— Ditto, Large Paper, Nett.				144	— 8°	0	16	0
	1s. 6d. per Book.				56	— largest 12° for Cambridge Com. Prayer	0	09	0
86	— 8° Pica	0	18	0	426	— 12° for Brev. C. Pr.	0	08	0
502	— 8° Long-primer	0	08	0	493	— 12° for Min. C. Pr.	0	07	0
					1007	— 12° for C. Pr. 24°	0	07	0

	Per Quartern.	l.	s.	d.
225	Psalms in Small Quarto	0	12	0
54	— 8° Minion for Brev. Bible	0	12	0
254	— 8° for Minion Bible	0	08	0

These three following 26 to the Quartern.

		l.	s.	d.
1088	Psalms 12° Nonpareil for Brev. Com. Prayer	0	06	0
910	— 12° Pearl for Min. Com Prayer	0	06	0
676	— Pearl for 24° Com. Pr.	0	06	0

Per Quartern.	l.	s.	d.	
A B C	0	00	8	*1 Rm 149*
Horn-book Prints	0	00	6	*A Rm 128*
Psalters	0	07	0	*11875*

Per Gross.	l.	s.	d.
Assembly Primer	0	12	0
Child's Guide	0	15	0
English Primer	0	12	0

FIG. XII.—Broadside, 1766 (*reduced*).

Table shows the steps by which this policy was carried out and the effect on the Dividend:

Date	Number of shares				Capital	Dividend at 12½%
	£320	£160	£80	£40	£	£
before 1729	15	30	60	0*	14,400†	1,800
1729	15	30	40	40	14,400	1,800
1736	16	32	42	44	15,360	1,920
1747	18	36	46	52	17,280	2,160
1753	19	38	48	56	18,240	2,280
1756	20	40	50	60	19,200	2,400
1759	22	44	54	68	21,120	2,640
1763	24	48	58	76	23,040	2,880
1768	25	50	60	80	24,000	3,000
1770	27	54	68	80	25,920	3,240
1796	29	58	68	96	27,840	3,480
1799	33	66	72	120	31,680	3,960
1803	36	72	78	132	34,560	4,320
1804	38	76	82	140	36,480	4,560
1805	38	76	82	140	41,280‡	5,160

* None officially, but about two dozen in practice.
† From 1611, when the writing up, on the purchase of Abergavenny House and the share in the Londonderry Estate, was complete.
‡ By raising the value of 20 Assistants' shares to £400, of 40 Livery shares to £200, of 40 Yeomanry shares to £100, and of 80 half-Yeomanry shares to £50.

The first move, in 1729, was admirable; the varying number of Yeomanry shares held by two partners was stabilized at forty. The next eight alterations, up to and including that of 1770, were based on the ability of the Stock to pay out more in Dividends and brought in, as partners, 104 more Liverymen than had been able to participate in 1729. But the cost, though calculated, was high; 12½ per cent had to be paid to the new shareholders and 5 per cent was the most that the investments could earn. It would obviously have been wiser to put the new capital into new books or into land; the profits, however, were there and more members of the Company were sharing them. From 1796, on the other hand, the policy was continued for different reasons; cash was needed for the purchase of almanack stamps at twice the previous year's rate, and *no* profit, not even 3 per cent, could be earned on this money. Fortunately *Old Moore* paid handsomely and covered the additional Dividend of £1,920 which the course of action from 1796 necessitated. But rather too much depended on *Old Moore*.

This increase in the number of partners, from 125 in 1729 to 336 in 1804, was almost matched by the increase in the number of Liverymen over the same period;[1] and these interdependent developments are remarkable in two ways. The first is the sheer volume of Livery growth, which no other company could show in the eighteenth century. The second is a revolution in the trade pattern of share-holding and of clothing; the increase occurred in spite of a diminution of the bookselling element in the Company. Whereas at the beginning of the century 40 per cent of the Liverymen and 60 per cent of the partners were booksellers, by 1800 these percentages had fallen to 17 and 23. The proportions of bookbinders and printers (the handicraft elements) in each category had altered little and, apart from a slight increase in shareholding by Liverymen who were not working in the book trade (the result of the Osborne row in the 1740s), the defection of one of the commercial elements had been made good by the growing adherence of the other; the stationers, who were scarcely noticeable as a group in 1700, had taken the places of the departed book-sellers.

The expansion of provincial printing after 1695 and the develop-ment of the newspapers, along with the growing use of paper for general commercial purposes, opened up a vast new market and encouraged a considerable increase in paper manufacture in this country. The supplying of paper soon became a specialized and profitable commercial activity, rather than part of a wealthy book-seller's business, as it had been of George Sawbridge's, or part of the general merchandizing of a Draper or a Haberdasher. What kept within the Stationers' Company this growing body of well-to-do stationers, or induced the outsider like Theodore Janssen to come in, is difficult to decide, for there was no tradition, inherited from the seventeenth century, of external pressure; stationers did not necessarily handle books. The desirability of joint action among themselves and the need to co-operate with printers and booksellers against the duties imposed on paper in Queen Anne's reign may have suggested one advantage which stationers, as a group, might derive from membership

[1] In 1804 the roll of the Livery, including Assistants, totalled 488; the full tally of freemen was probably about 1,500. The shares held by widows—58 in 1804—and by Assistants account for the difference between the total number of partners, 336, and the Liverymen eligible, i.e. those who had fined or served as Renter.

of the Company; early acquisition of a share in the English Stock would provide an appeal to individuals. Several decades passed before the impact of the new body of tradesmen made itself felt in the Company; but when, from about the middle of the century, the pattern of promotion depended less and less on the votes of a Court dominated by booksellers and became more nearly a formality, it was only a question of time before the stationers[1] outstripped first the master printers, who were less strong economically, and then the booksellers, who—as a group—became progressively less interested in their Company.

Why did the London booksellers, whose numbers were increasing and who had as strong inducements as stationers had to become Liverymen and shareholders, drift away from the Stationers' Company? And why was the drift so strong that, at the end of the eighteenth century, there were fewer of them—both relatively and absolutely— who had taken up their freedoms? The first reason was that an apprenticeship of seven years, the standard period from early in the century, was an anomalous mode of entry into a business such as bookselling. There were first-rate men like the Innys brothers and the Longmans to whom parents were still willing to bind their sons for the full term and to pay 100 guineas, or even more, for the benefit of sound training and useful contacts; but the tendency, over the century, was for the premiums asked by booksellers to become smaller and for men to take up their freedoms as booksellers by the expensive method of redemption, even though they had been apprenticed in the normal way; they were probably staying longer at school and were therefore eager to set up on their own when their indentures still had three years or so to run. The Company was prepared, occasionally, to turn a blind eye to this practice and allow a man to take up his freedom by service even though he had married or no longer worked for his master. It gradually became apparent that success as a bookseller could be achieved without seven years' service and even without formal entry into the ranks of the Stationers.

This led to a hardening of attitude, towards outsiders, in a Court of Assistants where the booksellers still had a majority. The refusal,

---

[1] A stationer could be a small shop-keeper in a side street, who sold pennyworths of ink and writing-paper, or a prosperous wholesaler in Cornhill with shares in paper mills. The latter could ask an apprentice's father for a premium of £300 or £350; Thomas Field received £500 in 1775.

in 1752, to admit an orange-merchant, though he brought an order from the Court of Aldermen, is understandable; the refusal three years later to admit Thomas Carnan was probably a tactical error; the motion, carried on April 1, 1760, that service and patrimony were to be the only gates of entry to the Company might have been suicidal. Though the order was modified in 1762 to allow the admission by redemption of those who had served an apprenticeship in the book trade (but not to a Stationer), only six men came in under the rule in a dozen years. The Court at first stuck to this policy when, in April 1772, leading tradesmen—six booksellers and two stationers who were not free of the Company—put forward the common-sense arguments that the continuation of the by-law would increase still further the number of booksellers who were not Stationers (which surely enough occurred), defeat 'the original Intention of Incorporation' and ruin the Company. It took two years for reason to prevail; insistence on association with the book trade was retained but insistence on apprenticeship was dropped. When, in 1787, the wastage became more obvious and the fee was cut from 10 guineas to 5, the number of redemptioners increased; there were ten in 1793–4.

A third discouragement to booksellers was the failure of the Company to play what they regarded as an adequate part in the protection of copyright. Even before the Printing Act lapsed in 1695, London booksellers had begun to rely on their own devices—combinations among wholesalers and joint ownership of profitable 'copies',[1] and the booksellers were more active than the Company in lobbying for the Act of Queen Anne. When in February 1774 their interpretation of the Act was proved wrong they planned a 'United Company' of copyright owners 'for the preservation of the Trade, and the security of Literary Property'. The plan was not carried out in its original form but it shows the attitude of the enterprising booksellers. Printers and stationers were expected to form a small proportion of the 100 partners and were to be excluded from the committee of management. The overwhelming majority among the 100 were to be booksellers; but in the ten years from 1769 to 1779 only thirty-three booksellers bound apprentices at Stationers' Hall—fewer even than in the last ten years of the century. Men like John Murray and Joseph Lackington prospered in their businesses without membership of the

---

[1] For these 'Congers', see *The Notebook of Thomas Bennet and Henry Clements*, Oxford, 1956, pp. 67 ff. referred to above, p. 175, n.

Stationers', or of any other, Company; and out of forty-six partners whose names appear on the title-page of the *Works* of Samuel Johnson (1792), less than half were Stationers and only four of the rest were Liverymen of other companies.

APPRENTICESHIP

The gradual replacement of booksellers by stationers—among Liverymen, among partners in the English Stock and among masters binding apprentices—had reached, in 1800, the point where power in the governing body was almost equally divided between these two groups of tradesmen. Meanwhile the other two groups had been supporting the Company in their own ways. The bookbinders maintained their small pieces of ground and were the most consistent in demanding premiums (averaging about £10) with their apprentices; they never had a representative on the Court. The printers, on the other hand, though they preserved their small proportions in the Livery and the English Stock (which, even in 1700, were smaller than when the Printers' Company was mooted in the 1660s) lost ground on the Court; in 1800 there were only three. But they kept the apprenticeship system very much alive; in the last ten years of the century 167 different masters bound 489 apprentices, nearly half the total number. From at least as early as 1713 journeymen had been allowed to bind boys and from about the same date the old limitation in the number permitted to each master had not been strictly observed. With this second relaxation of the rules had disappeared the illicit use of scriveners' indentures. Moreover, so long as the letter of City custom were observed—the master must be a freeman of the City and an apprentice must not be presented for his freedom under the age of twenty-one—the Company permitted printers, as well as booksellers, a modest disregard of the spirit. Thomas Gent was bound in 1710 at the age of seventeen, the proper age according to William Bowyer; after three years he found work in various printing houses, not only in London but in Dublin and York; seven years almost to a day from the date of his indentures his master made him free by service. In 1757 John Nichols began working with Bowyer before he was quite thirteen; at fourteen he was formally apprenticed and a year before he could be free he was acting as Bowyer's right-hand man; on the day of his freedom his master returned half the premium of £20—a normal practice when apprentices had behaved well.

An increase in the number of apprentices, even though 60 per cent never took up their freedoms, inevitably led to an increase in the number of journeymen.[1] As in earlier periods this body of men was keenly interested in the strict observance of apprenticeship rules. After a petition in 1773 the Court condemned the practice (begun over thirty years earlier) of paying wages to an apprentice instead of housing and feeding him; and it ruled that no journeyman would be allowed an apprentice unless he were able to maintain him in accordance with the terms of the indentures. The number, however, of 'outdoor' apprentices grew, and with this growth went the recruitment of boys of inferior education from families which could afford no premiums. Four broad generalizations can be made about the apprentices of Stationers (and their origins) during the eighteenth century. The first is that the proportion of those from London steadily increased. The second is that the number of those whose fathers were dead declined to an equal extent. The third is that the marked connection, both consanguineous and professional, between the Church and the book trade in the seventeenth century had turned into a similar association between lawyers and the Stationers in Fleet Street and Chancery Lane. The fourth is that, whereas illiteracy among Stationers was almost unknown in the seventeenth century, in the eighteenth it was not uncommon among printers' apprentices. When Bowyer made his will in 1777 he bewailed 'that such Numbers are put Apprentices as Compositors without any share of School-learning, who ought to have the greatest'; and he bequeathed, besides £5,000 to provide nine pensions for aged printers, the dividend from £1,000 for a journeyman compositor who was able to construe Latin and read Greek. William Strahan, another printer, made no testamentary comments on the educational qualifications of printers, but left £1,000 to provide pensions for five English and five Scottish journeymen, the second group of whom need not be Stationers. These special provisions for printers were designed to offset the decision of 1769 (already referred to) by which all the pensions of £3 and above were to be reserved for Liverymen and their widows. The total pay-out for

[1] As early as 1734 the rules which governed the Chapels in printing houses acknowledged three classes of journeymen: (1) those free of the Stationers' Company; (2) those who had been apprenticed in the Company but who had not taken up their freedoms; and (3) those who had not even been bound. This document is quoted by Howe, op. cit., p. 32.

charity mounted steadily—with such legacies from successful printers like Bowyer and Strahan—and by 1800 was over £600.[1]

THE STATUS OF THE COMPANY

Only part of this passed through normal corporation channels, i.e. through the hands of the Under Warden. His accounts were recording receipts and payments of around £1,000 a year. Opposite is a sample from the middle of the century—the account for 1756–7 kept by Jacob Tonson, the great-nephew of one of the most famous of booksellers—in which less than 10 per cent of the expenditure shown is on charity.

The two important variations from the Wardens' Accounts for 1663–4[2] are the absence of loan money (which I shall deal with in the next chapter) and the presence of Renter Warden fines. The second item was exceptional even for the eighteenth century and accounts for the large credit balance. Four years later the balance was under £14; with the continued growth in the size of the Livery and the consequent rise in the cost of the Livery dinner (£221 was made up to the Renters in 1798) the Wardens were regularly overspent. With the English Stock behind it, the corporation saw no necessity to limit expenditure by receipts, and from 1798 the Treasurer was ordered to pay £200 to each new Under Warden; this was a less extravagant arrangement than the 'footing' of Company bills, which had cost the Stock over £2,000 in the previous eight years.

Once again the English Stock demonstrates its overwhelming importance in the life of the Stationers' Company. It reinforced the association between the corporation and the traditional trades by providing work for some printers and good business for some booksellers; it fostered a loyalty to the gild as the only means of entry into a trading partnership which earned the equivalent of its capital in eight years. Each of these pressures acted, in a qualitative way, to maintain a community of interest at a time when such a bond had almost ceased to exist in other companies; and the second worked,

[1] £200 from the English Stock; £180 from Bowyer; about £50 each from Theophilus Cater, Thomas Guy and Thomas Wright; £40 from Strahan; and various smaller bequests. The total in mid-century was something over £300. In addition, some apprentices were assisted through the payment of their premiums by parochial and private charities and from organizations like the Drapers' Company, Christ's Hospital and the Sons of the Clergy.
[2] Set out on p. 182 above.

quantitatively, to increase the number of Stationers at a time when the Liveries of other companies were in decline. On the strength of these two tendencies the Company began to play a part in City politics which would have astonished earlier Stationers. In the seventeenth century Thomas Davies was the only freeman of the Company to become Lord Mayor, and he had to be translated to the Grocers before he could serve his term.[1] In the following hundred years only

WARDENS' ACCOUNTS, JULY 6, 1756, TO JULY 5, 1757

Receipts	£	s	d
By balance from Warden's Accounts 1755–6	87	18	5
,, cash received from Renter Wardens		19	6
,, presenting of apprentices, 76 at 5s each	19	0	0
,, turning over ,, 9 at 2s 6d each	1	2	6
,, admission of freemen, 40 at 4s 6d each	9	0	0
,, Livery fines, 12 at £20 each	240	0	0
,, Renter Warden fines, 21 at £24 each	504	0	0
,, Warden fines, 1 at £11 & 1 at £6	17	0	0
,, interest on investments	25	10	0
,, bequest money	7	6	8
,, rents from corporation houses and warehouses	197	16	0
	£1,109	13	1

Disbursements	£	s	d
To wages, including barge master and crew	65	5	0
,, repairs to property	231	3	0
,, repairs to barge	7	19	0
,, contributions towards feasts	67	2	0
,, rates and taxes	75	11	0
,, legal expenses	5	0	6
,, entertainment	61	18	8
,, sermons	25	4	8
,, charity, from bequests (Theophilus Cater's, etc.)	55	17	6
,, parish dues and tithes	23	10	0
,, quit rents, etc.	2	1	4
,, annuities, on money received by the Company	22	0	0
,, miscellaneous expenditure	23	13	8½
,, balance paid to John Clarke, Under Warden 1757–8	443	6	8½
	£1,109	13	1

[1] 1676.

John Barber and Theodore Janssen held this office. But from 1785 to 1831 the Lord Mayor was a Stationer on nine occasions, an average of once every five years.[1] Such a succession of ambitious men, powerful enough and rich enough to achieve their ambitions, underlines the strength and prosperity of the book trade in London and the pre-eminence of the Company associated with that trade. Moreover, the Company was confident in its standing. The sixteen gentlemen from his own gild, who attended a Lord Mayor at his entering upon and concluding his year of office, normally proceeded on foot; in 1785 and 1786 the Stationers insisted on accompanying Thomas Wright in coaches, in spite of protests from the Joiners and the Bowyers. In 1788, when William Gill became Lord Mayor, the Glovers agreed to coaches without a murmur; if Thomas Carnan was accustomed to driving, so were the Assistants whom he nearly defeated.

[1] The Clothworkers' Company, by way of contrast, provided the Lord Mayor on fourteen occasions before 1676, but on only eight occasions since. (Thomas Girtin, *The Golden Ram*, 1958, p. 323).

CHAPTER XIII

SIGNS OF OLD AGE

THE Stationers' Company entered the nineteenth century on a wave of prosperity. Rents were rising and the almanack business flourished on the popularity of *Old Moore*. The dispute between the master printers and their journeymen boosted the intake of apprentices; in thirty months from March 1805 John McArthur alone bound forty-seven. Even booksellers were taking up their freedoms more frequently; in the course of 1815 three names which are famous in the book trade—William Simpkin, Richard Marshall and William Budd Whitaker—appeared in the register as freemen by redemption. Moreover, the Livery, supported in the main by tradesmen other than printers, grew so steadily that it was thought expedient in 1809 to raise the fine to £50, and in the following year the number of Liverymen reached the record figure of 517—a size 'productive of many inconveniences', the chief of which was that a large number of Liverymen never achieved more than a £40 share in the English Stock. Though it was deemed inadvisable to deny the clothing to those who were not in the book trade, these 'outsiders' had been asked, from 1803, to sign 'disclaimers' of any right of election as partners.[1] The legality of this practice was questioned from time to time but, up to 1825, an average of two a year chose to sign rather than to remain in the Yeomanry, and the last signature was in 1862. These Liverymen had also signed away their chances of election to the Court, for they were not called upon to serve or fine for the office of Renter Warden, the turnstile for shareholders; they formed, along with those who were not ambitious for, or too poor to pay for, promotion, that section of the Livery which is known as Rotten Row. Such treatment of potentially useful members of the Company was a sign of considerable confidence; further signs were increases, from 1817, in the fines paid

---

[1] See below, p. 258, for comments on this practice. Type-founders were not counted as members of the book trade until 1845.

by Assistants. On election[1] a new member of the Court had to contribute £20 to the Company and £3 to the poor box, and anyone desiring to avoid office had to pay £200 for all the offices still open to him—that is, no one could in future fine for either or both the Wardenships and then enjoy the honour of being Master.[2]

But old-fashioned prosperity and vigorous middle-aged vitality were no protection for the Stationers against an attack on the City companies generally. The first objectives of the assault were the charities which, it was said, were being incompetently—or even dishonestly—managed. To test the truth of the allegations, Commissioners were appointed by Act of Parliament[3] to enquire into and report fully upon the charities administered by the Livery Companies of London. On June 6, 1820, the Clerk explained to the Court of the Stationers' Company that he had had to give evidence before the Commissioners without being able to obtain proper authority; but, although nothing else recordable occurred (except the decision in 1822 to increase the Clerk's salary by £20 for his extra work on the Company's legacies) until the Report dealing with the Stationers was signed in 1829,[4] the intervening years were a period of anxiety because, as I hinted in the last chapter, there were misapplications of funds to account for.

The Commissioners found that the Stationers' Company was employing a high proportion of the money bequeathed to it in the ways laid down by the benefactors; but they had no difficulty in discovering that bequests from William Norton, George Bishop, John Norton, Christopher Meredith and Evan Tyler[5] had for a long time been absorbed in the general funds of the Company instead of being used for loans to young Stationers. The Commissioners did not include in their report an estimate of the Company's accumulated liability, but it would have been easy enough for them to calculate

[1] Apart from the opportunity of holding the highest denomination shares in the English Stock (£320 and £400) the rewards were meagre; the fees for Court or committee attendance went up from 10s 6d to 21s in 1820 and, after several temporary increases, to 42s in 1891. In spite of this, hardly anyone refused election in the first half of the century and only fifteen in the second half.

[2] For a dozen less prosperous years from 1851 this fine was reduced to £105.

[3] As part of a general survey of the relief of poverty. The Acts were 58 Geo. III c. 91, 59 Geo. III c. 81, 5 Geo. IV c. 58 and 10 Geo. IV c. 57, 1818 to 1830.

[4] Published in 1830, by House of Commons order of March 11th, as the 22nd Report.

[5] £6 13s 4d *per annum* from William Norton, through Christ's Hospital; £6 from George Bishop (part of the rent from Newton Farm); £50 from John Norton; £10 from Christopher Meredith, and a capital sum of £500 from Evan Tyler to lend to ten Stationers for four years each.

that, if the small annual sums had been credited to a loan account over a period of 150 years, the value of the account would have grown to over £11,000. What made the liability appear even greater was that the property in Wood Street which had been bought with John Norton's £1,000 (made up to £1,200 from other sources),[1] brought in £400 a year, eight times the original interest.

It is possible that there were grounds in the third quarter of the seventeenth century for discontinuing the loans, which were irritatingly difficult to recover; and it is understandable that the officers in the 1820s would do everything to suggest that the Company was paying more to its poor than it was legally obliged to do. In a list of 'Charitable Donations', reprinted by a Court order of December 18, 1818, the proceeds of John Norton's £1,000 are 'to be applied, by the Master, Wardens, and Assistants, at their discretion, for the benefit of poor members of the Company. This benevolent Testator's intentions are substantially fulfilled'. The Commissioners, since they did not discover that the English Stock was the source of the £200 paid in annuities to the poor, assumed that this money derived largely from the increased Wood Street rents, the future application of which 'seems to be a fit subject for the consideration of a court of equity'.

This was sufficient for the Attorney-General, Sir James Scarlett; in a petition to the Lord Chancellor of December 1829,[2] he summarized the particulars certified by the Commissioners, maintained that the appropriation of loan money by the Company was clearly a breach of trust, and prayed that, until orders were made by a Master in Chancery, separate accounts should be kept. The Master of the Rolls, at the hearing on May 29, 1830,[3] argued that it was impossible to tell, at this distance of time, what had happened to Tyler's £500, that the present governing body was acting according to the practice of its predecessors and that it would therefore be unfair to take into account the Wood Street rents (whatever their value) and the three other loan charities (at their original value) before the filing of the information on May 4th; with these premises he made his order in 1833 that the Company was to prepare a scheme for the making of loans out of the money as at present received.

[1] See above, p. 210.

[2] On a copy of this document at Stationers' Hall there is a pencilled note which suggests that one reader thought 170 years had passed since the terms of William Norton's bequest had been properly observed.

[3] City of London Livery Companies Commission, 1884, vol. v, pp. 278 ff., reprints the 1864 report of the Inspector of Charities, Thomas Hare, who quotes this opinion.

THE STATIONERS' COMPANY'S SCHOOL

Nearly twenty years passed before, on January 9, 1852, the Solicitor to the Attorney-General suggested that the establishment of a school, out of the ample funds then at the Company's disposal, would be more likely to meet with official approval than the building of alms-houses—the fashionable solution, towards which the Stationers had refused a gift of £300 in 1845 as being against their policy! At its meeting in February the Court accepted the idea of a school and appointed a sub-committee,which reported in March that £5,316 16s 1d was available from accumulated funds for building.[1] After this burst of activity the Company had to wait for over five years before it learned that the scheme would be approved.[2] The Court, having agreed that the school should be in the vicinity of large printing offices, resolved to give up to £6,000 for Mr Tyler's (late Bensley's) printing house in Bolt Court and on January 12, 1858, £5,750 was paid. On May 4th adjacent premises in Hole in the Wall Court (very close to the meeting-place of the journeymen printers in the dispute with the masters fifty years before) were bought at auction for £260. Later, the site was extended on the western side by the purchase of a freehold in Johnson's Court.

The Assistants, particularly under the Mastership of John Dickinson, responded generously, in both money and time, to extending the newly-acquired premises, to making them more suitable for educational purposes and to drawing up a set of rules. The school was intended primarily for the sons of Liverymen and freemen of the

---

[1] I am not clear how this figure was reached. The Wardens' Accounts for 1851–2 are the first to show a sum set aside under the Chancery order; this is calculated from Michaelmas 1850 and made up as follows:

	£	s	d
20/24 (i.e. that proportion of the original purchase price which was John Norton's £1,000) of the rents from 11, 12 and 13 Wood Street, less certain allowances	243	7	6
due from William Norton's bequest for loans	6	0	0
„ „ George Bishop's „ „ „	6	0	0
„ „ Christopher Meredith's „ „ „	9	1	8
	£264	9	2

If this sum had been set aside annually since the order of 1833, it would, with interest, have amounted to about £5,300.

[2] Formal approval did not come until February 11, 1858, when the annual income was laid down as £504 18s 5d; the proportion of Wood Street rents was given as £251 5s and the interest on £7,752 19s Consols (origin obscure) as £232 11s 9d.

6 *The barge near Syon House in 1829*

Company, 'not afflicted with any contagious disease or convicted of any crime' (the ambiguity is in the original scheme), and not less than seven years old, at a quarterly fee of 6s. Among the subjects to be taught were Land Surveying, Book-keeping, Drawing and Designing; the hours were to be from 9 a.m. to noon and from 2 to 4 p.m., with half-holidays on Wednesdays and Saturdays. On February 5, 1861, Andrew Kennedy Isbister, whose printed application is a most impressive document, was elected Headmaster with fourteen votes against a Mr Bensley's none; and on April 8th the school opened. From the beginning it prospered; in 1869 a third classical master was added to the staff and the annual fees for the sons of non-freemen were raised from £5 to £7. In thirty years the school outgrew the original premises and early in 1892 a two-acre site at Hornsey was bought for £3,375; plans for a building costing £13,000[1] were approved by the Charity Commissioners and on October 2, 1894, the present school was opened.

THE LIVERY COMPANIES' COMMISSION

While the Stationers were still, in 1833, trying to adjust themselves to the order in Chancery, made as a result of the first attack on the companies, a second general assault was launched on a wider front. As part of the movement for political reform, Commissioners were appointed[2] to enquire into the structure and operation of municipal corporations; and the Livery Companies of London, since they controlled the franchise for both City and Parliamentary elections, were also to be subject to enquiry. In October the Clerk and a sub-committee of the Court of the Stationers' Company waited on Sir Francis Palgrave, one of the Commissioners, and, on the strength of the discussion with him, made a return of the existing form and activities of the Company against the background of its original purpose and intervening history. On March 12, 1834, the Commissioners asked all the companies to furnish in writing a large number of particulars. The Stationers ignored both the circular request and a reminder to them on June 3rd, on the ground that they had already supplied the required information; and they refused to send a delegation to answer questions. Sir Francis found, however, on October 30th that, though

---

[1] £8,250 was found towards this by the sale of the Bolt Court buildings to the City of London Parochial Charities.   [2] By writ of Privy Seal, July 18, 1833.

the Master, Wardens and Clerk failed to appear before him, Mr Joseph Baker, an engraver and a member of the Court of Assistants, was there to answer for them.[1] Most of the time was taken up by a discussion of the 'disclaimers' to shares in the English Stock which those not in the book trade were expected to sign before being clothed. Mr Woodthorpe, the Town Clerk, complained bitterly, in giving evidence, that he was not able freely to join the Livery of the Company of which he was free by patrimony; and Mr R. G. Pead, referred to by Joseph Baker as 'a seller of ham and beef', wrote to *The Times* to explain that, having served his time with Richard Taylor, a printer in Shoe Lane, and presented himself in 1827 for the clothing, he was advised by the Beadle, in the presence of the Clerk, to say 'yes' when he was asked in Court if he worked in the book trade; and that he preferred forgoing the Livery to telling a lie.

At a meeting of the Assistants on November 4th, the Clerk was instructed to protest to Sir Francis Palgrave against his statements, reported in the press, that the Company had refused to appear before him, and to remind him of a previous attendance and the supply of information. This is the last reference to the Commissioners (except for one brief communication a year later) until the Report was published in 1837.[2] From this emerges the point I made in the last chapter, that the Stationers' Company had changed, in the previous three hundred years, much less in purpose and composition than most of the others. Only one—the Carmen's—was exclusively composed of men employed in the trade suggested by its name, but it had admitted only 108 freemen during the first thirty-three years of the nineteenth century.[3] The Apothecaries were the next most exclusive and were still very active; about 6,000 freemen had been enrolled during the same period—over twice as many as in the Stationers' Company; but of these only about two a year came in by patrimony and none since 1825 by redemption. Among twenty-two companies which still claimed the right, and the ability, to enforce membership on all those engaged in certain occupations in the City, were (besides the Carmen and the Apothecaries) the Innholders; but nearly half of these were not innholders and only seven of the twenty-four Assistants were; moreover,

[1] *The Times*, October 31, 1834.
[2] By House of Commons order of April 25th. The generalizations which follow are taken from pp. 18 and 19 of the Report.
[3] Thirty-two by service, 47 by patrimony and 29 by redemption. See Appendix I for the Stationers' Company's figures.

a high proportion of the freemen came in by redemption.[1] The Apothecaries and the Goldsmiths were the only companies to operate an efficient control over their respective trades. The Apothecaries, the Stationers and the Gunmakers alone exercised supervision which bore some relation to the purpose for which they had been founded; and the last admitted fewer than three freemen a year.[2]

INTEREST IN THE COMPANY'S HISTORY

The weakest part of the Stationers' section in the Report is the historical, but it may be that the most stimulating result of the Commissioners' enquiries—and, so far as I can discover, there was no harmful result beyond the unlooked-for publicity—was a renewal of an interest in the origins and ancient functions of the companies. Fifty years earlier scholars like Thomas Warton, Edmund Malone and George Steevens, who were curious about Elizabethan literature rather than about gild history, had obtained permission to study, and even to borrow, the first register of copies. But on July 4, 1780, three months after John Noorthouck—a Liveryman of the Company—had been voted £80 for indexing the Court Books and Liber A, William Herbert, who was working on a new edition of Ames's *Typographical Antiquities*, was allowed to take away the record books one at a time. He saw the value of studying Company policy and he transcribed, along with the entries in the registers, Wardens' Accounts and many extracts from the Court Books and Liber A.[3] He died in 1790 without writing anything about the Stationers, but John Nichols included a short account of his Company in *Literary Anecdotes of the Eighteenth Century* (1812–15). Interest then temporarily waned and was rekindled in a more general way. In 1834 another William Herbert, Librarian to the Corporation, hurriedly finished and published the first volume of his *History of the Twelve Great Livery Companies of London*, partly because he did not trust the Commissioners to check the accounts supplied to them by the clerks of the companies and partly because

[1] The average annual intake was about 70; in no year were more than 11 admitted by service or 7 by patrimony.

[2] In 33 years 51 by service, and 22 each by patrimony and redemption.

[3] The three little volumes of his transcript were in the possession of George Chalmers and at least one other scholar before finding their way back to Stationers' Hall, where they now are. But one of them, labelled C, was offered for sale just over twenty years ago by Galloway and Porter, from whom it was bought and generously returned to its home by William A. Jackson.

the publicity given to the Commission would help his book; he published the second volume in 1837, the year of the Report. On March 1, 1842, George Woodfall[1] proposed and Charles Baldwin seconded a motion that a committee be appointed to examine the records of the Stationers' Company and to report on publishing 'such Particulars of its Literary and other History as may be likely to prove interesting to the Reading Public and which may be found not injurious to the interests, or derogatory to the dignity of the Company'. An 'open' committee, which any Assistant was entitled to attend, was charged to look into this matter and to 'point out a Gentleman for Editor on whose experience, ability, integrity and honour the Court may place the most implicit reliance'. On May 3rd the Assistants, having debated the committee's report in which Charles Rivington, the Clerk, offered to do the work if no professional could be found, resolved that the history should be written and that the Clerk should write it. There is no evidence of the progress of this scheme, but in 1847 John Payne Collier made a second transcript of the register of copies, extracts from which he published through the Shakespeare Society in the two following years.[2] John Gough Nichols, the grandson of John Nichols, kept the antiquarian tradition alive with a paper read at Stationers' Hall on April 12, 1860,[3] and ten years later the Early English Text Society revived the literary approach with a proposal to publish a complete transcript of the registers up to 1700 under the joint editorship of F. J. Furnivall and C. R. Rivington, who had become Clerk in 1869 when Charles Rivington was elected to the Court. Furnivall and his Society soon gave up the monumental task and Edward Arber stepped in. His worry was not the magnitude of his own labour but the difficulty of publishing the results and, after a break of twelve months when C. R. Rivington worked alone on yet another transcript of the registers, Arber issued his proposals on October 8, 1873, for publication by subscription; this led to the five magnificent volumes which appeared between 1875 and 1894.

Unfortunately for Arber the governing body interpreted Woodfall's resolution of 1842 in too strict a manner and withheld from him

---

[1] In December 1827, he had obtained permission to borrow the Court Books one at a time.

[2] It is almost certain that Collier used his access to the registers for adding, in the originals, small pieces of evidence to support his theories of authorship; these additions had been missed by Herbert sixty-five years earlier! See Franklin Dickey, 'The Old Man at Work: Forgeries in the Stationers' Registers', *Shakespeare Quarterly*, New York, xi, 1960.

[3] Published in the *Transactions of the London and Middlesex Archæological Society*, vol. 2, 1861.

permission to transcribe the records of the Court and even to see the contents of Liber A; he was, however, allowed to reprint a paper by C. R. Rivington which draws on this material and which underlines— in various ways—the mistake of denying it to Arber. The original plan to bring the entries of copies up to 1700 was completed only when G. E. Briscoe Eyre, King's Printer and Master of the Company in 1912, printed, from a transcript made by H. R. Plomer, three further volumes.[1] It was not until 1930 that the proceedings of the Court to 1602 were published (under the editorship of Sir Walter Greg) and not until 1957 that the records, including the relevant portion of Liber A, were brought up to 1640 by William A. Jackson.[2]

BREAKS WITH THE PAST

I can find no evidence that the Company, after the initial burst of enthusiasm in 1842, showed any corporate interest in its own history— save in one quite unimportant part of it which was deliberately brought to an end in 1849. On December 4th the Assistants resolved that it was 'inexpedient to retain the use' of the Company's barge and in the following April accepted Mr Hall's offer for it of 100 guineas; it spent the remainder of its life as an Oxford college boat-house, moored on the Isis at the foot of Christ Church meadows. The story of this one and its predecessors can be briefly told. Not till after the restoration of Charles II did the Stationers' Company play an independent part in the river pageantry of the City;[3] in the summer of 1662 a barge was hired for Liverymen to accompany the King and Queen from Hampton Court to Whitehall; not until June 1679 did members of the Livery raise £187 to buy a barge of their own. Surprisingly little use was made of it during those months of the year when river trips might have been pleasant; it was usually at the October Court that orders were given for it to be launched and trimmed against the procession by water to Westminster on Lord Mayor's Day. From the early part of the eighteenth century the barge was used on the same occasion by

[1] 1913–14; the last entry is for March 1709, about a year before the Copyright Act of Queen Anne came into force.

[2] These two volumes were sponsored and published by the Bibliographical Society. Most of the entries in Liber A before 1603 have not yet been printed.

[3] The only previous reference to a barge is the following memorandum against a precept of October 28, 1629 (copied into Liber A), from the Lord Mayor about conduct on the river: 'The Statonrs neu' attended wth any Bardge.'

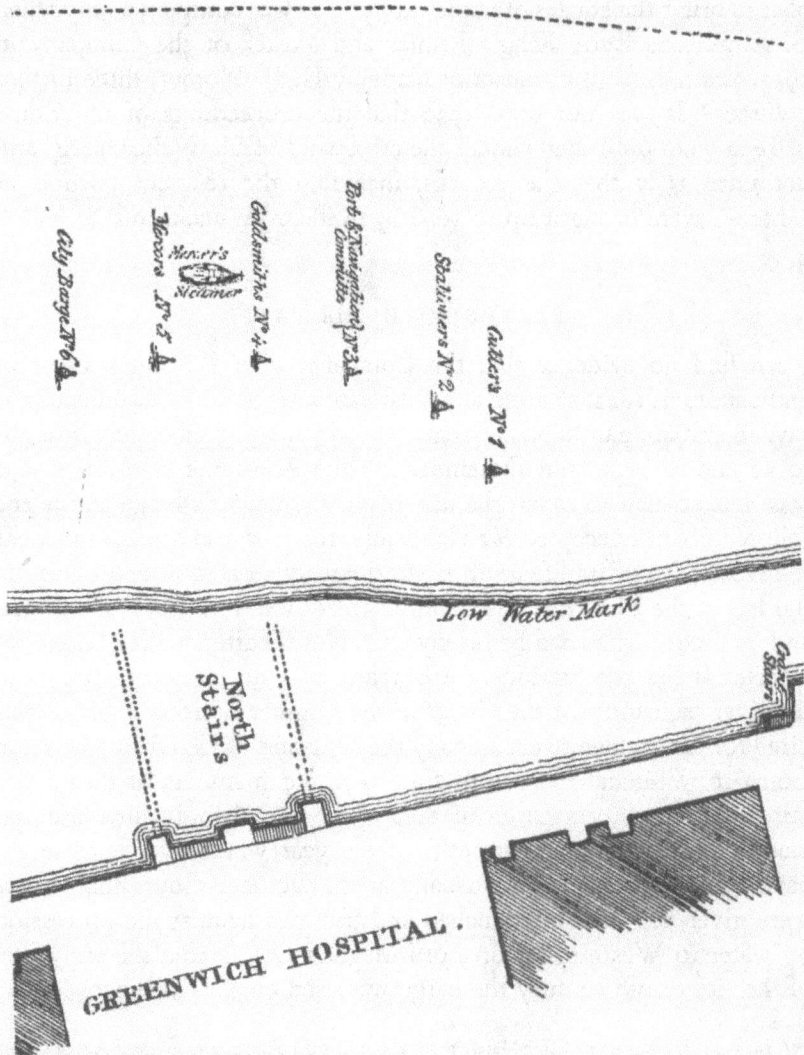

THAMES.

City Barge N°6

Havers N°5

Goldsmiths N°4

Havers Steamer

Lort K:Knightlon's Committee N°3

Stationers N°2

Gallies N°1

Low Water Mark

North Stairs

GREENWICH HOSPITAL.

FIG. XIII.—Part of the instructions, for the stationing of barges on the King's visit to Greenwich in 1835, issued by the Company of Watermen.

the delegation which waited every year on the Archbishop of Canterbury with copies of the new almanacks; in return the Archbishop sent down to the steps at Lambeth a hamper of wine for the Assistants and bread, cheese and ale for the Barge Master, his mate and the eighteen oarsmen. One further employment was found; from 1777 the Assistants and their ladies made an annual expedition by river in June to dine at the Star and Garter, Richmond. The expenditure of £700 on a new barge in the 1760s and the vast number of entries in the indexes to the Court Books indicate how important the subject appeared; it is therefore not surprising to find a resolution on July 2, 1825, 'That it is expedient that this Company shall continue to have and use a State Barge', followed by an order in August for a new one, estimated to cost nearly £2,000. On Saturday November 6, 1830, the Clerk of the Watermen's Company issued his usual printed instructions for the procedure on the following Tuesday. The Stationers were to lead the procession of twelve from Blackfriars Steps and anchor with five others on the Lambeth side, the rest anchoring on the Westminster side.[1] By 1834 the number of barges had dropped to six, and for the King's landing at Greenwich on August 1, 1835, there were only four; after 1849 even the Stationers had given up.

Seven years later an Act of Common Council formally ended another of the City traditions by abolishing all the laws and customs which put any limitation on the right to trade by retail or to exercise a handicraft. This, of course, merely regularized a disregard of rules which the expansion of London outside the City limits had made impossible to enforce; but it was a belated attempt to make adjustments for changed conditions. In 1858 the Court of the Stationers' Company, acting on the same principle, authorized the Clerk to obtain City approval for varying the length of service in apprentices' indentures to suit the parties concerned. I can, however, find no evidence of departure from the formal seven years, until, in 1889, another Act of Common Council legalized, for outdoor apprentices only, both the payment of

---

[1]
1. Stationers*
2. Apothecaries
3. Tallow-chandlers
4. Clothworkers
5. Vintners
6. Ironmongers

7. Merchant Tailors*
8. Skinners*
9. Goldsmiths*
10. Fishmongers*
11. Drapers
12. Grocers*

Those with * survived to 1834; the Merchant Tailors and Fishmongers had dropped out by 1835. In 1830 Sir John Key, a Stationer, was Lord Mayor.

wages and the shortening of their periods of service. For the first time, on May 7th, a young man was indentured as a 'stationer and printer' for five years, with a weekly wage which began at 10s and finished at 19s. The wages of seven-year apprentices varied from 4s to 8s in the first and from 16s to 20s in the last year, according rather to private arrangements than to the branch of printing to be learnt.

Although, as Appendix I shows, the number of apprentices bound at Stationers' Hall remained throughout the century at a remarkably high level, the number of those who took up their freedoms—through any channel—declined. As early as 1834, while the Commissioners were making their investigations, the Court was worried about this falling off and on May 6th decided that, in order to encourage more members of the book trade to buy their freedoms, the redemption fee, fixed at £15 in 1796, should be halved but that the rule about trades should still be observed.[1] What the Court acknowledged—by implication, at least—was that the old relationship between the number of apprentices and the number admitted to freedom had almost disappeared; that apprentices were, in the main, printers (stationers being a poor but steady second); that, as a result of the eighteenth-century attitude to the Yeomanry, it was not worth while for a compositor to take up his freedom by service unless he could afford, at some time, to be clothed;[2] and that the Livery, which had been considered uncomfortably high in 1801, might become uncomfortably low unless the number of redemptioners was maintained. The fear about the decrease in the Livery came out into the open in 1867 when the total had dropped to 333, and on April 2nd the Court decided that in future no Liveryman, whatever his trade, should be debarred from serving or fining as Renter Warden and thereby qualifying for election to a share in the English Stock. This relaxation at first slowed up the rate of decrease, and in 1880 the total was 312. Confidence was strong in that year for on May 4th the Court reaffirmed the ancient custom that Assistants (whatever businesses Liverymen might engage in) must be elected from active members of the book trade; and it also increased most of the fees which a man might be called upon to pay during his career as a

[1] As late as June 3, 1902, an order was made that applications for freedom by redemption would be considered only from principals in limited and other companies trading as booksellers, publishers, printers, type-founders, paper-makers, engravers, bookbinders and other cognate trades, and would be subject to Court approval.

[2] In spite of this there were, according to a return made to the Town Clerk in 1845, still 1,405 freemen outside the Livery; of these only 161 were householders in the City.

Stationer.[1] This second action once more accelerated the downward movement of the Livery, and by 1897 the number was 246, the lowest in the last two centuries; only twenty Liverymen stood below the Renter Wardens.

Parallel with these modifications in the structure of the Company went changes which brought to an end some part of the life of the Company and which mark the otherwise imperceptible slither into old age. I have already mentioned the sale of the barge in 1850; half a dozen years earlier the efficiency of the City Fire Service allowed the Company's fire-engine—but not the hoses—to be disposed of. In 1874 the City acquired the Dark House[2] for the Billingsgate Market development, and in the following year the Company sold to the Skinners its share in the Pellipar Estate, part of the seventeenth-century plantation of Londonderry; £48,000 was asked in June and £40,000 was accepted in September. In 1884 the Court formally abolished quarterage[3] and three years later relieved the Renter Wardens of their remaining obligations for the Livery dinner in November, on the grounds that they no longer had accounts to keep.[4] In 1835 the Court had, at the second attempt, decreed that new members of the Company, by service or patrimony, pay an additional 30s for their freedoms and be excused quarterage so long as they remained without shares in the English Stock. The arguments for this change were that the average amount collected by the Renters in recent years had been only about £100 and that over 750 members of the Company owed over £800 between them. By 1870 the quarterage paid up was £41 and in the last year of its life £32 16s.

A far more drastic and significant termination occurred in February 1883 when the Treasurership of the English Stock, as a full-time and salaried office, was abolished and Joseph Greenhill was pensioned off after sixty-four years of service at Stationers' Hall in one capacity or

---

[1] Freedom by service or patrimony, from £3 10s to £5
    „   „   redemption   „ £25 „ £30
Clothing   „ £60 „ £70
Assistant by ordinary election   „ £60 „ £80
    „   on election as Alderman „ £120 „ £150

[2] See above, p. 224.

[3] Still nominally 1s 4d a year for the Yeomanry, 2s for Liverymen and 2s 8d for Assistants.

[4] In October 1881 it had cut down the Court dinners from six to four (on the first Tuesdays in April, May and June and on December 1st), and had laid charges of £40 and £20 respectively on the Master and the Wardens instead of their paying for a dinner. The Livery dinners remained in July and November, and to the latter Liverymen could bring a guest each, according to seniority, until the number dining reached 150.

another.[1] He had succeeded his father in 1849 when the old man had retired after fifty-two years as Treasurer. Between them they watched the Stock slide from the table-land of prosperity around 1800 far down the lower slopes towards the bankruptcy of a profitable publishing business. There was little they could do about it; the vulnerability of the English Stock was apparent back in the eighteenth century and, among the Assistants, forces of conservatism—to give them their mildest description—were too strong in the nineteenth.

THE DECLINE OF THE ENGLISH STOCK

The first crisis came with the abolition of the Stamp Duties in 1834. On August 4th George Woodfall and Charles Baldwin (who were responsible for the proposal that the history of the Company should be written) were deputed, with John Richardson, to advise the Stock Board on future plans. The price of *Old Moore* for 1835 was reduced to 6d; the *Lady's* and the *Gentleman's Diaries* were increased by twenty-four pages each and White's by sixteen; and three new almanacks at 1s each were added to the list: the *Evangelical*, the *Medical*, and the *Family and Parochial*. The last contained, according to the advertisements, 'the Alterations in the Laws respecting the Poor; Abstract of the Beer, Weights and Measures' and Criminal Courts' Acts; Instructions for executors; an Account of Savings' Banks, &c., &c.' The results of the campaign cannot be gauged, because the detailed evidence has not survived; but it is possible that the raising of the Dividend in June 1838 from 12½ per cent to 15 per cent and twelve months later to 17½ per cent was due rather to successful marketing of almanacks than to moods of irresponsibility. The prosperity, if it occurred, was short-lived; in June 1847 the Dividend was reduced to 15 per cent and in December the dinner for almanack customers was discontinued. Six years later the sensible proposal was made that half the subscribed capital, which then stood at £41,280, should be repaid because the Stamp Duties, to raise cash for which the later increases in the capital were made, had long since been abolished and because, in addition, the costs of paper and printing had fallen. This proposal was defeated. In March 1859 a sub-committee was

[1] The family connection was maintained by the appointment as Honorary Chaplain in 1892 of the Rev. Henry Joseph Greenhill who had taken up his freedom on July 3, 1860, as the son of Joseph.

required to examine and report on a completely different proposition: the expediency of dividing some of the funded capital among the partners; at the Court held on April 5th John Dickinson proposed and Andrew Spottiswoode seconded a motion, based on the recommendations of the sub-committee, that a bonus of 150 per cent be paid! The debate which followed must have been exciting; Charles Baldwin (once again on the side of the angels and, at eighty-four, the doyen of the Court) moved and John Bowyer Nichols (the second generation of that fine family) supported the amendment which was passed in place of the motion.

No more was heard of this method of liquidating the English Stock but the partners were not happy about its management. In 1864 the Clerk was instructed to inform a shareholder who had applied for a copy of the by-laws—a sure sign of trouble brewing—that it was not customary to supply such information. The disquiet which prompted the request and which cannot have been lessened by its rejection, may have been the cause of the regular appearance in the Court minutes, from 1866, of the English Stock Accounts. Those for 1865-6 (given on p. 268) may not have seemed unsatisfactory to those who were permitted to examine them; the loss on the year's working was less than £20, the profit on almanacks was over £3,000 and the balance of assets over liabilities (as shown on March 31, 1870) was comfortable. But the downward movement, which was the inevitable result of an unrealistic Dividend policy and which is so vividly illustrated in the Table on page 270, must already have begun.

A little piece of unwelcome publicity did not improve confidence. In December 1870 C. H. Purday[1] complained to the Board of Trade that he had been prevented from freely searching the recent copyright entries in the registry at Stationers' Hall and in 1871 an anonymous writer[2] gave an account of this, or of a similar, incident. This would not have mattered if he had not gone on to pour contempt upon the Company for imposing on the ignorant and making vast profits from the publication of worthless almanacks—particularly Partridge's and Moore's. Some excuse is found for the author of the latter in that,

---

[1] Author of *Copyright. A Sketch of its Rise and Progress*, 1877.

[2] In *'Entered at Stationers' Hall'*, printed by M. Thomas, Franklin Press, Hanley Road, N., and sold by E. Truelove, 256 High Holborn, W.C., 1871, *Price One Shilling*. Neither Thomas nor Truelove were freemen of the Company. The pamphlet, of 32 pages, was reprinted in 1871 and reviewed in the *English Review*; its author announced *Stationers' Hall*, of 320 pages in 8vo, to be published by Truelove, but I have never seen it.

'having reached the mellow age of three hundred years, [he] cannot read the stars as clearly as in his younger days when, squatting on his haunches, he watched Venus and the tail of the Dragon on the roof of STATIONERS HALL'; but the Court took the hint and told Mr Woolhouse, the editor, to supply four pages of popular scientific information to replace the usual four pages of astrological predictions, in Moore's *Almanack* for 1872. At the same meeting it was decided to embark on a considerable programme of rebuilding in order to provide, besides office accommodation for the Company, a separate room where the public could conveniently consult the registers; fifteen years passed before the alterations were finished.

The atmosphere in which it was possible for the Education Act of 1870 to become law was not one in which the old almanacks—even in modified forms—were likely to maintain their widespread popularity.

ENGLISH STOCK ACCOUNTS, 1865–6

	£	s	d
By dividend on £15,631 Bank Stock	1,601	3	1
„ „ „ £42,000 3% Consols	1,239	0	0
„ rent from houses & warehouses, with Land Tax, less Income Tax (£40 15s) and rent to Merchant Tailors' Company for 38 Ludgate Hill (£210)	2,321	10	6
„ profit on Irish Estate, from the Skinners' Co.	219	15	11
„ from Wardens & Renter Wardens for wine & dinners	172	19	6
„ dinner money, on elections to shares	256	5	0
„ profit on 1866 almanacks	3,048	4	9
„ Dividend on 2 vacant shares	48	0	0
„ excess of expenditure over receipts	17	3	9
	£8,924	2	6
To Dividends to partners	6,192	0	0
„ pensions (including £125 to Guy's Hospital)	545	11	4
„ salaries	546	7	0
„ fees to Assistants and Stock-keepers	658	10	0
„ balance paid to Renter Wardens	171	14	1
„ income tax	59	2	8
„ insurance	57	9	0
„ sundries (wine, dinners, stationery, etc.)	693	8	5
	£8,924	2	6

ENGLISH STOCK: LIABILITIES AND ASSETS, MARCH 31, 1870*

	£	£	s	d
To Stock-holders for cash advanced		41,280	0	0
„ shares not paid out		350	0	0
„ sundries paid annually:				
pensions	418			
annuity to Guy's Hospital	125			
annuity to St Mary-at-Hill	5			
	548			
which at 25 years' purchase amounts to		13,700	0	0
„ amount to be charged against booksellers' balances, say		300	0	0
„ balance, over and above value of Hall, other property and copyrights		92,811	17	0
		£148,441	17	0

	£	£	s	d
By funded property:				
£39,200 3% Consols at 93½		36,652	0	0
£14,800 Bank Stock at 236		34,928	0	0
„ shares not paid up		246	0	6
„ rental	£2,273 0 0			
„ land tax	124 15 6			
	£2,397 15 6			
which at 25 years' purchase amounts to		59,944	7	6
„ Irish Estate £233 19s 8d at 50 years' purchase amounts to		11,699	3	4
„ cash at bank		418	12	6
„ bills at bank		3,407	14	9
„ cash with Treasurer		45	18	5
„ stock of wine, and of books & paper, say		1,100	0	0
		£148,441	17	0

* The earliest extant.

DECLINE OF THE ENGLISH STOCK, 1866–1900

Year	Dividends received £	Rents £	Sales of books, etc. £	Cost of books, etc. £	Dividend paid £
1866–7	3,084	2,322	3,188*	not shown	6,192
1867–8	2,503	2,312	3,180*	,, ,,	6,192
1868–9	2,524	2,288	2,979*	,, ,,	6,192
1869–70	2,458	2,780	5,450	3,113	6,192
1870–1	2,436	2,680	5,354	2,482	6,192
1871–2	2,412	2,658	5,205	1,939	6,192
1872–3	2,532†	2,425	4,829	2,108	6,192
1873–4	2,830	3,338	4,690	2,017	6,192
1874–5	2,851	3,118	4,386	1,887	6,192
1875–6	2,768	2,476	4,596	2,281	6,192
1876–7	3,113	2,384	4,605	1,508	6,192
1877–8	3,442	2,432	4,449	1,718	6,192
1878–9	3,626	2,488	4,060	1,675	6,192
1879–80	3,918	2,797	3,927	1,850	7,224‡
1880–1	3,928	2,318	3,728	1,161	8,256‡
1881–2	4,036	1,850	3,464	1,863	8,256‡
1882–3	4,039	1,205	3,139	1,501	6,192
1883–4	3,396	1,630	3,191	1,439	6,192
1884–5	2,872	2,912	3,004	933	8,256‡
1885–6	2,636	3,142	3,099	1,106	6,192
1886–7	2,454	3,284	2,590	1,187	6,192
1887–8	2,332	3,842	2,195	981	5,120
1888–9	2,260	3,924	2,393	1,045	5,120
1889–90	2,266	4,272	1,524	1,047	5,040
1890–1	2,232	3,421	1,796	989	4,950
1891–2	2,243	4,080	1,846	880	4,920
1892–3	2,083	4,128	1,865	950	4,920
1893–4	2,048	4,140	1,388	939	4,920
1894–5	1,610	4,115	1,262	855	4,870
1895–6	1,467	4,132	1,156	785	4,805
1896–7	1,462	4,122	436*	346	4,800
1897–8	1,548	4,127	63*	28	4,781
1898–9	1,491	4,112	279*	30	4,665
1899–1900	1,436	4,440	362*	33	4,650

* Profit only, except for last four years when sales of *Gradus* and royalty from Letts were lumped together.

† Investment of payments by the Skinners' Company for the Pellipar Estate begin to show a return.

‡ Years in which a bonus was also paid to the partners.

The inevitable decrease in sales increased the uneasiness of the partners and the secretiveness of the Assistants. In 1874, when Arber was appealing in vain for permission to make copies of decisions taken three hundred years earlier, the Court at last, and only as the result of further appeals, decided that the English Stock by-laws should be printed and distributed; but four years later this concession amounted to no more than permission for one of the partners, on behalf of his fellows, to inspect the rules under the eye of the Clerk. Not until 1893 was the resolution of 1874 implemented. Meantime the receipts from investments increased[1] because the proceeds from the sale of the Pellipar Estate were not all used for paying Dividends to partners. After 1882, however, the use of capital for maintaining Dividends (and even for paying a bonus) again shows itself in the figures, and it was not until February 1887 that a report of the Stock Board drew pointed attention to the short-sightedness of recent policy. On May 3rd the Court ordered one set of shares to be annihilated, as opportunity arose, and in June it accepted the recommendation that the annual Dividend be reduced to 12½ per cent. These measures, however, were not nearly severe enough to balance the accounts without resort to the sale of investments. By 1895 only six almanacks[2] were published from Stationers' Hall and the sales of these were about half what they had been ten years before; even *Old Moore* was down to 50,000, and the withdrawal of the Government as a customer had killed Wing's and reduced to 530 the printing number of the *British*, which had been bought from Charles Knight in 1868 for £750. On March 24, 1896, the Company made an agreement with Charles John Letts by which he took over the production and publication of the five remaining almanacks—Moore's, Goldsmith's, *Stationers'*, *Clergyman* and *British*—on payment of a royalty of 6 per cent. This arrangement, which was not very profitable for the Company and disastrous for Letts, virtually brought to an insignificant end three centuries of publishing at Stationers' Hall.[3]

The increasing prosperity of most of the City companies during the nineteenth century—prosperity which the Stationers enjoyed rather as privileged individuals than as a corporation—did not escape envious attention and, largely as a result of accusations made by

[1] See the Table opposite.
[2] The only *book* available at Stationers' Hall was the *Gradus ad Parnassum*, reprinted from plates cast in 1834.   [3] For the postscript to the story, see below, p. 281.

J. F. B. Firth, M.P. for Chelsea, a Royal Commission was set up in July 1880, under the chairmanship of Lord Derby, to enquire into the constitutions and administration of the companies, into their income and expenditure, and into the degrees to which the purposes of foundation were still carried out. The behaviour of the Stationers towards this Commission was remarkably like that of fifty years before. Answers were made under protest to the original circular of August 1880 but no replies were given either to the Secretary's complaint, in February 1882, that the answers were incomplete or to his reminder in July. In November, however, the Clerk wrote to protest that the first draft of the Report had been printed without further reference to the Company, and to reply to eight specific questions asked in July. These additional facts and the information given to the Commission by a deputation of the Master, Wardens and Clerk were embodied in the final Report, printed in 1884.

Four relevant points emerge from the enquiries and the Report of the Commissioners.[1] The first is that the Stationers', though far from being among the wealthy companies, had—even in its depleted state— the fifth largest Livery.[2] The second is that the number of apprentices bound at Stationers' Hall was still relatively high and that the apprenticeship system was still intended to provide a craft training instead of being, as in many companies, 'colourable'—a cheap way of obtaining a freedom. The third point is that the Commissioners drew attention to the danger from 'alienation' of assets in favour of existing members of a company—the sort of manœuvre proposed for the English Stock in 1859. The last point concerns the circulated question: 'Is there vested in the company . . . any right of exercising superintendence over . . . any . . . art, trade or business?' The Stationers' answer was: 'The company elect the registrar of copyrights under the provisions of the Copyright Act.'

COPYRIGHT

The Act of 1842 extended the term of copyright protection in books to seven years after an author's death or to forty-two years from the

---

[1] Sir Sydney Waterlow, Master of the Company in 1872, was a member of the Commission and signed the majority Report. William Spottiswoode gave evidence as President of the Royal Society. The minority Report is a well-argued defence of the companies, but it contains nothing specific about the Stationers.

[2] Only the Fishmongers 452, Loriners 386, Haberdashers 373 and Spectacle-makers 356 had bigger Liveries.

7 *The southern end of the hall in 1941*

8 *The hall in 1952*

date of publication—whichever term was longer; and it made formal entry at Stationers' Hall, on a prescribed form and for a fee of 5s, a prerequisite for a suit in defence of copyright. On July 5th, four days after the passing of the Bill, the Court appointed the Treasurer of the English Stock as the 'Officer of the Company' under the Act and ruled that he should meet the expenses out of the fees. Accommodation was provided at the eastern end of the Hall buildings, 'a narrow box-like room, the part of which assigned to the public not above a dozen feet in length and breadth. A counter runs all around the sides, and behind the counter sit a couple of lads of seventeen, or eighteen, whose look suffices to show that they deem themselves very important personages.'[1] The anonymous author describes his cold reception, and his request to search the registers so as to avoid using, for his book, another author's title. 'What an idea! You had better first search a London fog for sunlight', and he is told that the charge is 1s for each entry examined. As he crosses the courtyard on his way out, turning over in his mind—perhaps—the letter he is going to write to the Board of Trade, 'he hears the sound of festive music and clinking of glasses. . . . The members of the registering brotherhood are dining together. . . . How merry the old gentlemen are up-stairs.'

The picture is possibly not far from the truth. When C. R. Rivington, the Clerk, took over Greenhill's responsibilities on the latter's retirement in 1883, he found that there were still two men working in that 'inconvenient' upper room and that he could afford to pay his predecessor a pension of £500 a year out of the fees. The work gradually increased and the clerical staff had grown, after the registration of musical copyrights in 1902, to five (with some part-time assistance) and the income to over £2,500; the office moved briefly to 13 Ave Maria Lane and then returned to part of the rebuilt Treasurer's house. When the Copyright Act of 1911 came into force on July 1, 1912, registration, though it did not cease, dropped to a trickle which could be managed by the Beadle,[2] and the old staff had to be dismissed and compensated; Mr Jobbins, who must have been one of the two

[1] 'Entered at Stationers' Hall', p. 3.

[2] Registration under the 1842 Act did not fully end until December 31, 1923, the date chosen by Canada for the 1911 Act to come into force. Registration today is 'for the purpose of record and for assisting in the proof of the existence of a work on a given date in case of infringement'. The fees are 6s for registration on a form costing 2d; a certified copy costs 6s and searches 3s an entry. As late as 1922 the Company collected £195 15s 10d in copyright fees, and in 1924 the Registry at Stationers' Hall earned a profit of £70 2s 9d on a turn-over of £301 7s 10d for 669 entries, 606 certificates, 51 searches and 1,061 forms.

'important personages' in 1870, received £300 from the Government as a reward for forty-four years' service. And so ended a practice which the Stationers of the sixteenth century had invented for their mutual protection, which Parliament had adopted and modified by a series of Acts extending over two centuries, and which has in modern times given the Company a small but unique piece of international fame; 'Entered at Stationers' Hall' has grown into the English language.

The change in the official attitude of the Stationers' Company towards copyright—the official attitude being articulated in the resolutions of the Court of Assistants—epitomizes the alteration which the Company slowly and almost imperceptibly underwent in the century before 1911. When a new copyright Bill was before the House of Commons in 1813, the Court appointed a committee to watch the Company's interests; these were the interests of a corporation which was itself an owner of copyrights and which included, among its members, many of the biggest private owners. After about 1875 the corporate interest in the protection of copyright had almost ceased to exist and many publishers were not members of the society; but a vested interest in formal registration had taken its place. One of the awkward questions which the author of *'Entered at Stationers' Hall'* had asked was why the registry was not located at Somerset House, and the fear of losing a source of profit was persistent. In 1879 a deputation waited on Lord John Manners, chairman of the Royal Commission on Copyright, to plead for the retention of the registry; in 1891 a petition with the same purpose was sent to the House of Lords; in 1903 the Council of the Publishers Association was persuaded to appeal[1] to Balfour, the President of the Board of Trade, to allow registration—perhaps with reduced fees—to remain at the Hall; and the Court's discussions of the 1911 Bill never went deeper than a murmur at the loss of £500 a year in rent for the offices of the registry.

At the beginning of the eighteenth century Stationers' Hall was still a meeting place for masters and journeymen working in the different branches of the book trade, and it was still possible for a man to move from the ranks of the employed to those of the employers. By the beginning of the nineteenth century worth-while membership of the Company was denied to wage-earners until they were old

---

[1] Signed by C. J. Longman, president, Sir Frederick Macmillan, vice-president, and John Murray, treasurer.

enough to become pensioners; and when the two sides in the London printing dispute appealed to the Court no Assistant made any attempt to settle the differences within the framework of the Company to which a very large number of both parties belonged; the appeal of the masters, voiced by Luke Hansard and George Woodfall in March 1805, that the Treasurer, as the head of a big wholesaling organization, should sign the resolution of the booksellers against the journeymen printers, was unsuccessful but the masters were encouraged to bind additional apprentices, without the normal extra fees, at the Pension and Election Courts later in the month. The sympathy of the Assistants, and probably of most of the Livery, lay with the master printers but, in spite of restricting membership of the Company to those in the book trade and the sons of freemen—applications from others were not even referred to the Court, according to the Clerk's reply to a question from the Commissioners in 1883—in spite of this limitation, no organization in the trade, whether of master printers, of bookbinders, of stationers, of booksellers or of publishers, developed out of or had any direct association with the Stationers' Company. The disputes about published prices in the 1850s and the 1890s caused no stir in the Court Room—except perhaps across the dinner table—and the closest relationship was that of landlord and tenant; in 1896 the Publishers Association rented rooms at the Hall and employed the Beadle, William Poulten, as its part-time secretary; in 1901 the Council of Associated Booksellers was permitted to hold its monthly meetings there on the strict understanding that the Hall was not to be regarded as its office; in 1912 the Booksellers' Provident Institution made arrangements similar to those of the Publishers' Association; and since 1921 the office of the Royal Literary Fund has been at the Hall.

To this day the Company has remained, in spite of its usefulness to printers, uncommitted to any branch of the trade; but it has not, on the strength of this, become a Chamber to which all branches might look for guidance and for settlement of differences. It was during the nineteenth century that the Stationers' Company 'retired' from the book trade.

CHAPTER XIV

THE WORSHIPFUL COMPANY OF STATIONERS
AND NEWSPAPER MAKERS

———

THE retirement of the Company from the book trade has been followed by a general retirement of the book trade from the vicinity of St Paul's; and the fires at the end of December 1940 hastened this centrifugal movement. But if one is minded, from curiosity or piety, to pay a visit to the old centre of the trade, it is best to approach it from the west—by way of Fleet Street, where Wynkyn de Worde and other early printers were in business. A walk from St Dunstan's, the parish church of so many Stationers and the site of Lord Northcliffe's memorial bust, will take one past Bolt Court (where the Stationers' School was opened in 1861), past the new offices of the *Daily Telegraph* and the *Daily Express* (at the back of which were the Spottiswoode printing works) and down the hill to the line of the Fleet river. Across the street is the bust of T. P. O'Connor on the *News Chronicle* building, and almost next door are the headquarters of Reuters, bounded on one side by Salisbury Court (leading to Salisbury Square where Samuel Richardson had his printing house) and on the other side by St Bride's Lane which gives a glimpse of the restored church and tiered spire. Eastwards it is all St Paul's. Before crossing Ludgate Circus one can see the memorial plaque to Edgar Wallace, who is remembered here as a Fleet Street man and a founder member of the Company of Newspaper Makers. Away to the south, but out of sight behind the railway arches, lie the offices of *The Times* and Printing House Square, once the property of the Black Friars and, in the seventeenth century, the site of the King's Printer's printing house. Half-way up Ludgate Hill one crosses Old Bailey and a few yards further on one passes St Martin's, whose parishioners had worshipped at Stationers' Hall while their church was being rebuilt; then comes Stationers' Hall Court (Cock Alley), with a sight of the east wing of the Hall. On reaching Ave Maria Lane one is almost opposite the corner of St Paul's Churchyard where stood Peter's

College, the second Hall of the Stationers' Company. A dozen steps along Ave Maria Lane and the present Hall comes into full view across the open cellars of the old Simpkins building; to the east are the equally open cellars of the old Longmans offices and the other devastation, thick with buddleia and bracken, on either side of Paternoster Row.[1]

In Warwick Square, to the north of Amen Court, Oxford University Press and Hodders actively maintain the tradition of the locality; but Stationers' Hall stands like a once busy and handsome little port which, through changes in economic conditions and a failure to keep the channels dredged, the tide of commercial life has left high and dry. The routines of the past are still followed; apprentices are bound, freemen admitted and Liverymen clothed on the first Tuesday in the month; a few pensioners are still paid; the annual elections of officers are made according to the pattern established in the eighteenth century (although there are now twice as many Renter Wardens each year); formal visits are paid to the school; cakes and ale, the bequest of John Norton, are provided on the morning of Ash Wednesday, and in the afternoon the little procession wends its way to the service in St Faith's under St Paul's. But a Master of the Company, when he comes to write the report on his year of office, finds little new to say about the occasions over which he presided and he is glad to be able to link the life of the Company with that of the City or the nation, to describe the contribution of the Stationers to the Festival of Britain celebrations or to record that the Lord Mayor was his Under Warden.[2]

There has, however, been one development during the last quarter of a century which has done something both to strengthen the Stationers' ties with the western side of the City and to re-establish a lost association. The Company of Newspaper Makers was incorporated in 1931 and received a Royal Charter on July 19, 1933;[3] it had a membership of 162, of whom 130 were annual subscribers and the rest honorary or life members. Even before it had received the Charter it had approached the Stationers' Company with a suggestion for amalgamation. The former looked to gain a Hall and a part in the tradition of an ancient corporation; the latter welcomed a body of keen new members, some of whom were both rich and distinguished. After a canvassing of the pros and cons, it was agreed to join forces, and on

[1] This was written in August 1959.
[2] Sir Denis Truscott.
[3] Surrendered October 25, 1935.

May 22, 1933, the Court of the Stationers' Company approved the steps by which complete integration was to be achieved.

The big day was October 16th when eighty-seven Newspaper Makers were admitted to the Stationers' Livery and welcomed at lunch.[1] Though they could be given no seniority in their new Company, five of them became Assistants the same day (with the understanding that R. D. Blumenfeld, their Master, having been specially admitted a week earlier, should be added to the Court on his return to the country) and a further three were promised places in 1939, 1945 and 1951. Sir Percy Greenaway, who was both Lord Mayor and Master of the Company in May, was by agreement re-elected with his two Wardens in July 1933. He was to have made way for Blumenfeld after six months, but on December 5th he announced that the Prince of Wales had agreed to accept the honorary freedom and Livery of the Company and to serve as Master. On December 20th a Special Court was held at York House for the installation, but Greenaway continued in office as Deputy Master. There was no election the following July but Blumenfeld, with the old Wardens, took over in December. The first Newspaper Maker to be elected Under Warden—in 1936, as agreed—was Lord Iliffe. The Prince of Wales resigned the Mastership a week before he succeeded to the throne in January 1936, and for the next five years the Masters were elected for six months only. On January 25, 1937, the new Charter to the Worshipful Company of Stationers and Newspaper Makers was granted. The only alterations formally made by this grant were in the name and in the increase to £10,000 of the annual value of property permitted to be held in mortmain; but the union with the Newspaper Makers gave women equality with men on the Livery. Since most of the printers, publishers and proprietors of early newspapers and periodicals had been Stationers, the action of their successors was in the nature of a reunion.

The new members of the Company must sometimes have wondered, from their lowly places in the list of Liverymen, what they had gained by this 'home-coming', for the question had been asked by earlier Stationers. It is a question which is still valid. On October 2, 1917, the Court debated certain suggestions for extending the activities of the Company which E. J. Layton, one of the Wardens, had put forward. On January 8, 1918, it appointed a special committee (with power to co-opt four members of the Livery) to devise a scheme which would

[1] Others came in, by fours and fives, at succeeding Courts.

increase the revenue and, at the same time, make the Company of more use to its Liverymen. This committee, after meetings with the Federation of Master Printers and the London Master Printers' Association, made its recommendations in a printed memorandum of October 8th. A Society connected with printing, publishing and cognate trades should be formed and the Federation should take a building lease of the garden site; on this, and over the hall and the Court Room, the Federation should build offices for its own use and for the use of other bodies; plans had been prepared and the estimated cost was £25,000. In addition, it should have the use of the Company's premises on Mondays, Wednesdays and Fridays and of the hall twice a year (for exhibitions lasting three weeks) at an annual rent of £1,000. The advantage to the Company would be an increase in the Livery, through the proximity of the offices, and the reversion of a valuable building when the lease fell in. At its meeting on November 12th the Court first of all voted that messages of congratulation be sent to the King and to the Lord Mayor on the Armistice and then referred back the committee's report with the assurance that the Assistants approved the general idea of making the Hall a centre for the printing and other trades. On January 14, 1919, Sir Thomas Vezey Strong moved the modified suggestion that the managing body of the new Association should be formed only from those members of the federating societies who were also Liverymen; the scheme was then approved in general by the Court and referred back to the committee for opening negotiations. It is easy to see where the fears lay; nothing more is heard either of the Association or of the plans of the Federation of Master Printers.

But the problem of devising ways to keep the Livery in touch with the Court was not allowed to die and on June 3rd the General Purposes Committee was instructed to report on the subject with particular reference to the revival of the Livery Dinner, the old Venison Feast. On July 1st the Court approved the recommendations that there should be a tea-party for everybody and that four times a year a quarter of the Liverymen should be invited to a Court lunch at which some topic should be introduced for discussion. The Under Warden, Edward Unwin, did not think that these proposals went far enough and proposed that another committee should give deeper thought to the problem; but he was defeated by seven votes to four. In November J. R. Riddell asked to be allowed to put a case personally to the

Assistants and called a meeting of Liverymen who elected a committee. At its meeting on December 2nd the Court called in Riddell, G. W. Jones and R. A. Austen-Leigh, but was content to ask for a written statement of their views, which, in January, was referred to the sub-committee of the committee appointed two years earlier. At its February meeting the Court turned its attention to a letter which Sir William Waterlow had written on Christmas Eve, and 'turned down his sugges-tion that four representatives of the Livery, chosen each year in rotation by their fellow Liverymen, should sit on the Court: by-laws were difficult and expensive to change, the Court was already big enough and Liverymen not chosen would be disappointed. But it was agreed that there should be a Livery Committee of six which could act as a go-between and on which printing, publishing and paper-making interests should be represented. At a meeting on March 29th the Livery chose S. J. Sandle, R. A. Austen-Leigh, William Will and William Penman (all future Masters of the Company) along with W. C. Corke, J. L. Greaves, H. D. Singer and G. W. Jones; J. R. Riddell was appointed Secretary. On April 13th the names, and even the number, were approved; on St George's Day 1920 the Livery Committee met for the first time.

This may not appear to be an achievement of much importance; a committee of the Livery had organized dances at the Hall as long ago as 1878. But the Assistants had formally recognized that Liverymen were interested in the Company long before they were senior enough to calculate how many more years they would have to wait before they could be called to the Court—though this interest was not keen enough to sharpen tempers as it had sharpened them in the eighteenth century. Moreover, on April 13, 1926, the Court so far adopted Water-low's suggestion as to agree that it would choose two Liverymen—out of four elected by the Livery—to sit as Assistants for twelve months and then revert to their old seniority. This arrangement—modified in 1929 to give the representatives two years on the Court—exists to this day and has two advantages: there are always two men on the governing body whose ages are likely to be somewhere near the average age of Liverymen and whose interests, should there be a division of feeling between the Assistants and the rest of the Company, will remain those of the almost powerless majority. The Livery still has no say in the governance of the Company but it does have the means, if it cares to use them, of making its ideas or its wishes known to the governing body[1]—whether the ideas are those of the whole body of the Livery or of that group of Liverymen who are partners in the English Stock and own two-thirds of the share capital.

This unique organization, though it has ceased (like the Company) to perform the functions for which it was created, still survives and still plays a part in the life of the corporation. At the beginning of the century Charles Letts[2] was publishing the surviving almanacks on behalf of the Stock and finding the business far from profitable; but the Court continued the old policy of ordering a 12½ per cent Dividend for the partners. In 1903 the Stock Board strongly recommended firstly a reduction of Dividend to 10 per cent in order to save the investments which barely covered the capital contributed by the partners, £37,200; and secondly a further reduction in the shares both in size and in number, until the total liability was down to £28,000; at this level the income from investments and rents, £5,600, would cover the expenses, about £2,600, and leave enough for a respectable Dividend of 10 per cent. The Court ignored the recommendations. By 1907 Letts had had enough and put the Company in touch with Cassell who on March 26th signed a five-year agreement (which lasted twenty). The Stock paid £250 for editing and £250 for advertising; Cassell bore the costs of production and returned half the published price of each copy sold and 80 per cent of the revenue from advertisements carried by the almanacks. There were five of them left. Moore's at 6d had a sale of 25,000 but the *British*, selling 8,500 in its three editions, was feeling the competition from Whitaker's and from the *Daily Mail Yearbook*; the sale of the *People's* was down to 6,000 and only about 2,000 were sold of the two Sheet Almanacks, Goldsmith's and the *Stationers'*. The first and the last of these were the sole survivors of the war of 1914–18, and *Old Moore* was still selling nearly 25,000 at 1s. This figure rapidly fell to 16,000, and in spite of dropping the second colour (red) in 1925 and of reducing the number of pages by 32 to 96, the loss on the two almanacks (now borne by the Company) continued to run at about £180. In 1927 *Old Moore* was handed over to Cassell because, in the words of J. R. Riddell, 'it does not enhance the reputation or dignity of the Company', and a Diary for the trade, on the lines of *The Stationers'*

---

[1] The governing body can, of course, ignore the wishes of the Livery, as it ignored the printed Resolutions passed at the annual meeting of Liverymen on May 26, 1930.
[2] See above, p. 271.

and Newspaper Makers' Company's Pocket Diary for 1960, was published. For two years de la Rue handled this and the respectable Sheet, but early in 1929 Charles Letts came back into the story and took them over. Each was published at a small loss to the Stock and the Sheet was discontinued in 1941. The Diary, after a brief intermission during the war of 1939–45, survives to this day; from it one can still calculate how many sheets of paper (without allowing for waste) should be given out for 100 copies of a book to be printed in 64mo (and even in 15mo), and in it the English Stock is still described as 'a trading partnership of publishers'.

In this phrase the only accurate word is 'partnership', the profits for which derived mainly from the property acquired in 1606;[1] the rents in 1939 amounted to £4,600. On October 15, 1940, between one and two o'clock in the morning, incendiary bombs fell on the roof of the lobby to the Court Room; the fires which these started wrecked the western wing of the building and almost completely destroyed the roof of the hall. As a result, many movables of historic interest— including most of the records—were stored in the strong room under Cunard House or at the Public Record Office, and the screen at the southern end of the hall was carried away to Lady David's house at Henley. After the fires which began on the night of December 29–30th, the property between the Hall and Ave Maria Lane was reduced to rubble and Simpkins, with its great stock of books and its incalculable usefulness to the book trade, ceased to exist. The Hall received little further damage, apart from that to the windows of the Stock Room, but the income both of the partners and of the Company dried up; for the property in Wood Street was destroyed by the same raid and on January 14, 1941, the Court received not only disclaimers for all leases but notices from the Publishers Association and the Booksellers' Provident Institution that they were quitting on Lady Day.

For the next eighteen years the Company lived largely on its remaining capital; the partners received no Dividend until 1949 and then only 2½ per cent. When rebuilding was possible, it was decided not to replan the site (as had been suggested in 1918) nor to rebuild the eastern wing and extend the hall (plans for which, at a cost of £60,000, had been approved in 1935, soon after the amalgamation with the Newspaper Makers, and never carried out) but to restore the Court Room and the hall to their former beauty, and to redesign

[1] See above, p. 228, for an account of the additions.

the kitchen, offices and cloakrooms. The first major function in the refurbished Hall was, appropriately, the dinner on May 4, 1957, to celebrate the four hundredth anniversary of the granting of the first Charter. For an occasion like this, the screen and panelling and seventeenth-century chiffoniers are as fine as ever they were, and amongst the silver—which is not remarkable by Livery Company standards—are fine standing cups and basins and candlesticks of the seventeenth and eighteenth centuries. The view of St Paul's more than compensates for the lack of stained glass in the eastern windows.

But the days of this view are numbered for in April 1959 the Colonial Mutual Life Assurance Society Ltd acquired the site bounded by Ave Maria Lane and Ludgate Hill for its City office. The disposal of this piece of property is the most exciting—and potentially the most significant—event of the last, somewhat featureless, fifty years in the history of the Stationers' Company. If the great sum received from the sale is invested with imagination and the income used with discretion, if the traditional ties with the book trade are maintained and the recent association with Fleet Street fostered, the Company may be, in the years to come, not only prosperous but once again of service.

APPRENTICES BOUND AND TURNED OVER, FREEMEN PRESENTED, LIVERYMEN CALLED, AND IMPORTANT EVENTS,
1557–1959

Apprentices b'd.	t.o.	Freemen total	pat.	red.	tra.	Bro-thers	Livery	Date*	
7	–	13†	1	1	–	–	–	1557	May 4th, grant of Charter.
13	2	9	–	–	–	2	–	1558	
27	–	11	–	–	–	6	–	1559	November 10th, Charter confirmed; Injunctions.
31	–	9	1	1	–	–	6	1560	February 1st, grant of Livery.
67	–	6	1	–	–	16	2	1561	
25	–	4	–	1	–	11	–	1562	Ordinances approved.
19	1	5	–	–	–	–	2	1563	
52	1	9	1	–	–	10	1	1564	
43	1	9	1	–	–	8	1	1565	
26	–	7	1	–	–	5	–	1566	June 29th, Star Chamber
19	–	12	–	–	–	13	2	1567	Decree.
34	–	9	1	–	–	1	2	1568	
19	–	14	–	2	–	–	5	1569	
26	–	14	–	2	1	4	2	1570	
27	–	‡	–	–	–	–	–	1571	
37	–	–	–	–	–	–	2	1572	
48	–	–	–	–	–	–	2	1573	
33	–	–	–	–	–	–	–	1574	
55	–	–	–	–	1	–	–	1575	
65	1	12	–	–	–	–	1	1576	
34§	2	19	1	–	1	3	6	1577	August, complaint against monopolies.
26	5	19	3	1	–	–	–	1578	? June 5th, petition of poor
34	6	19	–	–	1	3	–	1579	printers.
31	4	14	1	–	–	1	–	1580	
43	2	10	2	2	–	–	5	1581	
17	2	22	1	3	–	–	–	1582	December, Barker's report to Burghley.
37	8	20	3	–	–	–	–	1583	July 18th, Report of Com-
42	2	27	1	2	2	–	4	1584	missioners.
25	3	18	3	–	1	–	2	1585	
27	2	27	–	–	–	–	–	1586	June 23rd, Star Chamber
20	2	19	1	–	–	–	2	1587	Decree.

* The columns to the left cover the gild year beginning in July of the year shown; the column to the right covers the calendar year beginning on January 1st. The figures given by D. F. McKenzie (*The Library*, 5th ser., xiii, 1958, pp. 294–5) are for calendar years.

† Those free by service are those in the 'total' column less those free by patrimony, redemption or translation.

‡ Since admission fees varied, no calculations can be made from the totals in the Wardens' Accounts for this year and the four succeeding years.

§ In the course of this year the fee was increased from 6d to 2s 6d.

Apprentices b'd.	t.o.	Freemen total	pat.	red.	tra.	Bro-thers	Livery	Date	
28	3	26	3	2	2	–	1	1588	
50	4	13	–	1	–	–	2	1589	
25	1	15	3	–	–	–	2	1590	
26	3	9	–	–	–	–	5	1591	October 12th, first recorded
31	2	18	2	–	–	–	–	1592	meeting of partners.
36	1	8	1	–	–	–	4	1593	
59	2	14	–	–	–	–	–	1594	
38	2	15	1	–	–	–	2	1595	
26	3	20	1	–	1	–	–	1596	
46	2	25	–	1	–	–	18	1597	
42	1	19	2	–	3	–	1	1598	
36	2	30	4	–	13	–	–	1599	
51	3	22	3	–	–	–	–	1600	
54	4	35	5	2	–	1	6	1601	
58	2	14	1	–	1	–	2	1602	
42	4	21	10	2	–	–	7	1603	October 29th, first grant of
84	7	15	3	–	–	–	–	1604	monopoly in Psalms, etc.
54	3	29	3	1	–	1	2	1605	
51	3	20	5	–	–	–	–	1606	Acquisition of Abergavenny House.

Apprentices b'd.	t.o.	Freemen total	pat.	red.	tra.	Livery	Date	
56	2	27	3	–	–	6	1607	
39	2	25	2	–	–	7	1608	
67*	6	29	1	2	–	1	1609	
71*	2	28	1	–	–	1	1610	
66*	6	34	5	–	1	18	1611	
56	5	30	3	2	–	–	1612	
48	5	30	2	3	1	–	1613	May 16th, petition of fifty-four
58	3	42	6	–	–	–	1614	journeymen printers.
58	1	30	3	–	1	21	1615	
62	4	34	2	–	–	–	1616	January 3rd, Latin Stock floated; March 8th, second grant of
45	5	31	–	–	1	–	1617	monopoly.
60	1	48	4	–	–	4	1618	March, Irish Stock floated.
64	4	34	4	2	–	5	1619	
59	5	36	7	–	1	2	1620	
33†	2	24	3	1	–	–	1621	
58	4	30	2	–	2	3	1622	
51	1	37	3	2	–	–	1623	December 10th, concession to Cam-
60	5	21	3	–	–	6	1624	bridge printers.
61	4	24	1	–	–	5	1625	
78	1	43	5	2	2	9	1626	
66	4	37	5	1	–	2	1627	June 27th, Latin Stock wound up.
74	–	29	3	1	–	14	1628	August, Aspley–Parker row.

* Including one disallowed.   † A plague year.

Apprentices b'd.	t.o.	Freemen total	pat.	red.	tra.	Livery	Date	
77	3	17	2	–	1	1	1629	April 16th, further concession to
56	1	30	7	1	1	–	1630	Cambridge printers.
61	1	31	10	2	–	12	1631	July 22nd, first Cambridge agree-
63	3	23	5	1	–	–	1632	ment.
68	2	59	6	2	–	10	1633	
82	1	49	3	1	–	6	1634	
62	4	40	2	–	–	–	1635	
31*	3	50	7	1	1	2	1636	
112	4	46	3	1	–	19	1637	March 12th, Oxford agreement;
78	3	44	2	–	–	1	1638	July 11th, Star Chamber Decree.
58	2	41	6	–	–	4	1639	September 5th, new Cambridge agreement; October, Irish Stock wound up.
65	2	37	5	–	–	–	1640	
67	3	49	8	1	–	2	1641	July 5th, abolition of Court of Star
35†	1	22	3	–	–	1	1642	Chamber; *Scintilla* published.
24	3	21	1	–	–	3	1643	
40	–	24	3	–	–	2	1644	
89	1	33	5	–	–	1	1645	January 23rd, Underhill's demonstration.
104	1	58	5	–	1	10	1646	Bibles printed for English Stock.
88	4	40	7	1	–	–	1647	March 1st, purchase of Scotch
50	2	42	6	1	–	–	1648	Patent.
68	3	38	8	1	–	–	1649	September 20th, Act for regulation
47	3	28	10	–	–	2	1650	of printing.
68	–	21	6	1	–	–	1651	First attempt to form Company of
57	1	46	9	–	–	30	1652	Printers.
77	–	65	8	–	–	–	1653	Purchase of Cambridge printing
86	–	55	7	–	–	–	1654	materials.
114	–	37	6	–	–	2	1655	
97	1	44	5	–	–⌉	‡	1656	
76	–	41	7	–	–		1657	
72	1	37	4	–	–⎬	30	1658	
45	–	29	4	–	–		1659	
66	–	43	7	–	–⌋		1660	
56	1	61	7	–	–		1661	October 1st, new agreement with Oxford.
56	–	51	6	–	–		1662	May 19th, Printing Act.
63	–	61	9	–	–	30	1663	Second attempt to form Company of Printers.
43	–	43	5	1	–		1664	
27§	2	34	4	–	–		1665	October 11th, new patent for school books.
46¶	1	26	7	–	–		1666	September 2nd–6th, Fire of London.
59	–	29	2	–	–		1667	August 10th, *inspeximus* Charter.

* A plague year.   † Only eleven bound in second half of the year.

‡ On October 22, 1656, the Court initiated the practice, which lasted for nearly fifty years, of opening the calls to the Livery for a period of years; the length of the calls varied considerably. See above, p. 159.

§ No entries between June 28, 1665, and February 5, 1666, because of the Plague.

¶ This year a girl was bound, for the first time.

Apprentices b'd.	t.o.	Freemen total	pat.	red.	tra.	Livery	Date	
68	1	26	4	–	–		1668	
114	1	45	4	–	–		1669	
81	–	41	9	–	–		1670	April 21st, agreement with John Hayes, the Cambridge printer.
85	1	31	7	1	2	89	1671	
58	1	22	9	2	–		1672	
61	1	29	5	·	3		1673	
63	–	36	9	3	–		1674	
64	1	52	8	5	–		1675	
68	–	52	2	3	–	32	1676	
92	1	55	7	4	–		1677	
54	–	41	3	–	2		1678	February 16th, new by-laws approved; June 28th, agreement with Seymour.
70	–	53	6	1	–		1679	June 10th, lapsing of Printing Act.
84	1	38	6	3	–	43	1680	
83	–	38	8	1	–		1681	October 5th, new by-laws of English
101	–	48	9	–	–		1682	Stock approved.
80	–	50	4	6	–	–	1683	
56	–	37	3	3	–	–	1684	March, *quo warranto* proceedings against Charter.
49	5	43	7	–	3	–	1685	Printing Act revived.
59	3	48	3	1	2	24	1686	
65	2	59	3	5	4		1687	
45	–	43	4	1	1	36	1688	
68	1	52	3	1	1		1689	
58	2	50	7	3	1		1690	
67	1	41	4	2	–		1691	
59	1	34	8	1	–		1692	January 27th, trade printing at Oxford taken over.
53	–	33	6	1	–	64	1693	October 6th, New Stock formed.
60	1	39	8	–	1		1694	
53	–	29	1	–	–		1695	April, final lapsing of Printing Act.
54	–	33	5	1	–		1696	
53	–	39	6	–	–		1697	
63	1	24	5	–	–	49	1698	
84	–	26	6	–	–		1699	
72	–	33	3	–	–		1700	
61	2	31	4	–	–		1701	
67	10	30	4	–	–	29	1702	
69	16	30	4	1	–		1703	
60	15	41	7	1	–	5	1704	
58	7	39	4	–	–	4	1705	
56	15	43	5	–	–	7	1706	March 11th, new agreement with Cambridge.
74	4	45	6	1	–	9	1707	
65	10	33	6	–	–	12	1708	
64	5	21	5	–	–	13	1709	
65	7	22	2	1	–	13	1710	
55	10	40	7	–	–	8	1711	Stamp Duties on almanacks introduced.
48	13	60	16	–	–	–	1712	Agreement with Baskett over Oxford privilege.
61	9	27	4	–	–	6	1713	
51	11	25	3	–	–	5	1714	
57	6	29	3	–	–	7	1715	
53	10	30	5	–	–	5	1716	

Appendix I

Apprentices b'd.	t.o.	Freemen total	pat.	red.	Livery	Date	
65	11	37	2	1	18	1717	
75	17	32	8	–	1	1718	
69	7	34	9	–	7	1719	
63	14	25	4	1	6	1720	
55	12	28	6	1	23	1721	
60	10	38	8	1*	7	1722	
61	9	34	9	1	9	1723	
65	22	28	7	1	13	1724	
57	16	41	8	–	7	1725	
68	13	29	6	–	6	1726	
57	11	25	2	–	9	1727	Renewal of Cambridge agreement.
43	11	31	5	2	6	1728	
52	10	33	4	1	2	1729	Alteration in number of Yeomanry shares.
51	7	34	8	1	11	1730	
47	8	29	7	1	5	1731	
66	7	32	3	–	9	1732	
58	10	39	5	4	7	1733	
64	9	28	8	1	5	1734	Renewal of Baskett (Oxford) agreement.
63	10	38	8	3	5	1735	
66	6	32	10	1	7	1736	First increase in total number of E.S.
56	11	36	6	1	3	1737	shares.
59	10	39	6	6	15	1738	
57	15	48	8	1*	6	1739	
57	15	39	2	6	7	1740	
42	12	33	7	1	6	1741	
47	13	32	3	2	7	1742	Attack on Court by Osbornes and Nutt.
50	10	44	7	2	4	1743	
59	11	40	9	2	6	1744	
48	9	29	7	1	8	1745	
46	6	35	4	4	11	1746	
74	16	29	7	1	4	1747	Renewal of Cambridge agreement.
67	13	49	7	6	4	1748	
69	4	42	2	3	8	1749	
62	7	29	4	–	7	1750	
66	10	46	13	4	11	1751	
68	6	23	1	1	12	1752	
48	13	31	5	1	9	1753	
68	14	38	4	5	16	1754	July 2nd, offices (of Mr, etc.) to be held
53	12	37	4	3	8	1755	for one year only.
76	9	40	2	2	11	1756	
65	15	40	6	4†	13	1757	
60	9	40	3	4	11	1758	
70	20	43	6	1	6	1759	
80	16	41	9	–	8	1760	
86	12	31	1	–	9	1761	
65	17	33	5	1	7	1762	Ilive's attack on the Court.
72	15	40	5	1	10	1763	
75	16	38	4	–	11	1764	
91	10	37	2	1	12	1765	
91	20	47	9	1	15	1766	

* Not free by redemption but translated to the Stationers' Company.
† Two of these were translated.

Apprentices		Freemen			Livery	Date	
b'd.	t.o.	total	pat.	red.			
97	19	36	1	–	12	1767	Renewal of Cambridge agreement.
94	22	29	1	–	9	1768	
100	14	52	5	–	16	1769	
96	27	41	5	–	16	1770	
68	22	43	4	1	14	1771	
67	26	37	3	1	10	1772	
41	21	59	4	3	16	1773	November 18th, Chancery injunction
63	15	63	5	–	13	1774	against Carnan.
72	11	46	6	2	14	1775	May 29th, Judgment against almanack
71	17	42	4	1	14	1776	monopoly.
89	14	66	4	5	14	1777	
58	9	44	4	1	8	1778	
55	4	40	6	3	10	1779	
57	4	30	4	3	1	1780	July 4th, William Herbert permitted to borrow early records.
67	9	26	2	1	11	1781	Stamp Duties on almanacks increased.
81	6	32	7	2	5	1782	
64	12	44	7	2	3	1783	
79	6	32	4	1	5	1784	
82	7	40	9	1	14	1785	
98	8	37	4	1	14	1786	
102	9	38	6	4	24	1787	
92	9	36	7	4	17	1788	July 29th, death of Carnan.
115	10	50	10	9	27	1789	
104	19	40	4	2	20	1790	
122	11	38	5	4	18	1791	
125	21	32	4	7	19	1792	
164	7	45	5	10	16	1793	
90	7	27	3	3	7	1794	
102	24	42	9	3	16	1795	
98	8	50	5	1	13	1796	
65	12	56	4	1	17	1797	
67	7	40	4	6	18	1798	
105	18	58	5	6	28	1799	
98	8	45	9	3	17	1800	
103	6	47	5	1	13	1801	
104	8	50	10	3	22	1802	
96	10	48	2	6	15	1803	
167	12	47	7	7	20	1804	
180	14	30	4	4	10	1805	
231*	7	51	7	4	13	1806	
180	8	52	12	4	21	1807	
172	9	55	9	11	19	1808	
189	10	53	9	8	8	1809	
175	11	39	6	1	6	1810	Livery numbered 517, the highest ever.
147	23	41	6	3	15	1811	
139	17	47	8	3	3	1812	
152	8	57	7	–	11	1813	
122	6	43	7	6	9	1814	
127	7	47	10	4	13	1815	
104	16	56	9	2	17	1816	

* 142 bound to printers.

Apprentices b'd.	t.o.	Freemen total	pat.	red.	Livery	Date	
131	16	57	7	4	14	1817	
157	11	69	12	9	17	1818	
160	12	51	4	2	10	1819	
152	7	42	8	3	8	1820	
167	10	57	10	4	11	1821	
141	8	57	12	3	13	1822	
145	7	67	20	7	19	1823	
220*	9	58	16	6	23	1824	
207†	16	60	12	–	12	1825	
110	13	44	8	–	9	1826	
127	21	67	14	2	16	1827	
128	3	65	12	2	13	1828	
103	12	51	9	–	9	1829	Charity Commissioners' Report on Stationers' Company.
119	10	46	11	2	10	1830	
133	7	45	7	–	12	1831	
138	42‡	48	4	8	15	1832	
139	8	40	11	3	11	1833	Order of Master of the Rolls *re* loan charities.
126	7	42	5	–	5	1834	Abolition of Stamp Duties on almanacks.
158	5	31	8	2	6	1835	June 1st, fees for freedom increased by 30s.
155	10	42	10	2	4	1836	in lieu of quarterage.
137	5	37	11	1	6	1837	Commissioners' Report on Companies.
137	22	41	7	3	16	1838	
134	6	40	10	1	11	1839	
110	8	41	7	3	13	1840	
97	10	39	10	3	11	1841	
88	7	32	7	–	9	1842	May 3rd, proposal for history of Company;
124	4	34	10	2	12	1843	Copyright Act.
132	6	39	8	–	9	1844	December 9th, Registration as Joint Stock
127	7	28	8	–	5	1845	Company.
105	6	29	6	1	5	1846	July 7th, General Purposes Committee
87	2	22	9	–	10	1847	first appointed.
66	11	23	3	–	5	1848	
87	5	26	8	3	11	1849	
109	2	32	6	3	9	1850	April 9th, sale of barge.
95	12	26	9	1	4	1851	
106	5	34	11	–	6	1852	
116	4	15	2	3	4	1853	
83	2	9	1	–	3	1854	
93	3	11	4	1	4	1855	
73	7	8	3	1	7	1856	
80	2	16	7	–	9	1857	
75	3	13	6	1	9	1858	
97	1	13	7	2	6	1859	
95	3	24	9	3	9	1860	
93	–	14	2	2	6	1861	April 8th, opening of School.
52	1	13	3	–	4	1862	
81	3	20	2	1	7	1863	
54	3	14	2	3	10	1864	

* 122 bound to printers. † 121 bound to printers.
‡ 26 were the apprentices of the late Robert Spottiswoode.

Apprentices b'd.	t.o.	Freemen total	pat.	red.	Livery	Date	
85	5	27	10	3	10	1865	
77	–	16	6	2	10	1866	
77	–	13	4	3	5	1867	
90	–	19	2	4	3	1868	
79	–	15	6	5	7	1869	
81	–	19	5	1	5	1870	
101	4	19	3	5	8	1871	'Entered at Stationers' Hall' published.
104	1	18	6	4	10	1872	[Transcripts.
74	2	18	5	3	6	1873	Arber's proposals for publishing his
97	1	22	6	6	8	1874	Sale of Dark House.
92	–	31	6	7	11	1875	Sale of share in Irish Estate.
105	5	17	5	1	3	1876	
137	26	17	5	2	6	1877	
120	1	31	11	4	15	1878	
105	3	23	7	4	9	1879	
121	–	24	6	2	6	1880	
111	8	12	2	4	6	1881	
125	2	33	14	2	8	1882	
140	65*	20	4	–	4	1883	February 6th, Treasurership, as salaried office, abolished.
115	6	13	3	–	5	1884	June 10th, abolition of quarterage; Report
110	2	12	3	–	3	1885	of Royal Commission.
99	3	17	3	2	6	1886	
107	1	15	4	2	4	1887	
101	–	15	3	1	6	1888	
123	34	11	3	–	1	1889	Act of Common Council varying apprentice-
124	29	8	1	3	5	1890	ship regulations.
150	11	12	3	2	5	1891	
101	1	12	2	1	4	1892	
75	–	19	1	3	7	1893	
67	3	9	–	1	3	1894	October 2nd, School reopened at Hornsey.
84	22	16	6	2	1	1895	
66	1	22	2	2	2	1896	March 24th, Agreement with Letts for almanack production.
79	–	21	3	15	19†	1897	Livery down to 246.
81	5	12	2	6	9	1898	
63	87‡	13	1	7	5	1899	
115	1	16	3	14	15	1900	
67	–	31	5	17	10	1901	
47	2	20	4	8	10	1902	
50	1	16	3	5	8	1903	
62	3	23	5	2	7	1904	
72	–	24	4	11	12	1905	
87	1	25	5	2	5	1906	
74	1	31	4	2	10	1907	Almanack publishing taken over by Cassell.
58	17	36	5	7	10	1908	
51	–	38	2	9	8	1909	
57	–	91	–	9	8	1910	

* 56 turned over to George Andrew Spottiswoode on the death of his father, Andrew.
† Among these were Frederick Macmillan, William Heinemann and Joseph Shaylor.
‡ 83 turned over to John Spottiswoode on the death of George Andrew Spottiswoode.

| Apprentices | | Freemen | | | Livery | Date | |
b'd	t.o.	total	pat.	red.			
52	–	44	1	3	4	1911	Copyright Act.
42	–	30	4	9	9	1912	
75	3	38	2	6	9	1913	
48	–	27	2	6	4	1914	
36	5	10	3	1	2	1915	
29	–	14	3	5	7	1916	
27	–	19	–	11	16	1917	Proposals to extend Company's activities.
27	–	34	4	14	17	1918	Master Printers' plan to build offices in Hall garden.
54	8	56	4	15	14	1919	Suggestions for increasing activities of the Livery.
47	1	66	2	29	25	1920	April 23rd, first meeting of Livery Committee.
37	–	32	1	8	14	1921	
40	52*	42	–	21	22	1922	
28	–	28	1	10	12	1923	
33	7	23	1	13	11	1924	
44	–	32	3	8	10	1925	
45	–	43	1	33	25	1926	April 13th, Court agrees to co-opt two Livery representatives.
38	–	48	2	12	22	1927	*Old Moore* sold to Cassell.
32	1	30	1	11	13	1928	
38	–	43	2	11	13	1929	
31	–	33	2	12	13	1930	
20	10	23	1	5	4	1931	Company of Newspaper Makers Incorporated.
16	1	33	2	6	4	1932	
37	–	151	–	140	146	1933	Companies of Stationers and Newspaper Makers agree to amalgamate.
31	–	37	4	6	6	1934	
46	–	40	3	7	9	1935	
47	4	35	2	10	11	1936	
39	–	28	1	10	11	1937	January 25th, new Charter.
35	–	17	–	3	7	1938	
7	–	6	–	3	3	1939	[enemy action.
8	1	3	1	–		1940	October 15th, Hall severely damaged by
16	2	7	–	1	3	1941	December 29th, Company's leased property
8	–	11	–	3	3	1942	largely destroyed.
16	–	15	1	9	4	1943	
17	–	26	1	20	8	1944	
13	–	34	6	16	27	1945	
17	1	34	3	11	12	1946	
19	–	43	4	9	19	1947	
13	–	53	6	20	17	1948	
21	–	24	2	11	16	1949	
33	–	13	1	3	8	1950	
34	–	22	1	8	7	1951	
24	–	22	5	7	12	1952	
14	1	16	2	2	1	1953	
18	–	20	1	7	6	1954	
11	–	11	–	5	5	1955	
36	–	18	1	10	9	1956	
24	–	35	–	15	14	1957	May 4th, quater-centenary dinner in restored Hall.
25	–	40	2	18	18	1958	
						1959	April, sale of Ave Maria Lane property.

* 51 turned over to Ronald Andrew Spottiswoode on the death of Edward Briscoe Eyre.

THE MILK STREET MYTH

W E must, I think, accept the tradition that the Company's first Hall was in Milk Street; but I can find no reason for believing in the 'myth' that the Company retained any claim to the Milk Street premises after the move to Peter's College in 1554. John Nichols is probably responsible for the survival of the myth. In a footnote on p. 545 in the third volume of his *Literary Anecdotes of the Eighteenth Century* (1812), he wrote: 'The Company still possess two houses in Wood-street, and three in Frier's-alley and Clement's-court in Milk-street, built, after the Fire of London, on the site of their original Hall.'

This statement has been accepted by Arber and others, and is given support by two entries in Court Book C. The first is dated August 17, 1607, and reads: 'Payd to the Collectors in mylkestrete for Two ffiftenes. xxiiij⁸. for the hall there.' The second, of May 26, 1611, is an order that the Master, the Wardens and Mr Norton 'shall contracte & bergayne for the sale of the lease of the hall in Milke-street' and it has the marginal note, 'The sale of the house in Milk-streete'. Nothing further is heard of a sale—in Milk Street or anywhere else. The first entry was made within twelve months of the move from St Paul's Churchyard to Abergavenny House and the second a few weeks after the formal purchase of the new property the Clerk, on both occasions, was writing in the *third* Hall, and he might, in referring to the old Hall, have had in mind the *first*—in Milk Street—instead of the *second*—in St Paul's Churchyard. My reasons for thinking that the Clerk made an understandable mistake when fair-copying the Court minutes are based on the following arguments.

1. There are no references to the Milk Street property anywhere in the records until late in 1606 (probably in November, after the Company had moved out of St Paul's Churchyard) when Mr Hyde was to have the Company's cellar 'in mylkstrete' for the storage of wine; it is strange that he is the first tenant to be mentioned in fifty years. The property, if it had remained as a freehold in the Company's possession, would have earned rent and fines for the renewal of leases; it is difficult to believe that no portion of these ever reached the Wardens' Accounts except as part of the Renters' balances. If the Company had retained the property as leasehold, there would have been payments of rent and periodic fines for renewal; the same argument applies to these hypothetical outgoings as to the hypothetical receipts.

2. In 1563 and 1571 the Company made returns to the City that it had no lands or possessions except a house in which to meet together, i.e. Peter's College (Liber A, ff. 7v and 17); and the Wardens, reporting to Burghley in 1583, wrote: 'We stationers are very poore and haue no land, but ye house we sit in'; but they might have had a leasehold in Milk Street.

3. The only entry in the sixteenth century comparable in its completeness to that of 1607 is for 1582 and reads: 'Paide to the collectors of St Gregories parishe

for the subsidye monney of the hall—vjs viijd.' (Register A, f. 233v, and one of the items omitted by Arber in his reprint, vol. i, p. 498.) Peter's College, the second Hall, was in St Gregory's parish.

4. In 1606 Richard Collins had been Clerk for over thirty years and had always thought of the 'Old Hall' as the one in Milk Street. From the autumn of 1606 there was a new 'Old Hall'.

But there is still Nichols's mistake to account for. The survey, made by Leybourn in 1674 and reproduced on page 211, will do this. Friar's Alley led out of Wood Street and became Clement's Alley before it debouched into Milk Street. (Clement's House and Morley House now obliterate this little dog-leg thorough-fare.) The property recorded by Leybourn was bought in 1619 with John Norton's money and lay in the parish of St Mary Magdalen, Milk Street. It was easy enough at the beginning of the nineteenth century to think of the eastern end of the property as being the site of the original Hall in Milk Street.

MEMBERSHIP OF THE COURT OF ASSISTANTS,
1556–76

THE Table of the names of the Ancients, which was hanging in the Council Parlour in 1557, has long since disappeared, and no complete list of them is given in Register A. There are, however, rolls of Stationers—in the Charter, for instance, and in subscription lists—and there are pages in the Register which carry the signatures of the Master, Wardens and their assistants. Following Mr Graham Pollard's lead (*The Library*, 4th ser., xviii, 1938, pp. 236 ff.), I have constructed the Table which appears below. The only generalizations I make in advance are:

(*a*) that, once a man becomes a member of the Court, he is a member for life unless he is formally dismissed, as James Holyland was in 1558–9, or unless he retires, as John Jaques probably did in 1560;

(*b*) that all Wardens, past and present, must be members of the Court;

(*c*) that the honorific 'master' was normally given, by the Beadle when writing up Register A, to members of the governing body only, but occasionally also to the Renter Wardens who at this time were closely associated with the Court and were in the running for election to it;

(*d*) that seniority, achieved by service as Renter Warden, has always been of great importance.

NOTES ON THE COLUMNS

1. Shows the place of each Stationer named in the Charter, which was probably compiled in the winter of 1556–7. It represents roughly the order of seniority established, among those at the top, by the first year of service as Warden or Renter, and, among the rest, by the date of freedom—perhaps of the City. Cawood and Cooke, as Wardens at the time of the Charter, achieved artificially high places in the list; Cawood (no. 2) had to wait his turn as Master until Kevall (no. 9) had held the office.

2 and 3. Require no further comment than that the six whose occupations are not known were probably not in the book trade and that two printers, Thomas Berthelet and Robert Toy, died just before the Charter list was made.

4. Numbers 4 to 8 must, I think, have been Wardens before 1551. The freedom dates are from the City records.

5. Shows the Master (possibly the first ever), the two Wardens and the six past-Wardens who were the Ancients at the time of incorporation, May 1557, and probably (with Berthelet and Toy until their deaths) as far back as December 1554 when the record begins. All except Dockwray stand, in my order (except for the interchange of Waye and Coston), at the head of a list of subscribers to Bridewell in the spring of 1556, and these eight appear as 'master bonham' etc., while no. 10, like all who follow, is plain 'John Turke'.

6. Shows the Court on the day John Walley became Under Warden early in July 1557; on the same day (almost certainly) a final list was made of those who had contributed towards the costs of incorporation. The first eight men are described as 'master Dockewray', etc., and are the nine original Ancients, without Bonham (dead or on his deathbed) and Holyland (a poor co-operator), but with 'master Wallye'. The next on the list is again John Turke.

The Court of Assistants

(1)	(2)	(3)	(4)	1557a (5)	1557b (6)	1557c (7)	1558 (8)	1559 (9)	1560 (10)	1561 (11)	1563 (12)	1563 (13)
1	Thomas Dockwray	notary		M	M	M	d	died 23rd June 15:				
4	William Bonham	printer		died summer 1557								
5	Richard Waye	—				s	M	d	d	s		M
6	Simon Coston	notary	free 1522				d	d	d	s		
7	Reyner Wolfe	printer	free 1536			s	d	M	d	s	s	a
8	James Holyland	bookseller	free 1541			s	dismissed 1558–9					
9	Stephen Kevall	—	free 1535 / W 1551			s	d	d	M	s		a
2	John Cawood	printer		W_1	W_1	W_1	d	d	d	M	M	a
3	Henry Cooke	tavern-keeper		W_2		s		d	d	? died sumn		
16	John Walley	printer	R 1554		W_2	W_2	d	d	d		s	
13	John Jaques	—	free 1535			s	W_1	d	d	? retired au		
10	John Turke	bookseller	" c.1536			s	W_2	d		? died sun		
12	Michael Lobley	"	" c.1531			s	d	W_1	d	s	W_1	a
17	Thomas Duxwell	"				s	d	W_2	d	s		a
18	Anthony Smith	"	R 1554			s	d	d	died early 156			
20	Richard Jugge	printer	free 1541 / R 1556			s	d	d	W_1		s	W_1
15	John Judson	"	free c.1533			s	d	d	W_2		s	a
14	William Riddell	"					d	d	? died autu			
21	William Seres	"	free 1548 / R 1556			s	d	d	d	W_1	s	a
22	Robert Holder	bookseller			R_1	d	d	d		s	
23	Thomas Purfoot	printer	?free 1542		R_2	$^dR_1$	d	d		s	? dis
28	Roger Ireland	—						d		s	W_2
67	Richard Tottell	printer	free 1547				$^dR_2$	R_1	W_2	s	a
47	Richard Harrison	"							W_2	die		
56	John Day	"	free 1550					L		R_2	R_1
74	James Gonneld	—									
79	William Norton	bookseller						L		R_2	
—	Humphrey Toy	"	free 1558					L	R_2	R_1	
—	John Harrison	w	" 1556							L	
60	William Cooke	—						L			
66	Thomas Marshe	printer							L		
—	Richard Watkins	"	?free 1557								

M......... Master of the Company
W_1......... Upper Warden
R_2......... Junior Renter Warden

s........... signed as a memb
d........... subscribed to the.

1564	1565	1566	1567	1568	1569	1570	1571	1572	1573	1574	1575	1576	(27)	(28)
59														
a		a	a	a	a	a	a	s	s	a				Richard Waye

? died summer 1564

| M | s | a | M | a | a | a | a | M | s | | | | | |

died late 1573

| a | M | a | | | a | a | | | | | | | | |

died April 1571

| a | s | M | a | a | a | a | a | | | | | | | |

died 1572

ner 1560

| W₁ | s | a | a | | W₁ | | a | s | s | a | | a | printer | John Walley |

:tumn 1560 ; living in Somerset 1571

nmer 1561

| | | | | died August 1567 | | | | | | | | | | |

| a | | a | died July 1566 | | | | | | | | | | | |

⁵0

| a | s | W₁ | a | M | M | a | a | | M | M | | | printer | Richard Jugge |
| a | | a | a | a | a | W₁ | a | s | | a | | a | " | John Judson |

mn 1560

| a | W₁ | a | a | a | a | M | M | s | s | a | M | M | printer | William Seres |

? died early 1565

missed early 1563

| a | | a | a | W₂ | a | | | | | | | | disappeared after 1575 | |
| | s | a | W₁ | W₁ | a | a | a | s | s | W₁ | | a | printer | Richard Tottell |

ed spring 1563

W₂	s	W₂	a	a	a	a	W₁		s	c	W₁	a	printer	John Day
	W₂	a	W₂	a		a	a	W₁		a		W₁	—	James Gonneld
R₁					W₂	W₂	a	s	W₁	a		a	bookseller	William Norton
							W₂	W₂		a		a	"	Humphrey Toy
								W₂	a			a	"	John Harrison
R₂	R₁								W₂			a	—	William Cooke
		R₂	R₁							W₂		a	printer	Thomas Marshe
			L					[?R₂]	[?R₁]		W₂		"	Richard Watkins
(14)	(15)	(16)	(17)	(18)	(19)	(20)	(21)	(22)	(23)	(24)	(25)	(26)	(27)	(28)

...er of the Court   a.......listed as a member of the Court

...Election Dinner   L.......called to the Livery

7. Opens a new phase. I believe that Walley was 'elected' Warden by a general meeting of the Stationers, in accordance with the ancient custom confirmed in the Charter, and that, within the next few weeks, the Ancients took a major decision (already taken in many other companies and embodied in the Stationers' by-laws of 1562) and co-opted nine of the most senior freemen to make up a Court of eighteen Assistants. All these (except Riddell and Coston) signed a survey, room by room, of the Company's movables early in the gild-year 1557–8, and they must have signed as members of the Court. Only by assuming two 'elections' within a short period can the differences in the two subscription lists and the tally of signatures be explained; only by assuming a change of policy (against which Holyland may have been too outspoken) can two 'elections' be reasonably accounted for. I have excluded Nicholas Taverner (no. 11, of whom nothing more is known) and William Powell (no. 19, who was certainly never on the Court); but I have included Riddell (no. 14) among those co-opted because he certainly was an Assistant in 1559 and was most likely to have been chosen at the same time as those of like standing. I assume that the change of policy affected also the choosing of Renters, those from March 1558 being nominated by the Court.

8. 'Master holder' appears in a list of subscribers to the 1558 election dinner; he had given up the office of Renter in March (after serving for one year) and had no need to subscribe, nor entitlement to the prefix, unless he had just been added to the Court. (I have omitted Renters from the Table if they never became Assistants.)

9. 'Master purfoote' is included in July 1559 for exactly the same reasons as Holder the year before. He was the first Renter to serve a second year as a result of the sensible arrangement for handing on experience—an arrangement I associate with the Court's assumption of the choice of officers. But Purfoot is something of a problem. He subscribed to the dinner in 1558 as Renter and to the dinner in the two following years as an Assistant, for he had no other reason. He was listed as an Assistant on January 22, 1563. Thereafter he appears in Company lists as the senior Liveryman. He was often in trouble for breaking the ordinances and was fined £6 13s 4d in 1565 for selling primers to the Haberdashers. Like Holyland, but for different reasons, he was not a co-operator and was probably dismissed from the Court.

10. In the 1560 dinner list neither of the Renters is mentioned. (John Whitney, no. 57, served as Renter in 1560 and 1561 but never became an Assistant.) What justification would 'Roger Irelonde' have for subscribing unless he were a newly chosen Assistant? He was certainly one in 1563.

11. Tottell, having served as Renter for the two previous years, becomes an Assistant as Under Warden in July 1561.

12. Shows the Master, Wardens and nine others who signed an ordinance as 'assestantes' on January 22, 1563, Harrison having been chosen in the previous July without ever serving as Renter. Both the Master and the Upper Warden this year had served the offices before.

13. Again the Master and the Upper Warden had served as such before. Ireland, the Under Warden from July 1563, had signed as an Assistant six months earlier, and no new election was made.

14. Day, like Tottell, became Under Warden (in 1564) three months after ceasing to be Senior Renter.

15. Gonneld, Under Warden from July 1565, was never Renter nor was he called to the Livery in 1560 with Day and the others.

16. One would have expected Norton to be added to the Assistants as Under Warden; but he had to wait four years. His treatment looks like the action of a printer-majority against a bookseller.

17 to 20. Require no comment.

21. In a list of those who subscribed in 1571–2 towards the cost of a new kitchen, etc. (Liber A, f. 139) the Master, Wardens and Assistants are put at the beginning with the prefix 'master'; there is then a gap followed by 'master Purfoote' and 'master Cooke', and then another gap followed by Liverymen with Christian names.

22 and 23. Require no comment.

24. In a list of those who subscribed for gunpowder on August 19, 1574 (Liber A, f. 29), the Master, Wardens and Assistants are listed separately and given the prefix 'master'.

25. Requires no comment.

APPENDIX III

26. Shows the Assistants, appointed September 3, 1576, to act as searchers of printing houses; they are listed in strict order of seniority and only Waye and Jugge (? sick; both died the following year) are absent. Each has a partner from the Livery; 'Thomas Purfoot', as the most senior, is paired with the Master.

From the co-option of Tottell in July 1561, the pattern is beautifully clear; entry to the Court is by service as Under Warden. When in July 1587 Richard Greene refused to serve, and was fined, as Under Warden, it was resolved (March 26, 1588) that 'he is to be an assistant in his place in sort as if he had taken ye wardenship vpon him'. The Ancients, after establishing, between 1557 and 1561, the principle that power of election—of officers and to the Court—lay in their hands and after having the principle written into the ordinances, resorted to the traditional practice of admission to their ranks through the Under-Wardenship gate.

A NOTE ON THE RECORDS AND ON SECONDARY
SOURCES

(a) *Records in print*

1. *A Transcript of the Registers of the Company of Stationers of London 1554–1640 A.D.* Edited by Edward Arber. Five vols., 1875–94.

   These volumes contain:

   > The Charter of 1557.
   > Wardens' Accounts, 1554–96 (from 1571 in summary only).
   > Entries of Copies, 1554–1640 (except 1571–6).
   > Enrolment of Apprentices, 1554–1605 (except 1571–6).
   > Admission of Freemen, 1554–1605 (except 1571–6) in full, and listed to 1640.
   > Calls to the Livery, 1560–1604.
   > Fines, 1554–1605.
   > Star Chamber Decrees of 1566, 1586 and 1637.
   > Balances of Renter Wardens' Accounts, 1600–27.
   > Letters Patents of 1603 and 1616, granting monopolies in almanacks, etc.
   > Ordinances of 1678, 1681 and 1683.
   > Many contemporary letters, petitions, reports, proclamations, licences, notes on printers, and other manuscript and printed material bearing on the book trade up to 1645.

2. *Records of the Court of the Stationers' Company 1576 to 1602.* Edited by W. W. Greg and E. Boswell. 1930.

3. *Records of the Court of the Stationers' Company 1602 to 1640.* Edited by William A. Jackson. 1957.
   This contains, besides the Court minutes:
   > Fines, 1605–40.
   > Liber A, 1604–40 (see (b) below).
   > Petition of journeymen, 1613.

4. 'A List of Printers' Apprentices, 1605–40', by D. F. McKenzie, in *Studies in Bibliography*, Charlottesville, xiii, 1960.

5. *A Transcript of the Registers of the Worshipful Company of Stationers; from 1640–1708 A.D.* [*1709*]. Three vols., 1913–14.

6. Indexes to Copyright Registry. Literary, 1842–1907, four vols.; Commercial, 1842–83, one vol.

(b) Principal Records still in manuscript

Liber A, 1559–1600[1] and 1641–1771. These are mostly copies of Mayoral precepts and returns made to the City, and ecclesiastical instructions; there are also a few important decisions of the Court. (A brief index was printed in 1902.)

Register of Bequests, from 1593.

Enrolment of Apprentices, from 1605. (To be printed up to 1640 by the Bibliographical Society of the University of Virginia. See (a) 4 above.)

Admission of Freemen, from 1605.

Calls to the Livery, from 1606.

Payments to the Poor, 1608–1856.

Minutes of Court Meetings, from 1641. (For many years from 1661 the 'waste' books also survive. There are manuscript indexes, with references to Liber A, up to 1919.)

English Stock Dividend Books, from 1644.

English Stock Treasurer's Journals, 1650–98, and from 1766.

English Stock Treasurer's Stock Books, 1663–1775.

Wardens' Accounts, from 1663.

Charters of 1667 (*inspeximus*), 1684 and 1937.

Register of Bonds for money lent, 1671–91.

William Leybourn's Survey of Property, 1674.

Receipt Books for share transfers, 1679–94 and 1702–1800.

By-laws of the English Stock, 1681. (Privately printed 1893.)

Entries of Copies, 1710–1842. (There is a printed index, 1710–73.)

Rental, 1773.

Survey of Manor of Pellipar, Londonderry, 1792.

Renter Wardens' Books, odd copies from 1851.

A 'Catalogue of Records at Stationers' Hall' was printed in *The Library*, 4th ser., vi, 1926.

Separate documents and papers, including leases and other records of property, agreements with the Universities, etc., petitions, legal advice, vouchers for Wardens' Accounts.

(c) Records known to have existed after 1554 but no longer extant

All records for 1571–6 (except summaries of Wardens' Accounts and a few entries in Liber A).

All Renter Wardens' Accounts before 1851.

Red Book of Ordinances (sixteenth century).

White Book listing printed books deposited (sixteenth century).

Account Book of '6d in the £ for the use of the Poor' (sixteenth century).

All English Stock books of account before 1650 and many—such as the Paper Stock Ledger—after 1650.

Book of Seizures (seventeenth century).

---

[1] Individual items have been printed by Arber (vol. ii, p. 62), by S. T. Prideaux (*An Historical Sketch of Bookbinding*, 1893, pp. 239–42), by A. W. Pollard (*Records of the English Bible*, 1911, pp. 313–22) and in *The Library*, 5th ser., x, 1955.

A Note on the Records

(d) *Printed works on the Company*

John Nichols, *Literary Anecdotes of the Eighteenth Century*, vol. iii, 1812, pp. 545–607.

John Gough Nichols, 'Historical Notices of the Worshipful Company of Stationers of London', *Trans. London and Middlesex Arch. Soc.*, vol. 2, 1861.

Reports of Charity Commissioners, from 1830.

Reports of Commissions of Enquiry into Livery Companies of London, 1837 and 1884.

'Introductions' by Edward Arber, W. W. Greg and William A. Jackson to nos. 1, 2 and 3 in (a) above.

'Introduction' by E. Gordon Duff to *A Century of the English Book Trade . . . 1457 to . . . 1557*, 1905 (reprinted 1948).

Graham Pollard, 'The Company of Stationers before 1557', *The Library*, 4th ser., xviii, 1938.

Graham Pollard, 'The Early Constitution of the Stationers' Company', *The Library*, 4th ser., xviii, 1938.

W. W. Greg, *Some Aspects and Problems of London Publishing between 1550 and 1650*, Oxford, 1956.

William A. Jackson, 'Variant Entry Fees of the Stationers' Company', *Papers of the Bib. Soc. of America*, 51, 1957.

D. F. McKenzie, 'Apprenticeship in the Stationers' Company, 1555–1640', *The Library*, 5th ser., xiii, 1958.

H. R. Plomer, 'Some Notes on the Latin and Irish Stocks of the Company of Stationers', *The Library*, 2nd ser., viii, 1907.

C. J. Sisson, 'The Laws of Elizabethan Copyright: the Stationers' View,' *The Library*, 5th ser., xv, 1960.

'Introductions' by Ellic Howe to *The London Compositor*, 1947, and to *A List of London Bookbinders 1648–1815*, 1950.

John Johnson and Strickland Gibson, *Print and Privilege at Oxford to the year 1700*, 1946.

Franklin Dickey, 'The Old Man at Work: Forgeries in the Stationers' Registers', *Shakespeare Quarterly*, New York, xi, 1960.

The following articles by me deal with particular aspects of Company history:

'The Accounts of the Wardens of the Stationers' Company [1557–96]', *Studies in Bibliography*, Charlottesville, ix, 1957.

'Book Trade Control in 1566', *The Library*, 5th ser., xiii, 1958.

'The English Stock of the Stationers' Company. An Account of its Origins', *The Library*, 5th ser., x, 1955. (With this are printed five items from Liber A, 1565–84.)

'Early Cambridge Printers and the Stationers' Company', *Trans. Cambridge Bib. Soc.*, ii, 1957.

'The "Company" of Printers', *S.B.*, Charlottesville, xiii, 1960.

'The Stationers' Company in the Civil War Period', *The Library*, 5th ser., xiii, 1958.

'The English Stock of the Stationers' Company in the Time of the Stuarts', *The Library*, 5th ser., xii, 1957.

A Note on the Records

'The Distribution of Almanacks in the second half of the Seventeenth Century', *S.B.*, Charlottesville, xi, 1958.
'Charter Trouble', *The Book Collector*, Winter 1957.
'The Stationers' Company in the Eighteenth Century', *Guildhall Miscellany*, 10, 1959.
'Thomas Carnan and the Almanack Monopoly', *S.B.*, Charlottesville, xiv, 1960.

INDEX

*Individuals are Stationers, widows of Stationers or apprenticed in the
Company, unless otherwise described.*
*References to City Companies include references to freemen of those
Companies.*

For Product Safety Concerns and Information please contact our EU
representative GPSR@taylorandfrancis.com
Taylor & Francis Verlag GmbH, Kaufingerstraße 24, 80331 München, Germany

www.ingramcontent.com/pod-product-compliance
Lightning Source LLC
Chambersburg PA
CBHW061130220326
41599CB00024B/4223

*9 7 8 1 0 3 2 9 0 5 7 2 3 *